THE TERROR WAR

The Terror War:
The uncomfortable realities of
the War of Independence

Joseph E.A. Connell Jnr

East_wood_

First published in 2021
Eastwood Books,
an imprint of the Wordwell Group.
Unit 9, 78 Furze Road, Sandyford Industrial Estate, Dublin 18
www.eastwoodbooks.com
www.wordwellbooks.com

Cover image—St Patrick's Street in Cork, Ireland on (or around) 14 December 1920. The image captures the aftermath of what's known as The Burning of Cork. Photographer: W.D Hogan. NLI Ref: HOGW 153. National Library of Ireland on The Commons @ Flickr Commons.

ISBN 978-1-913934-20-0 (Paperback)
ISBN 978-1-913934-26-2 (e-book)

British Library Cataloguing-in-Publication Data.
A catalogue record for this book is available from the British Library.

Typeset in Ireland by Wordwell Ltd
Copy-editor: Aoife Condit de Espino
Cover design and artwork: Wordwell Ltd
Printed by SprintPrint, Dublin

Contents

To Bob Clarke and David Fuquea
No better friends
And to Constance Cowley: Gone but never forgotten.
May God be good to her.

Acknowledgements

I must thank my parents for everything; without them I would have had no such love for Ireland. My brothers and sister and their families supported me at all times.

I am most grateful to Eastwood Books, and it has been a pleasure to work with Nick Maxwell, Dr Una MacConville, Ronan Colgan, Helen Dunne and everyone at the publishing house. Aoife Condit de Espino is a wonderful editor, and I cannot thank her enough. Everyone at Eastwood has given polish to my efforts and all their assistance is most appreciated.

Clare Cowley started helping with research, and helped on everything thereafter.

I am always grateful to Anthony Tierney for his continuing advice and suggestions.

Dr Patrick Geoghehan and Susan Cahill have given me the privilege of a recurring spot on their NewsTalk radio show, *Talking History*. I have been a guest several times of Myles Dungan for his RTE Radio show, *The History Show*. Dónal Ó hUallachain always finds time to have me on his show, *Looking Back*, on Radio Dublin. Carol Dooley has given me many opportunities to talk on her show, *Saturday Live*, on Sunshine Radio. It has been a joy to work with them all over the years, and I am most grateful.

Mícheál Ó Doibhilín is the editor of www.kilmainhamtales.ie and has let me submit articles for his site and published my books under his imprint. I am always pleased with his editing and guidance.

Tommy Graham of *History Ireland* has been most encouraging and helpful. I am indebted to him for allowing me to write a column, '100 Years Ago', in *History Ireland*.

All of them have a respect for those men and women of the revolutionary years, and have given me great assistance and support.

I have always been welcomed throughout Ireland with the greatest kindness and hospitality, and I thank everyone with whom I've spoken. I assure you that those feelings are returned with the deepest and most lasting affection.

Those who have helped and encouraged me are too numerous to mention and I thank them all; everyone I asked always gave me assistance, reassurance and direction: all heartened me when I needed that most, and have been generous with time and advice, too. At the risk of offending someone I omit, I must especially mention Mary Banotti, Ray Bateson, Áine Broy, Bob Clarke, Marie Coleman, Lorcan Collins, C.B. Connell, Briny M. Connell, Molly Connell, Revd Paul Connell, Carla Cowley-Ralph, John Dorney, Tom and Mary Duffy, Sgt Wayne Fitzgerald, Col. David Fuquea, Darragh Gannon, Liz Gillis, Marcus Howard, Debbie and Randy Jacobs, Lar Joye, Peggy Keating, Mary Mackey, Frank MacGabhann, Brenda Malone, Jim McIlmurray, David McCullagh, Barbara and Dominic Montaldi, Gregory O'Connor (RIP), Pól Ó Murchú, Nora Owen, Detta and Seán Spellissy, and Padraic Yeates.

And Pam Brewster for all things.

While I have been given a great deal of assistance, all mistakes are mine alone.

Abbreviations

BGOIA	(Better) Government of Ireland Act (1920)
BLPCI	British Labour Party Commission.
	The Party sent a delegation to Ireland in 1920 to investigate the effects of the war on the people.
BMH	(Irish) Bureau of Military History
COIN	Counterinsurgency operations
DMP	Dublin Metropolitan Police.
	It was an unarmed force and its jurisdiction included the city of Dublin, Blackrock, Dalkey, Kingstown, Pembroke and Rathmines. The 'A' to 'F' Divisions were geographical. 'G' Division dealt with serious crime, including surveillance of political suspects and subversive movements.
DORA	Defence of the Realm Act (1914)
GAA	Gaelic Athletic Association
GHQ	General Headquarters of the IRA (Dublin)
GOC	General Officer Commanding
GPO	General Post Office (usually in Dublin unless otherwise noted)
IGC	Irish Grants Commission
IO	Intelligence officer (used by both Irish and British forces)
IPP	Irish Parliamentary Party
IRA	Irish Republican Army (sometimes used interchangeably with 'Volunteers').
	It is difficult to pinpoint when the Irish Volunteers became the Irish Republican Army. Under the direction of IRB men like Collins and Richard Mulcahy, as well as Cathal Brugha who left the IRB, the Volunteers had been reorganised throughout the country after the Rising. The Volunteer newspaper *An tÓglach* (The Young Warrior/Soldier) stated that 'the Irish Volunteers are the Army of the Irish Republic' in December 1918. About this time the term 'Irish Republican Army' came into widespread use. The IRA was always distinct from the IRB, a secret society. Only in 1920, however, did British military

and police reports begin to refer to the IRA.
In Irish it is *Óglaigh na hÉireann*.
An individual member was usually called a 'Volunteer'.
During the War of Independence they were referred to as the IRA/Volunteers.
During the Civil War, those who were pro-Treaty fought in the Free State Army. The anti-Treaty forces took on the mantle of the IRA and were called the IRA/republicans. Some sources refer to them as the 'Irregulars'.

IRB	Irish Republican Brotherhood
IWM	(British) Imperial War Museum
MP	Member of (the British) Parliament
MSPC	(Irish) Military Service Pension Collection
NLI	National Library of Ireland
O/C	Officer Commanding
PRO	(British) Public Records Office, now the National Archive (TNA)
RIC	Royal Irish Constabulary.

It was an armed, semi-military force and its jurisdiction extended to the entire country, except Dublin. In 1913, however, members of the RIC were brought to Dublin to supplement the DMP during the Lockout.

ROIA	Restoration of Order in Ireland Act (1920).
SOE	Special Operations Executive (British World War II irregular forces)
TD	Teachta Dála. Member of Dáil Éireann, the Irish parliament.
WO	(British) War Office

Introduction

During 1919–21 the British and the Irish actions often reflected one another in fighting the Irish War of Independence. Both the Irish and the British did well in some areas, and were deficient in others. Further, it must be emphasised that both sides used terror – murder, burnings, shearing women's hair – to intimidate the Irish population, and both the British and the Irish were aware of the effects of terror and trauma. While the Irish Republican Army utilised terrorism as a means to resist British control, British forces employed terrorism in order to complete the conquest of Ireland and subdue the Irish nationalist movement. The aim of this book is to question some widely held convictions about terrorism and to demonstrate that each side used terrorism as part of its overall approach. Essentially, terrorism is a strategy based on psychological impact. The book invites the reader to approach the topic of terrorism from a new perspective – according to which terrorism is just one of the forms of political violence that was used in the Irish War of Independence.[1] The reader is asked to engage with and challenge actions of both the British and Irish and to examine them more closely – even to enquire who was the terrorist and who was the anti-terrorist?

The trauma of terrorism is a far subtler concept than many realise. It is not just a word for something extremely stressful. It doesn't always come from short, sharp shocks like terrorist attacks or firefights. And trauma isn't the same thing as post-traumatic stress disorder (PTSD). What trauma *is* about is events and their effect on the mind. But what separates it from something merely stressful is how we relate to these events on a deep level of belief. Trauma is not necessarily proportional to an event's intensity. Some people will process what has happened better than others. If trauma is about the interface of events and individual minds, what makes a mass trauma possible? Can groups themselves be traumatised? At its simplest level, a mass trauma (otherwise known as a 'collective trauma') takes place when the same event, or series of events, traumatises a large number of people within some shared time span. As an example of the trauma that is evoked by the actions noted here, newspaper accounts of the day often referred to such atrocities as 'acts of frightfulness'.

Perhaps more than anything else, though, the lasting social dangers of mass trauma consist in forgetting. When it goes unprocessed, undiscussed – perhaps it is actively repressed as it was by many of the Irishmen and -women who lived through the War of Independence – the group's social tissues remain disturbed and unhealed. Individual trauma builds up unrecognised and festers under the cracks. It is often thought that the terror that revolts us has no moral downside for the terrorist; as we shall see, however, those on both sides of the conflict who were engaged in acts that are deemed 'terrorist' acts often suffered along with the victims.

Terrorism is any organised set of acts of violence designed to create an atmosphere of despair or fear; to shake the faith of ordinary citizens in their government and its representatives; to destroy the structure of authority, which normally stands for security; or to reinforce and perpetuate a governmental regime whose popular support is unsteady. It is a policy of seemingly senseless, irrational and arbitrary murder, assassination, sabotage, subversion, robbery and other forms of violence, all committed with dedicated indifference to existing legal and moral codes or with claims to special exemption from conventional social norms. While many definitions of terrorism are discussed in Chapter 4, this book views terrorism as a mode of military struggle in conjunction with political aims rather than as a social, ethical or moral aberration. Terrorism here is a deliberate induction of fear in the belief that fear itself is sufficient to produce political results. The principal goals of terrorism as discussed here are to intimidate and demoralise. Terrorism essentially aims at influencing an audience, and in the Irish war there were several audiences to be influenced: the Irish police forces (RIC and DMP), the Irish people, the British people, international opinion, and politicians on both sides. Fundamentally, violence is a reciprocal construction: the intended victim's perception is integral to the perpetrator's act. Terrorism involves myriad reprehensible acts of violence, including fear, intimidation, coercion, destruction of property and killing. The reader is directed to acknowledge the suffering of actors, victims and survivors on both sides. History takes time to make or understand, and examination of contemporary and near-contemporary accounts as they become available enables us to view events with more nuance. Records and archives have three main functions in our society – evidence, accountability and defining culture. The distance of time should not allow us a sort of collective amnesia. Our 'one-sidedness' cannot allow our memories to be selective. This book posits that it has taken many decades for the emergence of a filtered and contextualised recollection of the War of Independence, when a 'safe' collective memory was formed, for there to be a broadly acceptable acknowledgment of the terror that characterised the war. Memory can sanitise all war, and sometimes our memory is cloaked in remembrance, and remembrance of the past tends to be highly politicised. We should always ask: what explains the excess of terror and counter-terror in the war? This is not always popular – but to understand conflict one must confront what people do when they set out to kill one another.

In a path-breaking early analysis of terrorism, Thomas Thornton offered five proximate objectives: morale building, advertising, disorientation (of the target population), elimination of opposing forces, and provocation.[2] Martha Crenshaw also identified advertising and provocation as proximate objectives, along with weakening the government, enforcing obedience in the population, and outbidding.[3] David Fromkin argued that provocation is *the* strategy of terrorism.[4] Edward Price wrote that terrorists must delegitimise the current regime and impose costs on occupying forces, and he identified kidnapping, assassination, advertising and provocation as tactics.[5] As we shall see, this book will illustrate all of these and demonstrate that both the British and the Irish used all of them.

The Irish War of Independence was notorious for violence, with a great deal of that violence being attributed to the Black and Tans, the section of the Royal Irish Constabulary (RIC) that was in large part composed of approximately 9,000 British ex-servicemen (about ten per cent were Irish-born), and the Auxiliary Division of the Royal Irish Constabulary (ADRIC or 'Auxies'), composed of approximately 2,200 mostly former officers in the British Army. The sole purpose of their terrorist actions was to 'make an appropriate hell for rebels' in an effort to reduce support for Sinn Fein and the IRA.[6] The common response by the Black and Tans and Auxiliaries to multiple deadly attacks was to burn houses, farmhouses and creameries in the immediate area of an IRA ambush. British Field Marshal Henry

Wilson said of the Black and Tans: 'reprisals were being carried out without anyone being responsible; men were being murdered, houses burnt, villages wrecked … It was the business of the Government to govern. *If these men ought to be murdered, then the Government ought to murder them*'.[7] Clearly, Wilson was not averse to reprisals *per se*, just that that they were being carried out by undisciplined individuals.

In 1919 Ireland had two separate police forces, the Dublin Metropolitan Police and the Royal Irish Constabulary. They both lacked an intelligence capability to effectively respond to the emerging insurgency. The reason for this is that the Irish had systematically attacked their experience. Specifically, the 'G' Division of the Dublin Metropolitan Police, and the Crimes Special Branch of the Royal Irish Constabulary suffered sustained attrition. These attacks and destruction of the smaller police stations were to cause serious gaps in intelligence capacity. Such was the terror of the Irish campaign that in the first three months of 1920 'over 400 isolated police barracks were destroyed, and the Constabulary was concentrated, and immobilized, behind steel shutters in the larger buildings; and by May of that year some eighty members of the RIC and detectives in the Dublin Metropolitan Police had been murdered without any assassin being brought to justice'.[8] A British Army report written in 1921 noted the consequences of the Irish campaign: 'in 1919, they commenced their attacks on the RIC; they murdered them, they boycotted their families, they drove them from small isolated barracks. With what result? Police were recruited in England, and the British Army was drawn into the fray.'[9]

It is important to note that action by and toward state agents can be terrorism just as actions by and toward non-state agents can be terrorism. Police officers could be the targets of terrorism by assassination just as the police could be the perpetrators of terrorism. For example, when Michael Collins determined that the DMP's G-Division men were the primary sources of British intelligence in Dublin, he first wrote to them all telling them to cease those activities. When they persisted, he had the Squad members chain constables to railings outside the police stations, and then had some beaten. Only when that was insufficient to get his point across, did he order the first killing of a 'G-Man', Detective Patrick 'Dog' Smyth. The terror campaign escalated to the necessary level of intimidation and fear and that subsequently exhibited itself when the DMP took a 'hands off' policy toward the Volunteers. Similar efforts against the RIC throughout the country resulted in many resignations from that force. All can experience intimidation, and causing others to change their lives is one of the foremost characteristics of terror.

Though he was a late-comer to the War, Sir Ormonde Winter, who was appointed Chief of Intelligence in Dublin Castle in May 1920, felt that force, coercion and terror were the ways to a British victory. He claimed that the British government used a degree of 'coercion' (e.g., the RIC, Black and Tans and the Auxiliaries) that was 'not sufficiently severe' – although he stated that they nearly succeeded. He identified what he determined was a cardinal weakness in the British policy-makers' approach and related it back to one of the leading theorists of war: Clausewitz said 'All kinds of philanthropy in war are a gross and pernicious error'.[10]

The British were unable to suppress the IRA by their military and police methods, and carried out security policies that gave ammunition to the Irish propaganda efforts. For the Irish, broadly speaking, the IRA[11] waged guerrilla war in the countryside, targeting police barracks and patrols, while in the cities its soldiers operated more as terrorists, killing off-duty policemen or civil servants.[12] Some of the recent writing on terror has attributed much of that killing by the Irish as sectarian-based.[13] All insurrections – however accepted the cause – are generally accompanied by ideological killings. This book, however, posits that while the IRA sectarian attacks killed some, most of the Irish terror was non-sectarian.

Terror became a part of the lives of those who lived throughout the country. There is a rippling effect to terrorism, the consequences of which impinge on lives and communities. Seeing death, seeing dead people, having people trying to kill you, maybe trying to kill other people, burning of property, beatings, rape and intimidation of women – all occurred throughout the country on a regular basis. George Russell (Æ) observed in July 1916: 'You see, it is not the shooting of 50 or 1000 people that moves public opinion, but the treatment of one person isolated and made public'.[14] The trauma was pervasive and became individualised – violence directed at or witnessed by a few led to widespread personal intimidation and trauma by many. Moreover, the war became one of tit-for-tat reprisals and counter-reprisals. Peter Hart has argued that the escalation of violence between the IRA and Crown forces can be explained by that tit-for-tat cycle involving 'the overriding motive of revenge, the ability of anonymous gunmen on either side to do what they liked, the frequently random or mistaken choice in victims, and their helplessness'.[15] High-profile reprisals by British forces received extensive coverage in the British press after mid-1920, and reprisals became a major political issue in Britain in the autumn of 1920, largely because of the activities of the Black and Tans and the Auxiliaries that were reported in the British press. That use and acceptance of reprisals by the British cost them key assets of discipline, prestige and legitimacy. The trauma that was being inflicted in these reprisal attacks was disproportionate punishment for individual actions, yet the actions of both the British and Irish erred toward the far edge of morally dubious. Much of the killing can be put down to retaliatory violence on both sides. In Dublin and Cork, conventional military casualties were not the norm – most deaths could be attributed to assassinations or reprisal killings. Each invited vengeance killings from the other side and thus all of Ireland was trapped in a cycle of mutually assured terror. The questions posed throughout this book are more about generating, rather than attempting to conclude, thoughtful discussion and debate. There can be no single answer to such questions: the answers are social constructs, shaped by the tolerances of the reader.

As the war moved from 1919 into 1920 and beyond, both sides increasingly used violence, leading to terror. The IRA were for the most part free to move in flying columns and operate in their native country with relatively little fear of significant reprisal to a column. Most of the IRA's attacks and ambushes were to obtain arms and disrupt the British administration of authority in every way possible. At first, those attacks were sporadic, and purely opportunistic, rather than systematic. While each action may not have caused the British much loss of life or matériel, the Irish assassinations and ambushes likely appeared to have such a significant effect as they were what, in essence, brought the British to the negotiating table. The Irish insurgent forces effectively used terror and assassination against the British forces, were devoted ideologically to the idea of a free Ireland, had well-developed military, political and intelligence organisations, conducted guerrilla warfare excellently and enjoyed the support of the majority of the Irish population – but they knowingly used targeted terror tactics when necessary.

By late 1920 Ireland was in a state of turmoil, in which shootings, house burnings, shearing women's hair and reprisals were commonplace. Collins wrote to TD James O'Mara, who was in the US administering the Dáil loan:

> events are moving rapidly here now. The policy of the English government is pure unvarnished assassination, and none of you need be surprised whose death you hear about next. Their actions remind me of the actions of a man who had only a limited time to live, giving that time to a mad orgy, before he dies.[16]

Irish terror was so effective that the British representatives in the courts, police, magistrates and local authorities all eventually ceded the authority of their positions to their Irish counterparts, who, with the support of Dáil Éireann, were already running large portions of Ireland.[17] Terrorism and brutality were at the very roots of the Irish independence campaign to present the Dáil, the Republican Courts and police as the *de facto* government of Ireland. The nature of the Irish campaign against the British establishment centred on confrontation, challenge and disregard for all authority deriving from Britain.

Stories of random British shootings of civilians, burning of creameries, and streets of looted shops through the south-west became commonplace in British newspapers. Destruction of shops and creameries was designed to hit both farmers and business people. Throughout Ireland that pattern emerged whereby attacks by the IRA on Crown forces were followed by British reprisals in which civilians were killed and injured and buildings destroyed or looted. Actions of this kind, when they are carried out systematically, constitute a distinct strategy of insurgency or counter-insurgency. This strategy should have a name, be it 'terrorism' or another, and retaining 'terrorism' has the advantage of familiarity for this book.

Many such reprisals took place around the country but the burning of the small town of Balbriggan in north County Dublin especially received worldwide attention because of its proximity to the capital, where national newspapers and foreign correspondents were based.[18] In addition to the death of two suspected IRA men, the local hosiery factory was burned down and houses and pubs were destroyed.[19] Further, in December 1920, the Black and Tans sacked County Cork and its capital, Cork City, in a 'wild orgy of looting, wrecking, burning, and drinking'.[20] They set fire to the whole of Patrick Street (the main business district in Cork City) and when the fire brigade came to put it out, the Black and Tans cut the hoses with bayonets and turned off the hydrants in order to ensure the complete destruction of the business district.[21] In total, the Black and Tans caused £3 million of damage in Cork alone, an amount equal to approximately £150 million today.[22] These examples demonstrate how the British forces further used terrorism in their attempt to crush Irish nationalism by illustrating to the Irish population the debilitating economic consequences of fighting Britain. Florence O'Donoghue wrote that the burning and looting of Cork was not an isolated incident, but the application of a policy initiated and approved, implicitly or explicitly, by the British government. He wrote the British actions were:

> a policy of subjugation by terror, murder and rapine, of govern-
> ment by force of arms, of the deliberate destruction of those in-
> dustries and resources whose absence would inflict the greatest
> hardship and loss upon the nation; of ruthless hunting down and
> extermination of those who stood for national freedom.[23]

Beginning in September 1920, that British terrorist-reprisal policy began expanding with the Black and Tan detachment burning the town of Balbriggan.[24] On 20 September two Black and Tans were shot in a public house, both of whom died. There was no evidence submitted to a court as to who fired the shots and one account said the shooting was the result of a quarrel. One of the IRA men, however, later described what happened in his witness statement:

> I ordered them [Black and Tan Head Constable Peter Burke and
> his brother Sergeant William Burke] to clear out, instead of doing
> so, they made a rush at me and I had no option but to fire. I shot
> one of the Head Constables [sic] in the head and wounded the
> other, who later recovered [Sergeant Burke died on the spot and
> Head Constable Burke died later], and then my pal and I cleared
> out the back door and got safely away.[25]

Black and Tans and Auxiliaries were based at the nearby Gormanstown Camp and up to 150 of them descended on Balbriggan that night, intent on revenge. While the raiding party consisted mostly of Black and Tans, some were also 'old RIC men'. Two local young men, Séamus Lawless and Seán Gibbons, were bayoneted to death on the street by the 'Tans', and a memorial today marks the spot where they were murdered.[26] The British forces proceeded to smash windows of shops and houses in the small town, and then set fire to a hosiery factory that was completely destroyed. They burned down forty-nine houses, forcing families to flee – some had to take refuge in the fields.

The foreign press covered the destruction of Balbriggan extensively, the *Manchester Guardian* editorialising about an 'Irish Louvrain' and continued:

> To realise the full horrors of that night, one has to think of bands of men inflamed with drink, raging about the streets, firing rifles wildly, burning houses here and there loudly threatening to come again tonight and complete their work.[27]

Hamar Greenwood stated in the House of Commons that the Balbriggan episode was regrettable, but proposed no punishments for those involved. He believed instead that 'the best and the surest way to stop reprisals is to stop the murder of policemen',[28] repeating a sentiment he expressed almost word for word twelve days earlier in the *Weekly Summary*.[29] Mark Sturgis wrote in his diary that if the Auxiliaries had simply 'confined themselves to the dignified shooting of the two prominent Shinners, notorious bad men, the reprisals would have been not so bad … worse things can happen than the firing up of a sink like Balbriggan'.[30] At the same time that individuals at various levels of the British administration were permitting and encouraging both reprisals and the killings of 'alleged Sinn Féiners', the press was beginning to recognise that these atrocities were taking place and to criticise the government for allowing them. The *New Statesman* editorialised on 25 September 1920 that the actions of the Black and Tans constituted authorised terrorism:

> In Ireland, under existing conditions it is inevitable that the armed forces of the Crown should at times get out of hand … There is

clear evidence that methods of terrorism are adopted less from passion than from policy.[31] [Emphasis added.]

Further to that, Sir John Anderson wrote to Mark Sturgis: 'It is quite clear from the evidence that the burning was organised, and countenanced by the officers in charge'. *The Times* went even further in an editorial:

in view of the wide area covered by the reprisals, it is difficult to believe that the occurrences in Balbriggan can have been entirely the result of a spontaneous outburst of resentment on the part of justifiably incensed policemen. There seems to be behind it a directing influence.[32]

After the reprisals at Tuam in July 1920, the *Galway Express* wrote:

When they throw petrol on a Sinn Féiner's house, they are merely pouring paraffin on the flames of Irish nationality.[33]

While *The Irish Bulletin*, which reported such acts throughout the conflict, gained greater credibility among the mainstream press, Dublin Castle's the *Weekly Summary*'s defence of reprisals made the newspaper increasingly infamous and unbelievable.

However much the Irish propagandists did embellish the story of the burning of Balbriggan, it was certainly effective in creating a worldwide view of the brutality and terrorist actions of the Black and Tans and Auxiliaries. The *New York Times* reported the story as 'two attacks' in 'a special cable to the *New York Times*':

The first onslaught early this morning lasted for two hours, and the second began in the afternoon.
... These reprisals followed quickly on the murder of Head Constable Burke and his brother Sergeant Burke.
When news of the outrage reached Gormanstown, where the RIC are stationed, a large body started off in motor lorries ... and the town was given over to ruthless reprisals.
Scenes of the wildest disorder reigned. Some of the inhabitants as-

sert that they were driven from their homes at the point of a bayonet. One woman only just succeeded in rescuing her baby from its
cot before the house was burned.
This morning the roads leading from the town were crowded with
fleeing women and children, some wheeling perambulators ...
In many cases they were bleeding as a result of being hit by flying
glass and debris. The Dublin hospitals are dealing with casualties.[34]

Six weeks later British reprisals took place in Granard, Co. Longford.
The IRA assassinated District Inspector Philip Kelleher there on 31
October, and on the night of 3 November uniformed men entered the
town and burned down a number of buildings. The same night, a convoy
of military and police was ambushed in the nearby town of Ballinalee and
forced to retreat.[35] *The Times* correspondent visited both towns the
following day and described Granard as a scene 'that can scarcely be
imagined in a town which is not in the throes of actual war. Most of the
businesses and the market hall were smoking ruins.'[36] Despite official
denials, the writer concluded that 'No reasonable man ... could come to
any other conclusion than that this terrible punishment had been inflicted
on the town by the R.I.C.'.
By late 1920 some Irish newspapers were risking official censorship by
their editorials. The *Irish Independent* declared 'Nobody in Ireland accepts
as truthful any statement made by the British Government'.[37] Even *The
Irish Times*, usually a loyalist paper, editorialised about the reprisals:

If only the people in Britain knew. Everywhere in Ireland today
you hear that cry 'why do these things happen?' Why are servants
of the Crown not charged with pillage and arson and what
amounts to lynch law even with drunkenness and murder! How
can the reign of terror be stopped?[38]

Despite the increasing wave of attacks, on 9 November 1920 David
Lloyd George assured a Guildhall audience in the City of London that
British forces were winning the conflict. According to the prime minister,
'We have murder by the throat in Ireland'. He described the rebel campaign
as 'a spectacle of organized assassination, of the most cowardly character'.

He then insisted 'There will be no peace in Ireland, there will be no conciliation, until this murder conspiracy is scattered'. After the reorganisation of the police, 'we struck the terror, and the terrorists are now complaining of terror'.[39] An editorial in *The Times* argued that the prime minister 'committed himself to war upon large sections of the Irish people and his government was engaged in an effort to scourge Ireland into obedience'.[40] In fact, just three days earlier, the *Montreal Gazette* had reported on raids, burning of businesses and Black and Tans running amok in County Kerry. The Tralee reprisals were in response to an IRA kidnapping of two RIC constables who were killed and their bodies secretly disposed. On 1 November 1920 the RIC and Black and Tans fired on crowds leaving Mass and terror was unleashed on the town:

> Volley after volley resounded to the terror of the people ... I do not remember, even in the [First World] War having seen people as profoundly terrified as those of this small town, Tralee.[41]

The resulting reprisals brought Tralee to the point of starvation, showing the British only maintained some control through terror:

> Each day, almost, also brings the record of 'reprisals', in which men in uniform, which show that their wearers' duty is to preserve order, raid villages, fire houses, destroy property and chase the in-habitants – men, women and children – from their homes into the inclement night. Men in high places who should understand the danger of irregular methods of lynch-law order, do not show a se-rious appreciation of the gravity of the situation; some give veiled excuses for the violence that almost amount to encouragement.[42]

The *Freeman's Journal* concurred in its editorial:

> War on women and children!
> How the cry thrilled Europe when the German jackboots tram-pled Belgium.
> England led the chorus of fiery protest.
> And Mr Lloyd George led England.

Baby-killer was the epithet that damned the Zeppelin raiders.
War on women and children!
The cry rises again today.
Not now from Belgian homes, but from the streets of a Kerry
town.
Tralee is at the point of starvation.
Starvation created for political purpose.[43]

The intensification of the reprisals and terror in general in late 1920 further stoked Irish national outrage, with the British campaign of 'unofficial reprisals' in particular energising already expanding Irish political networks. The atrocities of Crown forces at Cork, Balbriggan, Mallow, Tuam, Lahinch, Tralee and Trim not only caused great distress in Ireland, as those towns were economically prosperous centres, but also registered loudly among the Irish in Britain, impacting the wider British society. The British government acquiesced in a reprisal policy that not only brazenly broke the law itself, but also, by randomly destroying property, hit out indiscriminately precisely at the business and farming sectors that the government claimed were its natural supporters. British reprisals, whether provoked or not, undermined British law itself, and tarnished its reputation in Ireland and abroad. Reprisals in Ireland and the British government's broader Irish policy aroused disapproval among sections of British public opinion, concerned as they were with the First World War's potential legacy of 'brutalisation' and with the inversion of British 'peaceableness' with German 'Prussianism'.[44] Michael Collins and the Irish understood that the Irish could not get to their own governance by military means alone. The strategic function of the Irish warfare was to defeat the British psychologically and politically. Every IRA 'outrage' was used to provoke British reaction and was a blow to the British will to persist. Those British reprisals would serve two purposes: first, they would mobilise Irish opinion and, second, any British brutality in Ireland, freely reported in the British and international press, would be judged morally intolerable by Britain's liberal-minded political leaders. The British would contribute to their defeat by their own actions, and that was a part of the Irish strategy. Collins was playing politics with violence.[45]

Further, the American Commission on Conditions in Ireland in its 1921 report damned the conduct of Crown forces. It concluded that 'in spite of … the British Imperial Government ceaselessly attempting to terrorize the people and to paralyse the economic and social life of the country, the Republican government appears to be holding its own and establishing its right to be considered the only working government in Ireland'.[46] The British policy of reprisals was helping to legitimise the local Irish government, not dismantling it.

Reprisals – 'collective punishment' – were intended to coerce communities rejecting the British or the IRA, respectively. This was not confined to the burning of homes and businesses. When the British declared as hostile whole areas of the countryside, it pushed the public towards the Irish rebels, and made defeat of their insurgency more difficult. Nothing in the war had remotely the same effect on domestic and international opinion as did the British reprisals.

The British learned too late that burnings, reprisals and other forms of terror were unproductive. Major Bernard Montgomery (later Field Marshal), who served in the 17th Infantry Brigade in Cork, later wrote: 'Personally my whole attention was given to defeating the rebels and it never bothered me a bit how many homes were burned'.[47] In response, Tom Barry put the Irish strategy of retaliation for British burnings into effect in County Cork:

> what I did was to stop the destruction of our property by the British. It was [British Major A.E.] Percival [of the Essex Regiment] started it: they started burning up houses in the martial law area, small farmers' houses, labourers' cottages. Well, the only way you can fight terror is with terror, that's the only thing that an imperialist nation will understand. We sent a message to them that for every house of ours they burned, we'd burn two of the big houses, the Loyalist mansions.[48]

Barry and others burned the 'English Big Houses' to create enough of a storm in the House of Lords to bring about an end to official British reprisals and further nationalist house burnings. Charles Townshend wrote: 'The IRA could win an arson competition easily'.[49]

The propaganda apparatus of the IRA was well developed and efficient.

The pro-republican newspaper *The Irish Bulletin* was distributed freely to press correspondents and liberal-minded men and women in England,[50] and British atrocities were covered and criticised in leading British publications of the time such as *The Manchester Guardian*, *The London Daily Herald* and *The New Statesman*, as well as in many publications in the United States.[51] Information on Irish efforts and British atrocities found its way into every European capital and made its way to the US as well, framing the struggle firmly in a pro-Irish context. Nevertheless, the fact that the Irish were engaging in many of the same acts of burning, murders and hair cropping was not publicised – mostly unknown or ignored by that same press.

Coverage of reprisals by Crown forces provided evidence that an incompetent administration had become lawless as well as ineffective.[52] The British, Irish and foreign press were united in their condemnation of the Black and Tan reprisals. The *Freeman's Journal* compared Balbriggan to 'one of the Belgian towns that had been sacked by the invaders'.[53] The *London Daily News* editorialised on 'the barbarous "reprisals" now being systematically and openly carried out by the Black and Tans'.[54] *The Birmingham Post* commented in its editorial, 'it is not by means of reprisals that order can be restored'.[55] The terror tactics of the Irish did not, however, go completely unnoticed in the press. In March 1921 Henry Wickham Steed, editor of *The Morning Post*, wrote of the British correspondents' attitudes in Ireland:

> I have sent from time to time to Ireland men who constantly
> risked their lives as accredited correspondents of the British and
> Allied forces in France and in other theatres of war. But though
> they naturally went with feelings of loyalty and admiration for the
> Forces of the Crown, they returned with loathing at the manner in
> which operations in Ireland are conducted on both sides.[56]

As a result, it is true that correspondents from the major international and British newspapers focused on the British reprisals, and the IRA's campaign virtually escaped scrutiny, save for a periodic mention of 'outrages', a practice that gave the impression that assassinations and ambushes were merely an incidental backdrop to the reprisals themselves.[57]

The battle for public opinion was also carried on at the military level – Irish brigade-level officers were tasked to identify all reporters and journalists in their areas and to influence their coverage if possible.[58] Historian Thomas Mockaitis points out: 'In counterinsurgency an atrocity is not necessarily what one actually does but what one is successfully blamed for doing'.[59] There was hardly any attempt to explain IRA tactics or its practices of burning, murder and hair taking. For the most part, the foreign press framed the war in a pro-Irish context. The actions of the British and Irish frequently mirrored one another – an uncomfortable reality of the War of Independence.

Following the return of the Rising prisoners from Frongoch and other British prisons, Michael Collins, Florence O'Donoghue and the Irish leaders determined that an Irish intelligence operation was needed to combat the British presence in Dublin and throughout Ireland. Chapter 1 briefly outlines that Irish intelligence establishment and development.

To emphasise the critical nature of the intelligence war in the struggle, and the superiority of the Irish intelligence system, it is fitting that the pivotal event of the War of Independence was an intelligence coup. Collins's plans for Bloody Sunday were to be spectacular, to send many messages: to the British, to the Irish and to the wider world. It can be argued that both parties – the IRA and the British forces – committed terrorist acts on Bloody Sunday; while the former did so in an effort to resist conquest, the latter employed terrorism as a means of subjugating that Irish nationalist movement. (In current anti-terrorist analysis, counter-terrorists know that symbolism is only used if there are numerous casualties.) This display on the part of the IRA was designed to show the British that the IRA was an organised and effective fighting force capable of resisting British control. Bloody Sunday represented a microcosm of the War of Independence: the role of intelligence, shocking violence and an inextricable link with propaganda.

Three separate but connected events occurred in Dublin on Bloody Sunday, 21 November 1920. First came the killings of eleven suspected British agents in their Dublin lodgings that morning; two Auxiliary policemen were also killed; two civilians were killed, as well. Late that afternoon British units attacked the crowd at a Gaelic football match in Croke Park, killing thirteen innocent spectators and a player. Finally, in the early evening two high-ranking Dublin IRA officers, Brigadier Dick McKee and Vice-Brigadier Peadar Clancy, as well as a civilian visitor to Dublin, Conor Clune, were killed in Dublin Castle. In all, thirty-two people died within twelve hours.

The proposals for Bloody Sunday's morning raids came together over two months, and were finalised only a few days before the attacks. They were not, however, part of an Irish 'master plan' – they were a reaction to British intelligence agents getting closer and closer to the Irish leaders. Chapter 2 describes the events on Bloody Sunday itself.

The intelligence war in Dublin continued after Bloody Sunday, but it was irrevocably changed after that day. Recent research has shown, however, that British intelligence was not paralysed by the day, nor was Irish intelligence able to achieve complete control. Chapter 3 tells that story.

The War of Independence intensified as 1920 progressed – it became more brutal – and an increasingly ruthless IRA saw it necessary to provoke publicity and international sympathy for their cause. There was what some termed a 'descent into terror', and both sides used terror – and the trauma it caused – for their own purposes. The war, in Dublin as elsewhere, grew more savage – and every actor in the conflict became brutalised by the cycle of attack and retaliation. An examination of the men and women – both participants and victims – indicates that they were individually affected more than were the intelligence operations of Bloody Sunday. But that was the case throughout Ireland as the war continued. Each side blamed the other for what has been called the turn to terrorism. Many studies during the twentieth and twenty-first centuries have determined that the results of terror and trauma continue long after the events that caused them. The effects of violence in war are long-lasting – the trauma of terror is never ending. Only with these increased analyses will terror and trauma's more personal consequences be able to be considered. Any discussion of terror in Ireland, and particularly of Bloody Sunday, must consider the long-term human repercussions that the actions had on those who committed them, as well as on those upon whom they were committed and their families and whether the Irish killings should be classified as 'terror'. Chapter 4 considers the evolution and use of terror in the Irish War of Independence.

Chapter 5 uses witness statements and the words of those involved on both sides on Bloody Sunday, and throughout the country, to show that terror bred its own escalatory dynamics: excesses on one side produced excesses on the other side. The stories of the men and women are telling, terrifying and heart-rending. Questions abound regarding what those who participated in the period felt, and how much baggage they carried into the rest of their lives. Their life stories are not just tit-for-tat scores – their humanity is restored when they are remembered. Trauma lasts long after the events.

Finally, Chapter 6 discusses the end of the terror war – did the Irish win? Were the Truce of July 1921 and the Treaty of December 1921 results of either side 'winning' the war? Did military action – and terror – drive the British into a reluctant political engagement with those whom they had previously castigated as murderers? The British only negotiated with the Irish, and concluded a settlement, because of violence – politics and violence go hand in hand. Chapter 6 posits that neither side 'won'– both sides went to the bargaining table to make pragmatic compromises.

Notes

[1] A. Merari, 'Terrorism as a strategy of insurgency', *Terrorism and Political Violence* **5** (4) (1993).

[2] T.P. Thornton, 'Terror as a weapon of political agitation', in H. Eckstein (ed.), *Internal War: Problems and Approaches* (London, 1964), p. 87.

[3] M. Crenshaw, 'The causes of terrorism', *Comparative Politics* **13** (4) (1981).

[4] D. Fromkin, 'The strategy of terrorism', *Foreign Affairs* **53** (4) (1975).

[5] H.E. Price, 'The strategy and tactics of revolutionary terrorism', *Comparative Studies in Society and History* **19** (1) (1977).

[6] F. Pakenham, *Peace by Ordeal* (London, 1935), p. 50.

[7] Major Gen. Sir C.E. Callwell, *Field Marshall Sir Henry Wilson: His Life and Diaries* (2 vols) (London, 1927), p. 256. Emphasis added.

[8] Sir O. Winter, *Winter's Tale* (London, 1955), p. 291.

[9] 'General remarks on the rebellion in the 6th Divisional Area', Strickland Papers, IMW P3.

[10] Winter, *Winter's Tale*, p. 214.

[11] Though the term IRA, or Irish Republican Army, was commonly used during the period, the Irish forces never formally adopted the term.

[12] M. Boot, 'Kick the bully: Michael Collins launches the War of Independence', http://www.historynet.com/kick-the-bully-michael-collins-launches-the-1921-irish-rebellion.htm.

[13] See P. Hart, *The IRA and its Enemies: Violence and Community in Cork: 1916–1923* (Cork, 1998); C. Townshend, 'The IRA and development of guerrilla war', *English Historical Review* **93** (371) (1979); D. Fitzpatrick, *Politics and Irish Life, 1913–1921: Provincial Experience of War and Revolution* (Dublin, 1977); C. O'Malley, *The Men Will Talk To Me* (Cork, 2010); W. Sheehan (ed.), *British Voices From the Irish War of*

Independence 1918–1921: The Words of British Servicemen Who Were There (Doughcloyne, 2007); M. Ryan, *Tom Barry: Irish Freedom Fighter* (Cork, 2003); B. Keane, 'The IRA response to loyalist co-operation during the Irish War of Independence, 1919–1921', https://www.academia.edu/27954537/The_IRA_response_to_loyalist_co-operation_in_County_Cork_during_the_Irish_War_of_Independence.

[14] Russell letter to Mrs Philimore, 28 July 1916, Strathcarron MSS, Bod Dep. C, 714, folder 1.

[15] Hart, *The IRA and its Enemies*, p. 79.

[16] Collins to O'Mara, 25 September 1920, NAL, D/E5/57/14.

[17] T. Bowden, 'The Irish underground and the War of Independence 1919–1921', *Journal of Contemporary History* 8 (2) (1973); F. Costello, 'The republican courts and the decline of British rule in Ireland, 1920–1921', *Éire-Ireland* 25 (2) (1990); M. Kotsonouris, *Retreat from Revolution: The Dáil Courts, 1920–1924* (Dublin, 1994).

[18] *An Phoblacht*, 27 August 2010.

[19] M. Hopkinson, *The Irish War of Independence* (Dublin, 2002), p. 80.

[20] E. Holt, *Protest in Arms* (New York, 1960), p. 232.

[21] *Ibid.*

[22] M. Walsh, *The News from Ireland: Foreign Correspondents and the Irish Revolution* (New York, 2008), p. 70.

[23] F. O'Donoghue, 'The sacking of Cork City by the British', in G. Doherty (ed.), *With the IRA in the Fight for Freedom, 1919 to the Truce: The Red Path of Glory* (Cork, 2010); M.F. Seedorf, 'The Lloyd George government and the Strickland Report on the burning of Cork 1920', *Albion: A Quarterly Journal Concerned with British Studies* 4 (2) (1972).

[24] U. O'Connor, *A Terrible Beauty is Born: The Irish Troubles, 1912–1922* (London, 1975), p. 136.

[25] Michael Rock: Witness Statement 1399.

[26] R. O'Mahony, 'The sack of Balbriggan and tit-for-tat killing', in D. Fitzpatrick (ed.), *Terror in Ireland* (Dublin, 2012).

[27] *Manchester Guardian*, 23 September 1920.

[28] M. Seedorf, 'Defending reprisals: Sir Hamar Greenwood and the "Troubles", 1920–1921', *Éire-Ireland* 25 (4) (1990).

[29] *Weekly Summary*, 8 October 1920.

[30] M. Sturgis (ed. M. Hopkinson), *The Last Days of Dublin Castle: The Mark Sturgis Diaries* (Dublin, 1999), p. 43.

[31] *New Statesman*, 25 September 1920.

[32] *The Times*, 21 September 1920.

[33] *Galway Express*, 24, 31 July 1920.

[34] *New York Times*, 21 September 1920.

[35] *The Times*, 5 November 1920.

[36] *The Times*, 6 November 1920.

[37] *Irish Independent*, 20 October 1920.

[38] *The Irish Times*, 20 November 1920.

[39] *The Times*, 10 November 1920.

[40] *Ibid.*

[41] M. de Marsillac, London correspondent of the French newspaper *Le Journal* (T.R. Dwyer, *Tans, Terror and Troubles: Kerry's Real Fighting Story, 1913–1923* (Cork, 2001), p. 235).

[42] *Montreal Gazette*, 6 November 1920.

[43] *Freeman's Journal*, 7 November 1920.

[44] J. Lawrence, 'Forging a peaceable kingdom: war, violence, and fear of brutalization in post-First World War Britain', *Journal of Modern History* 75 (3) (2003).

[45] C.S. Gray, 'The Anglo-Irish War, 1919–1921: lessons from an irregular conflict', *Comparative Strategy* 26 (5) (2007).

[46] Report of the American Commission on Conditions in Ireland, p.105, https://www.corkcity.ie/en/cork-public-museum/learn/online-resources/2019-20-56-report-interim-the-american-commission-on-conditions-in-ireland-american-edition-1921.pdf.

[47] Sheehan, *British Voices from the War of Independence*, pp 145–52.

[48] Tom Barry, quoted in K. Griffith and T. O'Grady, *Ireland's Unfinished Revolution, An Oral History* (London, 1982), p. 221.

[49] C. Townshend, *Political Violence in Ireland. Government and Resistance since 1848* (Oxford, 1983), p. 352.

[50] *The Irish Bulletin* was an underground republican newspaper that was produced under clandestine conditions in Dublin throughout the War of Independence. It was published daily (except on Sundays and Bank Holidays) from 11 November 1919 until the Truce in July 1921. It offered the republican version of the war and challenged the official British version of events. In contrast, the *Weekly Summary* was equally a propaganda organ for the Crown forces published in Dublin Castle.

[51] Walsh, *The News from Ireland: Foreign Correspondents and the Irish Revolution*; F.J. Costello, 'The role of propaganda in the Anglo-Irish War 1919–1921,' *Canadian Journal of Irish Studies* 14 (2) (1989).

[52] P. Griffith, 'Small wars and how they grow in the telling', *Small Wars and Insurgencies* 2 (2) (1991).

[53] *Freeman's Journal*, 22 September 1920.

[54] *London Daily News*, 23 September 1920.

[55] *Birmingham Post*, 23 September 1920.

[56] *The Morning Post*, 20 March 1921.

[57] Walsh, *The News from Ireland: Foreign Correspondents and the Irish Revolution*, p. 190.

[58] Mulcahy Papers, University College Dublin Archive, P7/A/18.

[59] T.R. Mockaitis, *British Counterinsurgency, 1919–60* (London, 1991), p. 37; 'The origins of British counterinsurgency', *Small Wars and Insurgencies* 1 (3) (1990).

1. Irish intelligence is established in Dublin

One of the contacts referred to, who was invaluable to us was a girl named Miss Lillie Mernin. … This girl put us in touch with other members of the different staffs working for the British Military in Dublin. This girl worked mainly with Frank Saurin and is one to whom a large amount of the credit for the success of Intelligence must go.

Frank Thornton

For any government, intelligence is an absolute requirement. In this case, intelligence can be defined very broadly: intelligence is the gathering and processing of all information, whether open or secret, pertaining to the security of the state.[1] Clausewitz noted 'by "intelligence" we mean every sort of information about the enemy and his country – the basis, in short, of our own plans and operations'.[2] He went on to write: 'A great part of the information obtained in war is contradictory, a still greater part is false, and by far the greatest part is doubtful'. To Michael Collins, intelligence and tactics were one. Collins determined to push and provoke the British to the ends of their will, and the key to that was intelligence – and counter-intelligence: protecting the Irish secrets from British intelligence. He wrote:

> To paralyse the British machine it was necessary to strike at individuals. Without her spies, England was helpless. It was only by means of their accumulated and accumulating knowledge that the British machine could operate. Without their police throughout the country, how could they find the man they 'wanted'?

The destruction of the intelligence capacity of the Irish police and Dublin Castle was a deliberate strategy by the Irish, intimidating the members of the police and leading many to resign rather than be confronted with daily fear for their lives. Such intimidation was an example of terror directed at the British 'state forces' – the police. The War of Independence was an intelligence war because Collins and the Irish determined it to be so. Primarily, that intelligence war was between the British Secret Service, the Dublin Metropolitan Police (DMP) and the Royal Irish Constabulary (RIC) and Collins's network in Dublin. A like war was led by Florence O'Donoghue's intelligence operatives in Cork. It was a war of harassment, terror and reprisal in the country as well as the larger cities, and a war of propaganda. O'Donoghue ran intelligence and military operations in Cork that rivalled those of Collins in Dublin. As the war progressed, Collins, in Dublin, and O'Donoghue, in Cork, continued to organise and develop more Irish intelligence. Those living outside the capital often feel that no matter what the arena – politics, industry, history – Dublin exerts a magnetic pull in terms of resources and exposure; that feeling can become stronger the further one gets from the Liffey, and in a time of crisis it's easy to understand the grip that it exerts. O'Donoghue does not get the credit he deserves, and his operations were equally important to the Irish war effort, especially in south-east Ireland. His intelligence network was correspondingly successful in penetrating the British security forces as the IRA was in Dublin. In a humble, yet correct assessment, O'Donoghue wrote:

> For most of the formative period, and continuing up to the Truce, the Director was Michael Collins, and to his initiative, energy and resourcefulness, much of the success of the service is due. Nevertheless, he would have been largely powerless outside Dublin, were it not for the work done in the local brigades.[3]

Though Collins and O'Donoghue did not begin to collaborate formally until March 1920 – after the arrival of the Black and Tans – they routinely shared information after that. O'Donoghue said:

> Collins and I, each without the knowledge of each other, were trying to build up something similar but with this difference. I put down the basic organisation in the Companies and Battalions, but had made no progress in the intelligence aspect at that stage, where he had practically no organisation, but had made very considerable progress on the more valuable espionage aspect. Working in

Dublin, and with his contacts in London, his opportunities in this regard were much more extensive than mine. Out of the Quinlisk case [see below] there arose a comparing of notes and close contact that proved valuable.[4]

One of Collins's most important services was to pass on to O'Donoghue the RIC police cipher keys for Cork. O'Donoghue organised a team to intercept RIC messages, to decode them and transmit the information back to his Brigade Headquarters. Collins eventually provided funds to O'Donoghue to support local intelligence operations in Cork.[5]

Early in the war, the need for an organised Irish intelligence operation, in the cities as well as the country, became apparent. The Irish had to perfect their own intelligence systems, and frustrate and disorganise British intelligence services. Even small actions required the gathering of some intelligence in advance, which is the *raison d'etre* of all intelligence activity. Irish intelligence was divided into two areas: gathering of information on British forces, and gathering of information on British agents. Each company of IRA/Volunteers had its own intelligence officer (IO) and each of those was encouraged to recruit people in all walks of life who boasted of their British connections. The Irish recognised the essentiality of intelligence for survival and information (propaganda) for promoting and sustaining their ideology while building dissent against the British.

Collins and O'Donoghue each devised an Irish intelligence organisation consisting of two branches. One branch was composed of army personnel, comprising a representative from General Headquarters (GHQ) under the Director of Intelligence (Collins), a Brigade Intelligence Officer in each Brigade, sometimes with a limited staff, a Battalion Intelligence Officer in each Battalion, and a few men in each Company detailed for such work.[6] The other branch of intelligence included a wide variety of men and women, individually selected, who were engaged in duties or employed in positions where they could acquire valuable information about the enemy.[7] The main intelligence effort was directed toward penetrating and undermining all aspects of British government institutions, both civilian and military, including 'selective assassinations'.[8] From the efficient combination of the work of both branches, the Irish were able to partially counterbalance any weaknesses they had in military arms.[9] In recounting the factors that contributed to the success of the IRA in its operations, the admitted superiority of the Irish intelligence services, particularly in the first years of the war, must be taken into account. This first phase of the Irish intelligence undertaking, blinding the British, severely weakened Crown rule in many parts of Ireland and went a long way towards creating the Irish 'counter state'.[10]

When Collins was appointed Director of Intelligence, replacing Éamonn Duggan in January 1919, there were already three G-men feeding republicans intelligence – Éamon (Ned) Broy, Joseph Kavanagh and Eugene Smith – but their efforts were disorganised.[11] When Collins took over for Duggan, there really was no intelligence department as such. Duggan was a solicitor and kept the intelligence files mixed in his client's files – and, ultimately, the British captured those files anyway. The files were current press cuttings indicating the comings and goings of Castle and military personnel and had more social value than intelligence value. Collins undertook a policy of meeting face-to-face with these double agents, and recruited as many more of them as possible.[12]

Inexperienced personnel who had no rigid ideas about the kind of design needed, but who were entirely clear about what results they wanted from any scheme, built up the Irish intelligence organisation from nothing. As the war progressed the Irish continued to organise and develop more Irish intelligence capability.

Collins experienced a learning curve in his new position. Joe Kavanagh, who worked for Collins in Dublin Castle, gave the list of those to be arrested in the so-called 'German Plot' to another Collins man, Thomas Gay, who passed the list to Collins. In an indication of Collins's inexperience at the time, he gave Gay £5 to pay Kavanagh for the information. Gay knew Kavanagh would be insulted that Collins would think he would spy for money, so he never offered it to him. Collins had yet to learn that there were patriotic Irishmen even in the police and the Castle. Collins notified Éamon de Valera and the other leaders of the forthcoming arrests, but de Valera chose to ignore the warnings. It was an example of the efficiency of Collins's network that he seemed to have information even before the Castle had told the police. That series of raids on 17–18 May 1918 rounded up many, and these arrests were what brought Collins fully into the intelligence effort. Many of those arrested were more moderate republicans, leaving Collins, Harry Boland, Dick Mulcahy and other more hard-line republicans in charge.

Broy was an inside witness to the productivity of Irish intelligence until he was arrested in 1921, and he recognised the efficiency and proven methods the British police used in curbing anti-British activity. Ordinary citizens often attempted to deprive civil authorities of information pertaining to nationalist activities. Law enforcement officers were quick to adapt to such measures and deployed new tactics to improve results. Whatever the difficulties that police constables had in being accepted members of their respective communities after the Sinn Féin boycott of the police, they more than made up for in their abilities to surreptitiously glean information that would lead to satisfactory information and results. Recollecting his participation in the independence movement some years after the fact, Broy divulged some of the underhanded ways in which the police were able to obtain their information. In one instance, Broy wrote:

> When it was thought that members of a family had information which the R.I.C. needed, a constable would be sent on a bicycle to their house. When nearing the house he would deliberately puncture one of his tyres with a pin. Then he would call at the house for a basin of water to locate the puncture and, whilst carrying out the repairs, would enter into conversation with members of the family and gradually lead up to the subject in which he was interested. Members of the family would thus, quite innocently, supply the Constable with all the local gossip, and when the 'repairs' were finished the constable would have the information he needed to supply a very valuable report to Dublin Castle and perhaps also to supply the police with clues as to where to institute further enquiries.[13]

An Irish intelligence system was vital.

Even today, military intelligence has four parts: acquisition, analysis, execution and counter-intelligence. As crucial to the IRA's activities as the collection and analysis of intelligence, it was the productive efficiency of Collins's department in utilising the accurate surveillance on the British that ultimately allowed them to launch effective attacks while themselves avoiding detection.[14] One secret to effective intelligence is the sharing of ideas, and though there were some problems of communication between Collins, GHQ and the country units, for the most part the Irish understood what intelligence was needed, and utilised their intelligence better than the British.[15] What the British needed in 1917–18 was not so much tactical intelligence on the Irish Volunteers – they were acting mostly in the open. What the British needed was political intelligence on the shifts in Irish opinion. This they did not have or ignored. Britain's intelligence and security policy towards Ireland was always one step behind the developing political situation – which meant that their system was doomed.

In assessing the fundamentals of the IRA's overall strategy – and bearing in mind its evolving nature – some core elements emerge. The military and intelligence campaign was particularly focused on the police as the primary target, rather than the British Army, and this focus was arguably the crucial factor in the IRA's overall success. In Dublin, the G-Division of the Dublin Metropolitan Police (DMP) was neutralised – first by killing its most aggressive detectives, and then other detectives stopped helping the British. The trauma resulting from the beatings and killings of the G-Division constables had a telling effect. The Irish strategy of selective assassination, thus intimidating the police forces, was working. The British report after the war noted the effect of the Irish attacks on the DMP and RIC:

> Up to the summer of 1919, the military relied for their
> intelligence almost entirely on the DMP in the city and the RIC
> in the country, but these sources were practically closed by the end
> of 1919 by the murder campaign.[16]

By 1920 the DMP was no longer a threat to the Irish and both the DMP and the IRA followed a hands-off approach.[17] In the country, the RIC and their families were first ostracised, and then the RIC was forced back into barracks in larger towns.[18] Darrell Figgis wrote that wherever one travelled in Ireland after Easter 1920 one saw the roofless walls of burned-out police stations, sandbags still piled in windows.[19] Those actions left the British intelligence network in tatters. After the war, the British record indicated the extent to which the Irish terror and demoralising tactics had hampered the British:

There were spies everywhere and a very large percentage of the population were ready to act as extra eyes and ears for Sinn Féin and for the IRA even if they were not prepared to fight for them.[20]

The efficiency of intelligence was not just due to Collins and to the operatives working for him but to three things:

- an appreciation of the value of intelligence;
- efficient organisation and exploitation of sources;
- every member of the Irish forces regarded it as a duty – and many of those who weren't actively on patrol regarded it as such, too.

In essence, many of the Irish were unofficial intelligence agents.

In June 1920 the pages of *An tÓglach* provided not only a rationale for why the RIC were targeted by the IRA, but also what in retrospect proved to be a generally accurate assessment of the state the RIC had been reduced to by that stage:

[The British] front line in Ireland, his chief instrument of executive power was the R.I.C., an armed force of Irish mercenaries with elaborate local knowledge, situated in strongholds in every part of the country, even the wildest and remotest. The R.I.C. were his eyes and ears and his strong right arm in Ireland. A relatively small body of men as compared to the people of Ireland; they were able by their organisation and elaborate system of intelligence to dominate the unarmed citizens … To-day the first line of the enemy, the chief instrument of executive power has broken down and ceased to be effective. The R.I.C. have been driven from their outposts, nearly five hundred of their strongholds have been evacuated and destroyed, and they have been forced to concentrate only in certain strong centres, where, in some parts of the country they are in the position of beleaguered garrisons. They are no longer effective for the purpose for which they were intended … Demoralisation has set in their ranks …There are lists of resignations from the force daily, and the effort of the enemy to fill up the gaps by English recruits is a confession of failure. The English recruits [Black and Tans and Auxiliaries] will not be effective for the purpose for which the R.I.C. were established ... English soldiers have not the local knowledge of the Irish constables ... They are not likely to succeed where the R.I.C. failed.[21]

Any examination of intelligence in the period must review the performance of the British.[22] In its record prepared after the war, the British War Department identified three problems that the Department determined combined for its 'failures':

- a vacillating and negligent government;
- a hostile population;
- a jury-rigged intelligence system lacking unity, direction or leadership.[23]

One RIC Divisional Inspector complained: 'Before the war we knew everybody and what he was doing. Now we know nothing. The people are dumb!'[24]

Collins's Department of Intelligence Office was on the second floor of a building at 3 Crow Street, above J.F. Fowler, printers and binders, just 500 yards from an entrance to Dublin Castle. Along with his office at 32 Bachelor's Walk, this was technically Collins's main Department of Intelligence office but he infrequently came here. Sometimes his operatives called this 'the Brain Centre'.

It was, as I say, early in 1919, that Collins began to create a regular Intelligence Department. He was fortunate in getting the services of Liam Tobin as Chief Intelligence Officer. Tobin had been previously doing Intelligence work for the Dublin Brigade. Later the Assistant Quartermaster General, the late Tom Cullen, was drafted into Intelligence. Next in command came Frank Thornton. The Intelligence Staff was built up slowly, as suitable men were not easily found. A good Intelligence Officer is born, not made, but even the man with a great deal of natural instinct for detective work requires to be taught a great deal of the technique of the business.[25]

Immediately upon taking the position, Collins began assembling a staff, and he promoted Liam Tobin to lead it. The trio of Tobin, Cullen and Thornton acted as an equal triumvirate: Collins was the boss but the success enjoyed by IRA intelligence is as much attributable to their canniness as to his direction.[26] Under the name of Irish Products Company, Tobin, Cullen and Thornton operated and carried on the daily activities of intelligence analysis.[27]

Collins is often described as directing every minute detail of the Intelligence Department, but part of his success in managing as many projects as he did was his ability to delegate. His own interviews refer to 'the trustworthiness of my chief aides'.[28] In contrast, Tony Woods, a veteran of the Dublin Brigade, went so far as to say, 'Tobin, of course, was the real Intelligence man in Dublin in the Tan struggle, not Collins'.[29] This critique likely goes too far in attempting to shift credit for the intelligence war away from Collins, but it is important in that it emphasises the roles of his subordinates, and that there were differing views of Collins even in those years. Collins's personality often enabled him to attract people who were willing to turn over intelligence to him – his ability to make connections with people, to build personal bonds, was one of his greatest assets. It could also lead him astray, however, as it did with the spies Jameson and Quinlisk, and Collins was very fortunate to have Tobin, Cullen and Thornton turn their more sceptical eyes on some of Collins's 'conquests'.

Since the Irish wisely refused to engage the British in open combat, their war relied upon accurate, timely intelligence – it was absolutely vital to their success. Without it, the Irish had no chance of 'winning' the conflict, or even surviving long enough to wear down the British politically. To achieve their security, they ruthlessly rooted out British informants – for the first time in Irish history, the British had to rely almost exclusively on their own intelligence capabilities in lieu of paid informants. Terror patterns, including intimidation, ostracism and assassination, had dried up the British sources among the Irish citizenry. It was obvious to the British that they had a porous intelligence organisation, but it took until late 1920 for them to locate and stop the leaks.

The conduct of Collins's war depended upon intelligence and with all their faulty judgments and inaccuracies, Collins realised the British secret files still constituted Britain's greatest intelligence on Ireland. When Broy let Collins and Seán Nunan into the file rooms of the Great Brunswick Street police station on the night of 7 April 1919 to look over the G-Division files on the Volunteers, Collins determined that in order to defeat Britain they would have to eliminate their spies. Two days after this breach of security Collins was able to identify and moved to coerce all the junior detectives responsible for political crime. The IRA threatened that they would be murdered unless they agreed to desist from undertaking any further intelligence-gathering operations against the IRA. They were informed, however, that they could continue to undertake investigations into ordinary crime. A natural realist like Collins realised how essential it was to shut off the sources of knowledge and blind Dublin Castle. Collins said the British 'could replace the men, but couldn't replace what they knew'. Collins wrote in the *New York American* in 1922:

> England could always reinforce her Army. She could replace every soldier that she lost … But there were others indispensable for her purposes that were not so easily replaced … We struck at individuals and by doing so we cut their lines of communication and we shook their morale. Only the armed forces and the spies and criminal agents of the British government were attacked. Prisoners of war were treated honourably and considerately and were released after they had been disarmed.[30]

Collins told Broy: 'I am a builder, not a destroyer. I get rid of people only when they hinder my work.' Collins warned the detectives to look the other way or suffer the consequences. Detectives who ignored his warnings paid the price. Maybe his grasp of the need for intelligence in order to conduct the guerrilla war, and his willingness to use terror methods to gain it, was Collins's greatest contribution to that war.

In Dublin Collins needed a dedicated band of men to carry out his ordered killings. 'The Squad' was initiated on 19 September 1919 (though by that time it had been in operation for four months and had already carried out two killings). Collins and Mulcahy presided at a meeting at which the unit was officially formed. Its original meeting, however, was on 1 May 1919.[31]

We met Michael Collins and Dick Mulcahy at the meeting and they told us that it was proposed to form a squad. This squad would take orders directly from Michael Collins, and, in the absence of Collins, the orders would be given through either Dick McKee or Dick Mulcahy. Dick [Mulcahy] told [us] that we were not to discuss our movements or actions with Volunteer officers or with anybody else. Collins told us that us we were being formed to deal with spies and informers and that he had authority from the Government to have this order carried out. He gave us a short talk, the gist of which was that any of us who had read Irish history would know that no organisation in the past had an intelligence system through which spies and informers could be dealt with, but that now the position was going to be rectified by the formation of an Intelligence Branch, an Active Service Unit or whatever else it is called.[32]

William Stapleton was soon chosen to be a member, and he described the method of working in the Squad:[33]

[Bill] Tobin or [Tom] Cullen [from Collins's intelligence staff] would come down and tell us who we were to get. It might be one of the Igoe Gang or a British spy sent over to shoot Collins. Two or three of us would go out with an intelligence officer in front of us, maybe about 10 or 15 yards. His job was to identify the man we were to shoot. Often we would be walking in the streets all day without meeting our man. It meant going without lunch. But other times the intelligence staff would have their information dead on and we could see our quarry immediately we came to the place we had been told he would be at. The intelligence officer would then signal us in the following way. He would take off his hat and greet the marked man. Of course, he didn't know him. As soon as he did this we would shoot. We knew that very great care was taken that this was so. As a result we didn't feel we had to worry. We were, after all, only soldiers doing our duty. I often went in and said a little prayer for the people we'd shot afterwards.[34]

W.C. Forbes Redmond, Belfast RIC Assistant Commissioner of Police, was transferred to Dublin in December 1919 in an effort to bolster the British intelligence operations in Dublin and he was appointed as the Deputy Assistant Commissioner of the DMP in charge of the G-Division. He was completely unfamiliar with Dublin, so he was assigned a 'minder' by Dublin Castle: as luck would have it, the minder was Collins's operative, James McNamara. From then, McNamara was able to follow Redmond's movements and report to Collins.

Redmond led a raid on Batt O'Connor's home on 17 January 1920 and assured Mrs Bridget O'Connor he 'wouldn't bother her again'.[35] Collins's men made sure of it. Redmond stayed at the Standard Hotel before being killed on 21 January.[36]

> Redmond was stopping in the Standard Hotel in Harcourt Street, and Tom Cullen ... a man who was high up on the Intelligence staff and in the confidence of Michael Collins, was sent to stop in the same hotel in order to got all possible information regarding Redmond, particularly about his times of leaving and returning to the hotel, and what he did in the morning and at night.[37]

The Times wrote days later that 'the murder ... is accepted as final proof of the existence in Ireland of a criminal organisation of the most desperate kind. The crime must have been planned with much care and skill.'[38] Redmond was the highest-ranking casualty in DMP history.

Despite the murder of its G-Division chief Redmond, British intelligence in Dublin Castle succeeded in placing two secret agents close to republican intelligence. The first was John Charles (J.C.) Byrne, alias 'Jameson', who ingratiated himself with Collins by posing as a representative of a British soldiers' and sailors' union while Collins was trying to foment disorder in Crown forces by encouraging strikes. Jameson had come to the attention of the Irish while feigning Bolshevism as a member of British Labor circles, all the while performing in the role of *agent provocateur*. Jameson impressed Collins with schemes to obtain arms and money from the Soviet Government, and he arrived in Dublin with a letter of introduction from Art O'Brien, head of the IRB in London. An unsubstantiated report from Dublin Castle, and the near capture of Collins while engaged in a clandestine meeting with Jameson, provoked suspicions and the Irish prepared a plan to test Jameson's loyalties. With deliberate carelessness Collins permitted Jameson to see parts of a bogus document that referred to important papers held in the home of a pro-British ex-mayor of Dublin. Jameson in turn relayed this information to Dublin Castle and soon afterward the British raided the ex-mayor's home.

In another test, Collins's intelligence team lured Jameson to an office at 56 Bachelor's Walk. Jameson told them he brought revolvers and other hand guns from England 'for the cause'. He left the heavy portmanteau with Frank Thornton, and it was transferred out of the 56 Bachelor's Walk premises. When McNamara tipped off Collins that there would be a raid on the building later that day, it was more confirmation that Jameson was a spy. As the final straw for Jameson, in a briefing to his staff Redmond had foolishly ridiculed G-Division detectives in front of Collins's agent James McNamara, pointing out that he had an operative who made contact with Collins only a fortnight after arriving from London. Redmond boasted to the detectives that they, who knew Dublin so well, could not get close to Michael Collins, while a man who only recently arrived from England managed to meet him more than once.[39] When Collins agent Dave Neligan heard this, he realised the only suspect was Jameson, and Collins ordered the intelligence staff to stay away from him.[40] Neligan informed Collins through Éamon Broy, and Jameson was killed a few days later, on 2 March 1920.[41]

A further British agent was Timothy Quinlisk, a former member of Roger Casement's Irish Brigade, formed from Irish prisoners of war held in Germany during World War I. This affiliation gave him immediate nationalist credentials on his return to Dublin after the war, and the Irish National Aid Association paid his bills for several months. As a former member of the Casement Brigade he was denied back pay for his period of imprisonment and convinced Collins he was in dire financial straits. He was well educated and spoke French and German fluently, and after the war when he was discharged from the British Army he lived for a time in Dublin and then in Cork City. Always known by Collins and his men by the one name, 'Quinlisk', he was a British double agent. Collins and his men suspected him relatively quickly after his appearance, and, once, Collins gave him £100 to get out of the country. Quinlisk, however, came back for more and that sealed his fate. Quinlisk was an inept spy: after his reappearance Volunteer leaders quickly placed him under close surveillance and found more than enough reason to execute him. He was told Collins was in Cork and when he subsequently gave the Cork RIC this information and said it would be easy for the Cork RIC to capture him, it was clear to Collins that Quinlisk was a spy. The Cork No 1 Brigade Council agreed that he should be shot, and Quinlisk was killed on 19 February 1920 outside Wren's Hotel in Cork. The execution party from the Second Battalion consisted of Michael Murphy (O/C) and two others. Murphy coldly recalled of the not-quite-dead Quinlisk: 'I then turned him over on the flat of his back and put a bullet through his forehead'.

> I might here state that on the same evening that Quinlisk was executed, following a raid on the mails by some of our lads, one of the letters written by 'Quinn' (as he called himself) ... addressed to the County Inspector, RIC, was found. The letter said that Quinlisk 'had information about Michael Collins and would report again in a few days when the capture of Collins seemed imminent ... The Cork No 1 Brigade Commandant Seán Hegarty got in touch with GHQ, Dublin, immediately following the identification of 'Quinn' as Quinlisk, and word was received back from Mick Collins that Quinlisk was definitely a spy in the pay of the British.[42]

Quinlisk's family knew nothing of his spying activities and when his father came from Waterford to claim the body about two weeks later, he had a confrontation with Murphy, who had been informed by the clerk of the Cork poor-law union of the father's application to the workhouse authorities. At the time of the 1911 census the victim's father Denis had been an 'acting sergeant' in the RIC residing at 10 Cathedral Square in Waterford City.

Still another British spy who attempted to infiltrate Collins's intelligence organisation was Bryan Fergus Molloy when he was stationed at British payroll headquarters on Parkgate Street.[43] (Molloy was a former British soldier from County Mayo whose real name was Frederick McNulty.) He worked for the Chief Intelligence Officer at Parkgate, Colonel Stephen Hill

Dillon. Through a Sinn Féin TD, Dr Frank Ferran, Molloy was introduced to Batt O'Connor, and told O'Connor that his superiors wanted him to join the British Secret Service, but he'd do so only if he could pass information to Collins. Thereafter, Liam Tobin, Tom Cullen or Frank Thornton would meet Molloy in the Cairo Café or Kidd's, but they never trusted him.[44] His true identity was known almost from the start, having been revealed by Piaras Béaslaí's cousin, Lily Mernin, who was typist for Colonel Hill Dillon.[45] Molloy was killed on 25 March 1920 outside the Wicklow Hotel by a team led by Mick McDonnell.[46]

As a guerrilla army relying on secrecy and mobility, the IRA was rarely in a position to punish suspected spies by holding them prisoner. Instead the republicans inflicted a variety of other punishments on these suspects. Richard Mulcahy's claim, however, that 'none of these people would have been killed if they could have been otherwise effectively disposed of either as direct or indirect murderers, and a danger to our whole organisation' by simply keeping away from them seems highly improbable.[47] Collins justified the killing of those deemed to be informers by saying 'we had no jails and we therefore had to kill all spies, informers, and double-crossers'.[48] Florence O'Donoghue concurred: 'The absence of any facilities for the detention of prisoners made it impossible to deal with the doubtful cases. In practice, there was no alternative between execution and complete immunity'. (As discussed below, the Irish execution of 'spies and informers' has come under greater scrutiny in recent histories, and there are differing views whether some were executed for sectarian or societal reasons, rather than because they were actually spies. However classified, these executions and assassinations were forms of terror used by the Irish in order to exercise control over the population or those who may have considered helping the British. See the discussion of 'spies and informers' in Chapter 4.)

Dave Neligan was one of Collins's most reliable agents and his ability to place himself at the centre of the British administration is almost unbelievable. Originally, he joined the DMP 'to get away from a boring country life'; his DMP badge was No. 46. He hated the work and left the DMP on 11 May 1920; when he went home to Limerick, Collins sent word for him to return to Dublin. Neligan said he hated working for the British in the Castle; he 'would join a flying column, do anything but go back to the Castle'. At Collins's request, however, he returned to become the 'spy in the castle'.[49] Collins told him that there were plenty of men to join columns, but that his contacts and placement in Dublin Castle were vital for the intelligence operation. Neligan convinced his employers in the Castle that his life was in danger back in Limerick, and rejoined the service. Then he joined the English Secret Service in May 1921 and became Agent No. 68 assigned to the district of Dalkey, Kingstown (Dun Laoghaire) and Blackrock. When Neligan joined the Secret Service, he was warmly congratulated by the British major, who shook his hand and said 'Try to join the IRA, my boy, try to join the IRA!' Neligan was so successful in convincing the British he was on their side, that he later received pensions from the British as well as the Irish governments: an old IRA pension, one from the Irish Police, another from the Irish civil service, as well as still others from the RIC and British Secret Service.

Lily Mernin was 'identified' as one of Collins's most important sources, 'Lt G'.[50] She was able to recommend and recruit other typists in British military offices throughout Dublin, including Sally McAsey who married Frank Saurin. Mernin was supplying information to Collins on the British military just as Broy was supplying information on the DMP. She was employed by Colonel Stephen Hill Dillon in British offices in Parkgate Street and also worked for Major Stratford Burton, the garrison adjutant at Ship Street Barracks. Mernin would walk up and down the streets of Dublin on the arm of Cullen or Saurin, pointing out British agents who worked in Dublin Castle. She also went to matches at Lansdowne Road Stadium with Cullen and pointed out agents.

> One of the contacts referred to, who was invaluable to us was a girl named Miss Lillie [sic] Mernin. She was employed as Typist in Command Headquarters of Dublin District, the intelligence branch of which was under the control of Colonel Hill Dillon, Chief Intelligence Officer. This girl put us in touch with other members of the different staffs working for the British Military in Dublin. This girl worked mainly with Frank Saurin and is one to whom a large amount of the credit for the success of Intelligence must go. She is at present employed at G.H.Q., Irish Army, Parkgate Street.[51]

Collins, like the others in his intelligence department, often used the ploy of walking down a street linked arm in arm with a woman who worked in the British administration and who would squeeze his arm to identify a British officer.

Collins used his contacts everywhere to recruit more sources. He even developed an organisation in the prisons through which he successfully knew everything that happened to prisoners, and many of the gaolers were his sources. If they weren't his sources, they knew that many of their colleagues were reporting to Collins and that affected their actions. The Irish intimidation extended even into the British prison system.

Intelligence depends upon quick and dependable communications. Collins claimed that:

almost fifty percent of the telegraphists in Ireland were either active members of the IRA or employed as operatives in our intelligence department. From the telegraphists we got the code which was changed twice a day by Dublin Castle – immensely simplifying the work of our censor in his handling of Government messages. According to admissions made at Dublin Castle at the time, not one telephone message was sent or received that was not tapped by the IRA.[52]

Intelligence of this sort was not limited to Dublin. In County Cork, Charlie Browne wrote of their knowledge of British deployments before they were made:

Our intelligence staff at Macroom post office succeeded in deciphering a code message from the enemy pertaining to a large round-up in the Macroom–Ballyvourney area. Confirmation was soon received from Cadet O'Carroll at the Castle and almost at once, on June 2nd, the first enemy reinforcements moved into Macroom.[53]

Many of the most effective contributors to the War of Independence never fired a shot, nor were expected to. They were the unseen, all passing on dozens of tiny scraps of detail that allowed the IRA to build profiles of those they intended to kill. Collins and the Irish used every means available to acquire intelligence and keep in touch throughout Ireland: railway workers, clerks, waiters, hotel porters and telephone operators, policemen, sailors and dockers. The Irish Intelligence Department penetrated prisons, postal facilities and government departments from the British headquarters in Dublin Castle to Whitehall itself. Sympathetic postal officials in London, Dublin and generally throughout all of Ireland enabled the Irish service to intercept and decode many of the British cipher messages. Collins particularly used women in all their occupations as they created far less suspicion than men, and the women were not used just as secretaries or office workers, but as couriers for dispatches as well as weapons.[54] That women could be given such vital roles came as a surprise to many men of the time. Todd Andrews wrote upon later meeting Kay Brady that it:

> led me to a concatenation of minor surprises. I had never known anyone who had owned a car except a taxi driver. A car owned and driven by a woman was a complete novelty. Miss Brady and [Ernie] O'Malley [engaged] in much mutual leg-pulling. I had never seen men and women in that relationship before and was impressed by the fact that her mental agility was much greater than his. My education in the qualities of women had begun and it continued as we drove to Carrickmacross.[55]

Collins came from a family in which women were in the majority and where his mother, Marianne, was in charge after the death of his father when Michael was seven. He got used to the idea of strong, resourceful women early in life and he respected such women. He found it natural that women should care for him and he, in turn, appreciated and admired them. He was usually more comfortable in the company of slightly older women– Moya Llewelyn Davies and Lady Hazel Lavery, for example.[56]

Collins simply wouldn't have been able to operate without the aid of his female spies and dispatch carriers. He had a small army of them working for him as secretaries, typists, couriers and landladies of safe houses, and all were devoted to him, though many thought he was difficult to work with because he always concentrated on his work above all else. Lily Mernin, Nancy O'Brien, Molly O'Reilly, Máire Comerford, Eileen McGrane, 'Dilly'

Dicker, Sister Eithne Lawless, Moya Llewelyn Davies, Anna Fitzsimmons, Susan Mason and so many others were invaluable to him.[57]

The women working in clubs, post offices, railway stations, British military and civilian offices, boarding houses, hotels, Dublin Castle, and elsewhere, were in positions to monitor the activities of British agents. All reported to Collins directly, or through intermediaries, and he co-ordinated their disparate information. His detailed and methodical handling of the information meant that every piece of it, no matter how small or seemingly tangential, filled in a piece of the puzzle for Collins.

In 1929, then US Secretary of State Henry Stimson closed most of the American intelligence departments saying: 'Gentlemen do not read each other's mail'. Reading the British correspondence supplied by Ned Broy, Nancy O'Brien, Lily Mernin and others provided the lifeblood of Collins's intelligence incursions into the British civil and military operations.

Molly O'Reilly began working undercover in the United Service Club in 1918 and became a priceless intelligence source for Collins.[58] Molly gathered intelligence on British officers who frequented the Club, supplying Peadar Clancy with their names and private addresses. Things slacked off at the Club and Molly found out that the officers were now going for dancing to a club owned by Countess Markievicz and Charlotte Despard, the Bonne Bouche in Dawson Street, so she subsequently transferred there. She gathered information on officers and identified thirty to thirty-five secret service men, again supplying Clancy with names and addresses. It was a regular occurrence that officers hung up their guns in the gentlemen's room while dancing, and Molly passed that information to Clancy, who passed the weapons on to a porter who delivered them to the IRA QM Dinny O'Callaghan's shop on Capel Street.[59]

Sir James McMahon was director of the Posts and Telegraphs Office at Dublin's General Post Office (GPO) in 1918–19. In late 1919 he called in Nancy O'Brien, Collins's second cousin, who worked in the Post Office administration offices, and pointed out that the management knew of her dedication and work, and wanted to promote her within the department. He explained that they knew that Collins had information even before the officers to whom it was sent had it and they had to have someone they could trust do the work in order to safeguard the information. Because of her abilities, he was going hire her to decode messages in his office.[60] When told of her being given the job, Collins remarked 'Well, Christ, I don't know how they've held their empire for so long. What a bloody intelligence service they have!' Nancy had moved to London at the same time as Collins in 1906, and they were always very close. As a spy, she was invaluable to Collins and she would often spend her lunchtime in the ladies' toilet copying papers to give to him later. Once, when Collins berated her for not finding a message he was particularly interested in, she turned and gave out to him. Later that night, he cycled to her home in Glasnevin and apologised – leaving a present of her favourite 'bulls-eye' candies for her. On another occasion, when she was going to Cork because her father had passed away, Collins asked her to complete a mission for him. He had her carry a load of guns that had just come in from England in her luggage, and Nancy had a policeman help her with the very heavy case.

Eileen McGrane lived at 21 Dawson Street and was a lecturer at the National University (now UCD). Collins, Arthur Griffith and others came to her home for meetings at the flat. It became a part-time office for Collins and Ernie O'Malley during the War of Independence. She wrote:

> Shortly after I took my flat at 21, Dawson St. which was shared by Mary McCarthy and Margot Trench, the Republican government headquarters seemed to have great difficulty in getting suitable rooms for their work. I offered to Michael Collins the use of a small room in the centre of the flat which he was very glad to accept. Of course there was no question of rent. He put into it some office furniture and files of various kinds were deposited in the office. No official personnel were located there. Mick Collins, Tom Cullen, Arthur Griffith and others came from time to time for conferences or to collect or deposit papers. The principals had a key to the door of the flat and access to the key to the office which was in my custody. The only servant we employed was a cleaner, Mrs. McCluskey, whose husband was caretaker in the National Land Bank. He often did guard on the Street outside when Mick Collins came to the office and on one occasion at least gave warning of a raid in the neighbourhood.[61]

The house was raided on 31 December 1920, and McGrane was taken to Dublin Castle where she was interrogated by Colonel Ormonde de l'Épée Winter. He was sure she would talk to him but she spoke not a single word in one and a half hours.[62] Afterward she was imprisoned in Mountjoy Prison, then sent to England to Walton Prison in Liverpool, then returned to Mountjoy. A large bundle of Collins's documents was found in that raid after he foolishly left them there, including many of the documents taken from Dublin Castle, and those of the G-Division, as well as the DMP headquarters daybook that he carried from his foray into Great Brunswick Street police station. It demonstrated a weakness of Collins: he hated to part with files, even when they ceased to be useful, and he never took sufficient precautions to ensure that the people referred to in the files could not be identified. Some documents traced to Éamon (Ned) Broy were found here, leading to his arrest. This was the first intimation the Castle had of the effectiveness of Collins's recruitment within their own ranks, and they began a long process of elimination that led them to Broy.

Women in the intelligence war were not limited to Dublin. In 1919–21, Brigid Lyons Thornton was going to medical school in Galway, then was a doctor at Mercer's Hospital, but also was a courier to Longford and Galway, carrying weapons and ammunition, as well as documents. Whenever confronted on a train or at a roadblock she wrote 'I had recourse to a prayer and a piece of feminine guile'![63]

Josephine Marchmont Brown worked for the British administration in Cork and was as valuable as any spy in Ireland.[64] Her story began when her child was kept by her in-laws in Wales after the death of her husband in Flanders. Josephine had significant bargaining power – as the widow of a member of the British Army and a trusted senior clerk in Cork's Victoria Barracks, she had access to highly sensitive information: information O'Donoghue and his IRA comrades needed desperately. O'Donoghue was trying to build an army from scratch, establishing networks of safe houses, organising raids and sabotaging the British regime, but he was frequently coming up short on the greatest weapon in a guerrilla war campaign – intelligence. He was immediately interested in Josephine's potential as a spy. Josephine explained her role in the barracks and offered to become a spy.

As O'Donoghue set about getting approval to go to Cardiff to kidnap Josephine's son, she began smuggling sensitive information out of the barracks. In November 1920 the IRA executed five civilians accused of being British informers. In reprisal, British forces attacked Sinn Féin halls and burned safe houses. By now the British suspected that they had a mole in their midst. Realising the growing danger that Josephine was in, O'Donoghue asked Collins if he could lead the kidnap mission to Cardiff himself, and emphasised that it had to be done quickly. The abduction was a success and Reggie, who was now about seven, was smuggled back to Ireland and mother and child were reunited. When Reggie was returned, he stayed with Josephine's sister and she could only meet him in secret for the duration of the war.

Now that the IRA had kept their side of the bargain, Josephine resumed her espionage with renewed vigour. With the war growing dirtier by the day, Josephine's intelligence was of increasing significance to O'Donoghue and the IRA. She obtained details of troop movements, and the Irish were even able to obtain information on informers in their own ranks. Brown eventually rose to become Chief Secretary at British Sixth Division Headquarters with almost unlimited access to sensitive army intelligence information.

The Irish were not the only ones to collect intelligence, and though the British were at a disadvantage in many areas, their intelligence acquisition and analysis improved greatly as the war went on. Colonel Evelyn Lindsay Young served as Intelligence Officer with the Connaught Rangers from 1920–22, and knew how dangerous the 'game' was:

> The collection of intelligence was one of the most interesting and
> risky games over there. Our intelligence was not too intelligent
> and methods employed were sometimes unorthodox; the only rule
> was 'get the information' … the means was most often left to the
> individual.[65]

Throughout 1920 there was a terror and intelligence war between Collins and the Dublin Castle administration. While it never developed into 'open warfare' on the streets of Dublin, there were many killings and assassinations of individual operatives from both sides. It was a savage battle of wits between the Irish and British services, fought without mercy in the shadows. The Castle's efforts were headed by Colonel Ormonde Winter, Chief of the British Combined Intelligence Services in Ireland from the spring of 1920 until the Truce. Despite having no previous full-time experience in intelligence, Winter's brief was to re-organise the shambles that British intelligence in Ireland had become.[66] Winter's biggest contribution was a centralised document archive and the production of meta-data to allow the intelligence to be summarised and disseminated, a very modern concept for the time. Unfortunately, in the pre-computing era the meta-data were lengthy epitomes produced manually, and the procedures for dealing with captured documents were clumsy. The epitomes provided a summary or a quote that was judged to be of particular pertinence. They were a trigger mechanism whereby a military or police unit could call for the original document if they thought they would act as a basis for further action. Some idea of the amount of work involved may be gathered from the fact that in the Dublin District area from October 1920 to July 1921, 6,311 raids and searches were carried out, and over 1,200 epitomes of captured documents, some consisting of over 200 pages of foolscap were circulated.[67] Long delays could ensue, however, before the intelligence was shared with the operatives or forces who needed the intelligence in order to function.

The biggest problem for Winter was that, with the exception of Dublin, he did not control military intelligence. This reflected the poor command and control between the two parts of the British security forces. Earlier, the GOC in Ireland, General Nevil Macready, was given the opportunity to control both the police and the army, but turned it down. Thereafter, the police (including the Black and Tans and the Auxiliary Division) and the army often operated independently, with limited intelligence co-operation until the final months of the campaign.[68] In essence, the British intelligence effort under Winter addressed its intelligence shortcomings by deploying many more officers, while still failing to co-ordinate efforts with the War Office, and Army intelligence continued to act independently of the Castle administration. The net result was more and more British operatives, under separate military and civilian commands, never co-ordinating with each other, and the lack of an efficient organisation was telling. In desperation, the British even solicited informers by placing an advert in Irish papers:

During the last 12 months innumerable murders and other
outrages have been committed by those who call themselves

members of the Irish Republican Army. Only by the help of self-respecting Irishmen can these murders be put a stop to.

It is possible to send letters containing information in such a way as to prevent them being stopped in the post.

If you have information to give and you are willing to help the cause of Law and Order act as follows:

Write your information on ordinary notepaper being careful to give neither your name nor your address. Remember also to disguise your handwriting, or else to print the words. Put it into an envelope addressed to:

D.W. Ross

Poste Restante

G.P.O. London

Enclose this envelope in another. (Take care that your outer envelope is not transparent.) Put it with a small piece of paper asking the recipient to forward the D.W. Ross letter as soon as he receives it. Address the outer envelope to some well disposed friend in England or to any well known business in England.

You will later be given the opportunity, should you wish to do so, of identifying the letter and should the information have proved of value, of claiming a REWARD.

The utmost secrecy will be maintained as to all information received.

Notes

[1] P. McMahon, *British Spies and Irish Rebels—British Intelligence in Ireland: 1916–1945* (Suffolk, 2008), p. 2.
[2] C. Von Clausewitz (ed. and trans. M. Howard and P. Paret), *On War* (Princeton, 1984), p. 117.
[3] F. O'Donoghue, *No Other Law* (Dublin, 1986), p. 116.
[4] J. Borgonovo, *Spies, Informers and the Anti-Sinn Féin Society* (Dublin, 2008), pp 135–6.
[5] *Ibid.*, p. 139.
[6] S. Sharkey, 'My role as an intelligence officer with the Third Tipperary Brigade (1919–1921)', *Tipperary Historical Journal* 11 (1998).
[7] F. O'Donoghue, 'Guerilla warfare in Ireland', *An Cosantoir* (1963).
[8] S. Issacharoff and R.H. Pildes, 'Targeted warfare: individuating enemy responsibility', *New York University Law Review* 88 (5) (2013). See Chapter 4 for discussion of assassinations as a form of terror.
[9] J.F. Murphy Jr., 'Michael Collins and the craft of intelligence', *International Journal of Intelligence and Counterintelligence* 17 (2) (2010).

[10] A. Mitchell, *A Revolutionary Government in Ireland: Dáil Éireann 1919–1922* (Dublin, 1995); M. Kotsonouris, *Retreat from Revolution, The Dáil Courts, 1920–1924* (Dublin, 1994).

[11] Smith was also known as 'Smyth'. He was the one who smuggled out the information on the 'Castle Document' from Dublin Castle prior to the Rising. See D. White, 'The Castle Document', *History Ireland* 24 (4) (2016). Smith was also the brother of DMP G-Division Detective Patrick 'Dog' Smith, the first G-man Collins had executed. Eugene Smyth: Witness Statement 334.

[12] Éamon Broy and Eugene Smyth, in U. MacEoin (ed.), *Survivors: The Story of Ireland's Struggle as Told Through Some of Her Outstanding Living People. Notes 1913–1916* (Dublin, 1996), pp 52–4.

[13] Éamon Broy: Witness Statement 1280.

[14] M.R. Cremin, 'Fighting on their own terms: the tactics of the Irish Republican Army, 1919–1921', *Small Wars and Insurgencies* 26 (6) (2015).

[15] Murphy, 'Michael Collins and the craft of intelligence'.

[16] 'Record of the rebellion in Ireland in 1920–1921 and the part played by the army in dealing with it', Imperial War Museum, Box 78/82/2.

[17] Cabinet Memorandum: 'The present military situation in Ireland and the proposed military policy during the coming winter', General Macready, 6 August 1920. PRO CAB/24/110/50.

[18] See Chapter 4 for discussion of the trauma caused by the policy of ostracism.

[19] D. Figgis, *Recollections of the Irish War* (London, 1927), p. 282.

[20] 'Record of the rebellion in Ireland in 1920–1921', Imperial War Museum.

[21] 'Our duty', *An tÓglach*, 15 June 1920.

[22] R. Popplewell, 'Lacking intelligence: some reflections on recent approaches to British counter-insurgence 1900–1960', *Intelligence and National Security* 10 (2) (1995).

[23] 'Record of the rebellion in Ireland in 1920–1921', Imperial War Museum; Lt Gen. Sir Hugh Jeudwine Papers, Imperial War Museum, Box 72/82/2.

[24] *Ibid.*

[25] P. Béaslaí, *How It Was Done—I.R.A. Intelligence: Dublin's Fighting Story* (London, 1926), quoted by Frank Thornton: Witness Statement 615.

[26] P. Hart, *Mick* (London, 2006), p. 205.

[27] Liam Tobin: Witness Statement 1753.

[28] M. Collins, (ed. F. Costello), *Michael Collins: In His Own Words* (Dublin, 1997), pp 80–1.

[29] Tony Woods, in U. MacEoin (ed.), *Survivors: The Story of Ireland's Struggle as Told Through Some of Her Outstanding Living People. Notes 1913–1916* (Dublin, 1996), p. 322.

[30] P. Béaslaí, *Michael Collins and the Making of a New Ireland* (London, 1926), p. 319.

[31] Joseph Leonard: Witness Statement 547.

[32] General Paddy Daly: Witness Statement 387.

[33] W.J. Stapleton, 'A Volunteer's story', *Irish Independent*, 1916 Golden Jubilee Supplement (April 1966).

[34] U. O'Connor, *Michael Collins and the Troubles: the Struggle for Irish Freedom 1912–1922* (New York, 1996), p. 143; W.J. Stapleton, 'Michael Collins's Squad', *Capuchin Annual* (1969); William Stapleton: Witness Statement 822.

[35] Bridget (Mrs Batt) O'Connor: Witness Statement 330.

[36] C. Younger, *Ireland's Civil War* (New York, 1979), p. 99.

[37] General Patrick Daly: Witness Statement 387.

[38] *The Times*, 23 January 1920.

[39] Dave Neligan, quoted in K. Griffith and T. O'Grady, *Ireland's Unfinished Revolution, An Oral History* (London, 1982), pp 164–5.

[40] *Ibid.*

[41] David Neligan: Witness Statement 380; General Patrick Daly: Witness Statement 387.

[42] Michael Murphy: Witness Statement 1547.

[43] Dave Neligan named him Bernard Hugh Mulloy – D. Neligan, *The Spy in the Castle* (London, 1999), p. 72. Peter Hart named him Patrick Molloy – Hart, *Mick*, p. 238 *et seq.*

[44] Liam Tobin: Witness Statement 1753; Frank Thornton: Witness Statement 615.

[45] Lily Mernin: Witness Statement 441.

[46] Michael McDonnell: Witness Statement 225.

[47] R. Mulcahy, Béaslaí critique, Vol. 2, p. 46 (see explanatory note in Bibliography).

[48] Hart, *Mick*, pp 212–14.

[49] Neligan, *The Spy in the Castle*, p. 68 *et seq.*

[50] M. Ryan, *Michael Collins and the Women in His Life* (Dublin, 1996), p. 70; Lily Mernin: Witness Statement 441. Rex Taylor did not determine the identity of 'Lt G.', but he wrote, 'so far as the present writer could ascertain, Lieutenant 'G' was a member of the British Military Intelligence in Ireland. He [*sic*] was also one of Collins' chief agents as well as being a particular confidant of his': R. Taylor, *Michael Collins* (London, 1958), pp 126–9.

[51] Frank Thornton: Witness Statement 615.

[52] H. Talbot, *Michael Collins' Own Story* (London, 1923), p. 85.

[53] C. Browne, *The Story of the 7th. A Concise History of the 7th Battalion Cork No. 1 Brigade I.R.A. from 1915–1921* (Macroom, 1971), p. 156.

[54] See J. Connell, *Unequal Patriots* (Dublin, 2017).

[55] C.S. Andrews, *Dublin Made Me* (Cork, 1979), p. 240.

[56] See S. McCoole, *Hazel, A Life of Lady Lavery* (Dublin, 1996), *Guns and Chiffon* (Dublin, 1997), *No Ordinary Women, Irish Female Activists in the Revolutionary Years* (Dublin, 2003).

[57] See Ryan, *Michael Collins and the Women in His Life.*

[58] 'Remembering the past: Molly O'Reilly', *An Phoblacht*, 7 October 1999.

[59] Author's correspondence and documents from Clare Cowley, granddaughter of Molly O'Reilly, http://mspcsearch.militaryarchives.ie/docs/files//PDF_Pensions/R2/MSP34REF2032 5MaryTCorcoran/W34E4055MaryTCorcoran.pdf. See Molly O'Reilly, in T. Fagan (ed.), *Rebels and Heroes. Hidden Stories from Dublin's Northside* (Dublin 2016), p. 54 *et seq.*

[60] J.B.E. Hittle, *Michael Collins and the Anglo-Irish War: Britain's Counter-insurgency Failure* (Chicago, 2007), pp 78, 131–2, 152.

[61] Eileen McCarville (née McGrane): Witness Statement 1752.

[62] M.T. Foy, *Michael Collins's Intelligence War* (Stroud, 2006), p. 198.

[63] Dr Brigid Thornton (née Lyons): Witness Statement 259.

[64] A. Quinlan, 'The Mother who turned IRA spy to save her son', *Irish Independent*, 25 November 2012.

[65] T. Ryle Dwyer, *Big Fellow, Long Fellow*, pp 137–8.

[66] C. Andrew, *Her Majesty's Secret Service: The Making of the British Intelligence Community* (New York, 1986), p. 255.

[67] O. Winter, *Winter's Tale* (London, 1955), pp 307–8.

[68] G. Pattison, 'The British Army's effectiveness in the Irish Campaign 1919–1921, and the lessons for modern counterinsurgency operations, with special reference to C3I aspects', UK Ministry of Defence (1999).

2. The intelligence war leads to terror

The attacks caused complete panic in Dublin Castle. ... The attack was so well organised, so unexpected, and so ruthlessly executed that the effect was paralysing. It can be said that the enemy never recovered from the blow. While some of the worst killers escaped, they were thoroughly frightened.

David Neligan

The intelligence war continued to escalate with terror on both sides, and on 21 November 1920, in the quiet of a Dublin Sunday, small crews of IRA gunmen began the systematic assassination of a group of specially trained and recruited secret servicemen, mostly MI5 and SIS specialists, in the most noted intelligence coup in Dublin in attacks that became known as Bloody Sunday.[1] This British unit had been recruited in London the summer of 1920, and placed in the charge of Major C.A. Cameron. In all, sixty agents were trained and despatched to Ireland. It now appears certain that the majority of the men assassinated were British officers engaged in undercover work, although the Irish made some mistakes in identification, and court-martial officers and civilians were killed in error.[2]

Earlier that month, Prime Minister Lloyd George had confidently assured his audience at London's Guildhall that the IRA was on the verge of defeat, and that the British 'had murder on the run'.[3] The attack, coming as it did when the British forces felt they had the IRA breaking, was a momentous act of reassertion. Its timing was also crucial for the Irish, since it had become apparent to the police, and certainly to Collins, that the IRA boycott of the police was beginning to falter, and general allegiance to the Republican cause could be weakening. Hence, Bloody Sunday not only removed a major threat to the IRA but also simultaneously gave a warning to the Irish people that any weakening of their resolve to continue the struggle and support the guerrillas would not be tolerated.[4] The Irish were well aware of the need to use terror to intimidate their own people on occasion.

Intelligence chiefs in London were pragmatic: their goal was to locate Michael Collins, thus severing the head from the body of the IRA. Collins was aware of the intensification and knew that he would have to move soon to meet it. He received information from a contact in Scotland Yard that this group of men was coming to Dublin with the avowed intent to smash the IRA/Volunteers, and particularly Collins's intelligence operation. The Irish could not defeat the British in pitched battles, but they could 'put out the eyes and ears' of the intelligence service upon which the military relied.[5]

In late 1920 that special intelligence unit was organised by the British into one whose ultimate purpose was to break Collins's organisation. The strategy chosen by this group was simple: they intended to assassinate the political members of Sinn Féin who were moving openly in public, or who were involved in the military struggle. Having done this, they felt that the IRA would be bound to make some moves that would flush its other leaders to the surface. After September 1920 the number of raids increased and intense searches were carried out nightly in the city. The men effecting this policy became known as the 'Cairo Gang'.[6]

While the origin of the name 'Cairo Gang' is obscure, some of the British agents had served with military intelligence in Egypt during World War I. Captain Robert D. Jeune was assigned to the RIC Special Branch in Dublin and noted:

> After a short course at Hounslow, we were sent over to Dublin in the early summer of 1920. The first batch were instructed to pose, initially, as Royal Engineer officers, but this rather futile procedure was soon dropped and the work consisted of getting to know the town thoroughly, tailing 'Shinners' and carrying out small raids, with a view to collecting all possible information which lead us to eventually stamping out the revolt.
>
> In November, [1920] information was coming in well and we were beginning to get on top of the IRA, who were becoming desperate. I happened to receive information from three different sources to the effect that something was going to happen, but there was nothing definite.[7]

Jeune was on the Irish execution list for Bloody Sunday but slipped out of

28 Upper Pembroke Street just before the attacks, and said 'those of us who had survived were shut up under guard in a hotel where it was impractical to do any useful work'.[8] As to be discussed below, the attacks changed the British intelligence effort, but hardly 'paralysed' it.

Colonel Ormonde Winter controlled and activated the Cairo Gang in Ireland. The IRA/Volunteers knew him as the 'Holy Terror' because he was always prepared to descend to the most extreme methods to obtain information from prisoners. Some British held him in no higher regard, as he was known to Mark Sturgis as 'a wicked little white snake … probably entirely non-moral … knows several languages, is a super sleuth, and a most amazing original'.[9] In October Winter organised the Central Raid Bureau to co-ordinate the activities of his agents and the Auxiliaries. Soon they began to make their presence felt. The Cairo Gang was ruthless and efficient, and had been primarily responsible for tracking down Dan Breen and Seán Treacy, killing Treacy in Talbot Street on 14 October 1920.

Two men, Peter Ames and George Bennett, directed the so-called Gang. These individuals maintained liaison with three veterans of the campaign, Lieutenant H.R. Angliss (alias Patrick 'Paddy' McMahon), who had been recalled from Russia to organise intelligence in South Dublin; a mysterious Irishman by the name of 'Lt Charles Peel'; and D.L. McLean, the chief of intelligence at Dublin Castle. Besides being more experienced intelligence operatives than those working earlier in Ireland, the members of the Gang increased the threat to the Irish because they immediately reorganised the British intelligence effort, which until their arrival had been decentralised and unco-ordinated. They moved quickly to correct weaknesses.[10]

Although the Irish were aware that changes were taking place on the British side, it was some time before they ascertained the identities of members of the Cairo Gang. Their first break came following the execution of John Aloysius Lynch, a Dáil/Republican Court judge and county councillor from Killmallock, Co. Limerick. Lynch was mistakenly killed in the Royal Exchange Hotel on 23 September 1920 by a detail led by Capt. G.T. Baggalley, who was subsequently killed on Bloody Sunday. Some feel John was mistaken for Liam Lynch, but probably not.[11] John was much older than Liam, so they should not have been mistaken for one another. Lynch had just delivered £23,000 to Collins for the Dáil Loan, but that was his only connection to the IRA/Volunteers. After this episode, Lieutenant Angliss, drunk and despondent, divulged his participation in the execution to a girl, who inadvertently passed this information to an Irish informant. Further members of the group were identified after an unwitting landlady revealed to another Irish informant that several of her British guests regularly went out very late in the evening. At the time Dublin was under a strict curfew, and only authorised personnel were allowed on the streets. The Squad took the individuals in question under observation, and they determined that the men were in contact with previously identified members of the Gang. To the Squad, this meant that they were instrumentally involved with the Cairo Gang. In fact, the British had set up their organisation 'on proper continental lines with a Central Headquarters and other houses forming minor centres throughout the city'.[12]

For months Collins watched the British get closer and closer. From their first appearance in Dublin he began gathering information on them, and found they usually were living as private citizens in respectable rooming houses. He set his own spies to open their correspondence, had the contents of their wastepaper baskets taken by the housemaids, and had duplicate keys made for their rooms. Crucially, the IRA co-opted most of the Irish domestic staff who worked in the rooming houses where the officers lived, and all of their comings and goings were meticulously recorded by servants and reported to Collins's staff. Lily Mernin was then working at Ship Street Barracks for Major Stratford Burton, the garrison adjutant, and she was one of Collins's most valuable sources operating under her secret alias of 'Lt. G'.[13] Major Burton was in charge of court-martial proceedings, as well as being in charge of the billeting of the various military posts throughout Dublin, and Mernin would always make an extra carbon copy of all reports and documents for Collins. Mernin was instrumental in locating the residence addresses of the British military officers assigned to Dublin:

> Before the 21st November 1920, it was part of my normal duty to type the names and addresses of British agents who were accommodated at private addresses and living as ordinary citizens of the city. These lists were typed weekly and amended whenever an address was changed. I passed them on each week to the address at Moynihan's, Clonliffe Rd. or to Piaras Béaslaí. The typing of the lists ceased after the 21st November 1920.[14]

Locating and eliminating Collins had become the prime goal of all the British intelligence organisations, and they were getting close. In an October meeting in the Cairo Café on Grafton Street, a member of the Gang joined Tom Cullen, Frank Thornton and Frank Saurin as they were drinking and pretending to be British spies. The real British officer said to them: 'Surely you fellows know Liam Tobin, Tom Cullen and Frank Thornton – these are Collins's three officers and if you can get them we can locate Collins'.[15] If they knew the names of his intelligence officers – numbers one, two and three of his intelligence staff – though not knowing what any one of them looked like, the British were getting uncomfortably close. It boded ill for any of Collins's men who fell into their hands at that time.

It was not paranoia on the part of the IRA leadership in Dublin that the net was closing about them. British intelligence was mounting raids that yielded vital clues about the IRA's operations and were, it was feared, close to actually capturing the likes of Collins and Mulcahy. In the first two weeks of November the Gang detained some of Collins's closest advisors. They held Frank Thornton for ten days but he managed to convince them he had nothing to do with Sinn Féin. On 10 November they just missed capturing Richard Mulcahy. On 13 November they raided Vaughan's Hotel and questioned Liam Tobin and Tom Cullen, but let them go. Collins, Cathal Brugha, Mulcahy and the military and intelligence leadership felt they had no choice but to attack.

Mulcahy had almost been captured in that November raid, and commented: 'We were being made to feel that they were very close on the heels of some of us'. He made it quite clear about the responsibility of those against whom the IRA directed their operations on Bloody Sunday:

> They were members of a spy organisation that was a murder
> organisation. Their murderous intent was directed against the
> effective members of the Government as well as against GHQ and
> staff at the Dublin Brigade.[16]

The entire Irish intelligence organisation was mobilised to track down the British agents, and Frank Thornton and Charlie Dalton exploited every source in Dublin. Individuals reported British who were out after curfew, DMP Constable Patrick Mannix identified suspects living in Upper Mount

Street, and David Neligan and James McNamara worked all their sources in the Castle. There was even a source in the Auxiliaries 'F' Company, where Sergeant John Charles Reynolds sold information to the IRA.[17] Collins waited and accumulated evidence before he went to the cabinet to seek authorisation for his operation.[18] Because of the scale of the operation, Collins needed the approval of a Dáil cabinet and government that ordinarily distanced itself from IRA actions. The design was developed in absolute secrecy, with meticulous planning and ruthless execution.

On Wednesday, 17 November 1920, Collins sent the following memo to Dick McKee, brigadier of the Dublin brigade: 'Have established addresses of the particular ones. Arrangements should now be made about the matter. Lt. G is aware of things. He [sic] suggests the 21st, a most suitable date and day I think. M'.

Collins had devised a codename for the targets: 'the Particular Ones'. The plan was brutal and simple. Surround the buildings with scouts, lookouts and gunmen. For each building, eight to ten men to rush the entrance, two to four men left outside to act as scouts and lookouts. Take the carpeted stairs two at a time, kick in doors, identify the target, and shoot to kill at point-blank range. Any incriminating papers found with the dead would be a bonus.

Collins, Brugha, Mulcahy, McKee, Peadar Clancy and others examined the cases of over fifty British officers at their 35 Lower Gardiner Street meeting on 20 November. The names of fifteen out of the fifty men selected for assassination were turned down because of insufficient evidence.[19] Brugha, as Minister for Defence, was very conscientious and adamant in his judgment – if there were the slightest loophole for uncertainty about an agent or spy, then that individual would be removed from the submitted list. It is a measure of the discipline of the supposed 'murder gang' run by Collins that Brugha's opinion held sway and was obeyed. Nevertheless, while earlier historians accepted that each man killed passed through a rigorous process of elimination before being placed on the list for execution, more recent research questions whether some of the men killed might not all have been intelligence officers and some were less experienced than previously thought.[20] Further, at least two of those killed were innocent civilians. Fate also had a part to play. Many of the targeted men were simply not at home when the IRA raided. Some were, in fact, out on raids of their own that morning.

The operation was to start at 9.00 am sharp. Collins told them all 'it's to be done exactly at nine. Neither before nor after. These whores [the British] have got to learn that Irishmen can turn up on time.'[21] Paddy Daly, leader of Collins's Squad, was not one of the men assigned to carry out the attacks on Bloody Sunday, but he was intimately involved in the organisation and planning. In fact, there was a member of the Squad in each group. Daly recalled in precise detail how the attacks were planned:

The four Battalions of the Brigade were engaged, and the O.C. of each Battalion was responsible for a certain area, not his own area because most of the spies were grouped in certain districts. If the 2nd Battalion Volunteers had been confined to their own area, they would not have done anything but the Gresham Hotel job. All other operations allotted to the 2nd Battalion were outside their Battalion area, in fact they were in the 3rd Battalion area.

Seán Russell picked the men for the various operations, and in every case he appointed a member of the Squad in charge of the various groups.

There were five operations allotted to the 2nd Battalion and five different groups were appointed to carry them out. In other words, the 2nd Battalion had 13 spies to deal with. One operation, on the east end, did not come off as the spies had left that address the previous day and there was nobody in the home when the Volunteers went there. The other eleven were all accounted for.

Joe Leonard was in charge of Baggot Street; Tom Keogh was in charge of 22 Lower Mount Street; I cannot remember who was in charge of Upper Mount Street, it was probably Seán Doyle; Paddy Moran was in charge in the Gresham Hotel. Paddy Moran was not a member of the Squad but he volunteered for the work. He was Captain of 'D' Company of the 2nd Battalion, and on that account Seán Russell did not put a member of the Squad in charge of the Gresham Hotel operation, knowing that he could not improve on Paddy Moran. Paddy Moran was not in Mount Street on Bloody Sunday. The evidence that was sworn against him was that he was in Mount Street and was sentenced to death for the Mount St. job. The arrangements for the Bloody Sunday operations were made by Dick McKee.

… The four Battalions were represented at this meeting in the Printers' Hall, and I was there as O/C of the Squad. Details were given to us about the various houses that were to be raided and we got detailed descriptions of the individuals who were to be eliminated … At this meeting Dick McKee questioned every officer in charge of operations as to their reconnoitring of their positions and the arrangements they had for getting their men back to the North side of the city, because the operations were taking place on the South side. He impressed on them that they were to be careful of the bridges on the way back. The 2nd Battalion had arranged to commandeer a ferry-boat to take the men across the Liffey to get back to the North side.

At this meeting Seán Russell put me in charge of all the operations, instructing me to have some first-aid people at No 17 North Richmond Street, the house of Mrs. Byrne. He also told me that I was to take up my position there and make any arrangements I could to go to the assistance of anyone who might be wounded during the operations. I did not like this because it would be the first time since the Squad was formed that the men would be going into action without me, but I was told that I was not going because I had other business to do. Dick McKee turned and said 'Paddy, I'm not going either. Have you not full confidence in the men appointed?' Of course I told him I had. He explained to me that Seán Russell got instructions to appoint all the officers for all their various operations in the city, and he paid the Squad the great compliment of putting them in charge of the various groups even outside their own Battalion area.

Operations were timed for nine o'clock on Bloody Sunday, and at about 8.15 a.m. I saw each group leave for its objective.

The first to return to North Richmond Street was Tom Keogh, bringing with him Billy McClean [sic] who had been wounded in the hand. They told me that when they were coming out of 22 Mount Street on the completion of their task, a lorryload of [Black and] Tans, who had heard the shooting, pulled up and started to dismount. Tom Keogh immediately gathered his men in the hall and told them they might not get time to attack. 'We must attack first', said Tom. He swung open the hall door, absolutely charged the Tans, and succeeded in wounding or killing one of them. The lorry then drove off and left some Tans on the ground, but the party did not wait to see whether they were alive or dead.

… As the various reports came in we discovered that Frank Teeling was missing. Tom Keogh said that Teeling had not been shot coming out from the house in Mount Street. He also said that all the men left the house but that Teeling may have gone out the back way. A few hours afterwards, toward mid-day, we heard that Frank Teeling had been wounded and captured. This was a big disappointment to everybody.

Teeling and McClean were the only two casualties we had in the four operations.

There was an all-Ireland match in Croke Park that Sunday and all Volunteers who had taken part in the operations spoke about going to it. I advised them to keep away from Croke Park because I knew there were bound to be spotters and spies round the turn-stiles. There were servant girls and landladies in the houses our men had visited that morning and we had no guarantee that they were friendly. The obvious place to find anybody of an Irish-Ireland outlook that day would be Croke Park.

Tom Keogh jokingly remarked that it was a good-looking maid who opened the door for him and that he made a date with her. That was Tom's attitude.[22]

Seán Russell was the 27-year-old commandant of the 2nd Battalion, and shared McKee's organising intensity. His contribution to 2nd Battalion operations is not adequately recognised, and while Collins and McKee devised and produced this operation, Russell was its unacknowledged director. It was Russell who determined that the British were most vulnerable on Sunday mornings when most of them slept late and the assassination units were most likely to surprise armed and experienced enemy soldiers. In recounting life in Dublin, one British officer wrote disparagingly:

No one is ever astir before ten o'clock, and the vast army of RI constables, DM police, ex-officers, servants and lady clerks which had been assembled in the Castle to put down the Sinn Féin rebellion did not take long to capture the careless rapture of Irish slothfulness, and used to remain abed until the sun had warmed the day.[23]

Russell reduced the risk of leaks and the time for doubts by waiting until the last few days to brief those going on the raids. Each group would be led by a Squad member, and each group would be accompanied by GHQ intelligence officers to seize papers and other documents. Russell planned simultaneous attacks so no British could take defensive measures, and the Irish would escape straight home if they lived on the south side, or immediately back to the north side of the Liffey before the British closed the bridges.

On the morning of 21 November the operation began at 9am, exactly as planned. Some of the men targeted refused to come out of their rooms and were shot in bed. Others came to the door and were shot as they opened it. The killings were finished by 9.30. That Sunday marked the starkest and most shocking point in the War of Independence, a struggle defined by guerrilla tactics, formidable intelligence, terror, selective assassination, intimidation and ruthless execution. Members of the IRA/Volunteers from all the Dublin units took part, and some would never recover completely from the nerve-shattering work of that morning.[24]

Collins's men went out to kill thirty-five that Sunday, but some of them could not be found. The publicised and 'official' figures stated that eleven officers were killed and four escaped. The dead included British Intelligence officers, British Army courts-martial officers, two Auxiliaries, Temp Cadet F. Garniss and Temp Cadet C.A. Morris,[25] an RIC constable, a number of soldiers in the wrong place at the wrong time and two civilians. In fact, eleven British officers, two Auxiliary Cadets and two civilians (T.H. Smith and L.E. Wilde) were killed in eight locations:

92 Baggot Street Lower: Captain W.F. Newberry (a courts-martial officer).
119 Baggot Street Lower: Captain George (Geoffrey) T. Baggally (a one-legged courts-martial officer.)

28 Earlsfort Terrace: Sergeant John Fitzgerald (he was in the RIC and was probably killed for that alone, as the Squad asked for 'Colonel Fitzpatrick').

117–119 Morehampton Road: Captain Donald L. MacLean (an intelligence officer at Dublin Castle); T.H. Smith (a civilian land-lord not engaged in intelligence).

22 Lower Mount Street: Lieutenant H.R. Angliss (alias Patrick 'Paddy' McMahon; he was a British intelligence agent); Auxiliary Cadets Carniss and Morris.

38 Upper Mount Street: Lieutenant Peter Ashmunt Ames; Captain George Bennett. (Ames and Bennett were leaders of the intelligence unit.)

28–29 Pembroke Street Upper: Major C.M.G. Dowling (a British intelligence officer); Colonel Hugh F. Montgomery (a staff officer 'in the wrong place' who took three weeks to die from his wounds); Captain Leonard Price (a British intelligence officer).

Upper Sackville Street, Gresham Hotel: Captain Patrick Mac-Cormack (almost certainly buying horses for the Alexandria Turf Club and not engaged in intelligence activity at all); L.E. Wilde (a civilian).

Colonel Wilfred James Woodcock DSO, Lancashire Fusiliers, Lieutenant R.G. Murray, Royal Scots, and Captain B.C.H. Keenlyside, Lancashire Fusiliers, were all wounded at 28 Upper Pembroke Street. Woodcock was not connected with intelligence and had walked into a confrontation on the first floor of the Pembroke Street house as he was preparing to leave to command a regimental parade at army headquarters. He was in his military uniform and, when he shouted to warn the other five British officers living in the house, he was shot in the shoulder and back, but survived. While he was not an intelligence agent, Woodcock certainly knew that many of the British staying in the house were engaged in intelligence activities. His wife Caroline wrote of those she called 'hush-hush men', who 'came in and out at odd hours'.[26] As Keenlyside was about to be shot, a struggle ensued between his wife and Mick O'Hanlon. The leader of the unit, Mick Flanagan, arrived, pushed Mrs Keenlyside out of the way and shot her husband. John Caldow, MacLean's brother-in-law and a former soldier with the Royal

Scots Fusiliers, was wounded at 117 Morehampton Road. 'Lt Charles Peel', the alias of an unidentified British agent staying at 22 Lower Mount Street, escaped unscathed, amongst others.

Of those killed by the IRA, Ames, Angliss, Bennett, Dowling, MacLean and Price were intelligence officers. Baggally and Newberry were Courts Martial officers not involved with intelligence. Fitzgerald was a policeman, who was probably mistaken for someone else. Smith was the landlord of a house where some of the army men were staying and was killed by mistake. Morris and Carniss were Auxiliaries on their way to warn the barracks, as was Montgomery, who happened to be in the wrong place at the wrong time.[27] McCormack and Wilde appear to have been incorrectly targeted or possibly were innocent ex-officers.

Captain Patrick McCormack was staying in room 22 of the Gresham Hotel and was most likely killed by mistake. (The IRA/Volunteers had asked for room 24. Hugh Callaghan was the doorman who led the IRA to the rooms, and he mistakenly took them to room 22 instead of room 24.) McCormack was really a member of the Royal Medical (Veterinary) Corps and was probably in Dublin to buy polo horses for the garrison in Egypt. Unlike the other British officers, McCormack, a Catholic from Castlebar, was buried in Dublin at Glasnevin Cemetery. Also killed was L.E. Wilde (staying in room 14) who probably had no connection with the army or intelligence.

Paddy Kennedy was one of the Squad:

Seán Russell took charge for that night, and he gave us our instructions for the following morning. He explained that a big swoop was to be made simultaneously on all British agents residing in private houses throughout the city and that the operation was to be carried out at nine o'clock sharp. He detailed Paddy Moran to take his party to the Gresham Hotel and eliminate three British Intelligence Officers who were stopping there. Lieutenant-Colonel Wilde and Captain McCormack were two of the British agents; I cannot remember the name of the third man. I arranged with Paddy Moran to meet him next morning in North Earl Street. I met him as arranged and we proceeded to the Gresham Hotel. As we entered the hotel the other members of our party, who were in

the vicinity, came in after us. Our first job was to disconnect the
telephone. As we knew the rooms in which the Intelligence agents
were located, our party split up, as pre-arranged, and proceeded to
the rooms allotted to them by Paddy Moran. I remained with
Paddy Moran while the shootings were taking place. There were
people in the dining-room and we took up position at the door
and held them there. Two British agents were eliminated that
morning, the third man escaped. He was a Catholic, I believe, and
had gone out to early Mass. The whole operation lasted less than
ten minutes.[28]

The Volunteers in the Gresham were under the command of Patrick
(Paddy) Moran.[29] He was hanged on 14 March 1921 in Mountjoy Prison
for participation in the Bloody Sunday executions at Baggot Street Lower.
He was not actually there, and while he was a prisoner at Kilmainham Gaol
he had an opportunity to escape, but refused it knowing he was not guilty
of the crime with which he was charged.

James Doyle was manager of the Gresham at the time:

At about 9 o'clock in the morning of 'Bloody Sunday' I was in
bed in my room and was awakened by noise. It was a muffled sort
of thing like the beating of a carpet. The porter called up to my
room afterwards and I asked him what was the noise I had heard.
He said that Captain McCormack, who was occupying a room
quite close to me, had been shot dead. I got out of bed and
entered Captain McCormack's room and I saw that he was then
dead.

The porter also told me that another man had been shot dead in
a room on the next floor over Captain McCormack's. I went to
this room also and saw the dead man. His surname was Wilde. I
was totally ignorant of what took place or why these men were
shot at the time.

I questioned the porter and he told me that a number of armed
men had entered the hotel and asked to be shown to the rooms
occupied by these two men.

McCormack had been staying here since September and had

made purchases of race horses. He had booked his passage back to Egypt for December by the Holt Line. Although he had been a Veterinary Surgeon in the British Army there would appear to have been grave doubt as to his being associated with British Intelligence. While he was here I never saw him receiving any guests. He slept well into the afternoon and only got up early when a Race Meeting was on. When I found him shot in his room, 'Irish Field' was lying beside him.

I mentioned to Collins after the Truce that there was a grave doubt as to Captain McCormack being a British Agent. He said that he would make inquiries into the matter, but after this the matter was never referred to again.

Mr. Wilde had been here for a considerable time before 'Bloody Sunday'. When Archbishop Clune visited this hotel again subsequently, I mentioned the shootings to him and he told me that Wilde had been put out of Spain; that he was well-known there as a British Agent.[30]

Archbishop Clune's statement notwithstanding, there is no further evidence that Wilde was a British agent.

In 1922 McCormack's mother petitioned the Irish government, claiming her son was a completely innocent victim. Collins wrote to Richard Mulcahy, in Mulcahy's role as Minister for Defence, telling him how the matter should be handled. Collins's letter to Mulcahy deflected the blame for the incorrect selection to the Dublin Brigade:

With reference to the case, you will remember that I stated on a former occasion that we had no evidence that he was a secret service agent. You will also remember that several of the names of the November 21st cases were just regular officers. Some of the names were put forth by the Dublin Brigade. So far as I remember, McCormack's name was one of these. In my opinion, it would be as well to tell Mrs McCormack that there was no particular case against her son, but just that he was an enemy soldier.[31]

Some of the targets escaped by not being home, and Collins's men were able to recover only a few papers of import. Groups of men were sent to all of the following addresses and either missed their quarries or they had previously moved:

Eastwood Hotel, 91 Leeson Street Lower: Colonel Thomas
    Jennings, Major Callaghan.
St Andrews's Hotel, Exchequer Street: Auxiliary Frederick Harper-
    Stove.
Shelbourne Hotel, 27 Stephen's Green North: Major William
    Lorraine King.
Upper Fitzwilliam Street: Captain John S. Crawford.
Harcourt Street: Captain Jocelyn Lee Hardy.
28 Upper Mount Street: Major Frank M.H. Carew.
28 Upper Pembroke Street: Auxiliary Captain Robert D. Jeune.
7 Ranelagh Road: Lieutenant William Noble.

Lieutenant William Noble, a British intelligence agent, had rooms at 7 Ranelagh Road and IRA/Volunteers led by Joe Dolan and Dan McDonnell were assigned to kill him, but he wasn't home.[32] Dolan was so angry that he wasn't there that he gave Noble's 'paramour' a 'right scouraging with a sword scabbard. Then he set the room on fire.'[33]

I was one of the organisers of that. I was in the Intelligence
Section and was sent round all the hotels and boarding houses
collecting information from waiters and footmen and others. I had
supplied 75% of the information for this job. I got all the
information I needed from the staff of the hotels I visited. There
were 40 men to be executed that morning. I was also actively
engaged in the operation. I was out in Ranelagh with Dan
McDonnell at the house of Lieutenant Noble at 9 o'clock but he
had left the house at 7 o'clock. The operations were carried out in
all the areas as arranged except the 1st Battalion area. Of the 40
who should have been shot only about 17 were actually [shot].
Coming back from Ranelagh we met Tom Keogh. He was
bringing along Bill McClean who had been wounded. They had

been in Mount Street. I helped Tom Keogh to bring Bill back to North Richmond Street where he lived.[34]

Also in the Volunteer team in Ranelagh were C.S. (Todd) Andrews, Francis X. Coghlan, Hubert Earle and James Kenny. Coghlan was so incensed at Dolan's behaviour that he remained at the house to put out the flames and see the children in the house to safety.

The British reports went into detail on the happenings at each of the houses that were attacked, using many wives' and girlfriends' testimony to describe the deadly efficiency and determination of the Irish. For example, the wife of Captain B.C.H. Keenlyside of the Lancashire Fusiliers watched as her husband was ordered out of bed and forced downstairs with his hands in the air:

> I protested and begged them not to hurt him, while tugging the arm of one of the IRA men. I followed them immediately out and saw another officer being taken downstairs with his hands up. They then placed him and my husband side by side and fired at them, wounding my husband in the jaw ... I ran down quickly and helped him to our bedroom. My husband noticed especially that only one man fired and he was quite young, but seemed cool, grim and determined.[35]

As reports came in to Dublin Castle that day, consternation and confusion turned to something close to panic as the list of those killed mounted up. Though not all the men targeted were home or were killed, and though some were misidentified, if every spy or agent in Ireland had been killed it could have not have caused greater consternation in the Castle. David Neligan stated that the incident: 'caused complete panic in Dublin Castle. ... The attack was so well organised, so unexpected, and so ruthlessly executed that the effect was paralysing. It can be said that the enemy never recovered from the blow. While some of the worst killers escaped, they were thoroughly frightened.'[36] Terror and intimidation were rife among the British living outside protected barracks. The anonymity of quiet Dublin lodgings was no longer a secure shelter for the British. Throughout the city, panicked British officers and their families packed their belongings and moved into the Castle. Within hours, the various small apartments and houses within the Castle's walls were filled with shocked men and women who had barely paused to pack a suitcase. Confusion was increased by the long procession of touts, spies, agents and their wives who fled to refuge in the Castle in taxicabs and military lorries. As the vehicles converged on the Castle gates, the guards became extremely wary as they were on the lookout for Irishmen attempting to attack the Castle from within. David Neligan reported:

> In the Castle, pandemonium reigned. An officer, whose pals had been wiped out, shot himself. The tragedy was hushed up. His body was taken to England with the others.[37]

In the British records, their review of the day concluded:

> The murders of 21st November 1920 temporarily paralysed the special branch. Several of its most efficient members were murdered and the majority of the other residents of the city were brought into Dublin Castle and Central Hotel for safety. This centralisation in the most inconvenient places possible greatly decreased the opportunities for obtaining information and for re-establishing anything in the nature of a secret service.[38]

The extent and cold-blooded nature of the killing of the British officers even stunned some of the Irish leaders. Desmond FitzGerald and William Cosgrave were shocked. Cosgrave was so intimidated he donned a priest's cassock and took refuge for a while in a Christian Brothers borstal at Glencree in the Dublin mountains. Arthur Griffith was horrified: 'In front of their wives on a Sunday in their own homes'.

On the morning, the British military were slow to realise the extent of what had happened. About 9.20 General F.P. Crozier was passing 22 Mount Street with a group of Auxiliaries when they heard some shooting. Crozier and the Auxiliaries jumped out and ran to the house. Tom Keogh, who burst through the soldiers as they surrounded him, shot two Auxiliaries who were in the back of the house. After Crozier saw what happened upstairs he went to the garden where he found an Auxiliary about to shoot Frank Teeling, one of the Squad who had been wounded. Crozier stopped the Auxiliary from his summary execution and saw that Teeling was taken to hospital, and then Crozier headed to Dublin Castle.

Later that morning, Collins discovered two of the IRA's most vital members had been captured. Dick McKee, Brigadier of the Dublin Brigade, and Peadar Clancy, Vice-Brigadier, had been captured the night before in Seán Fitzpatrick's house at 36 Lower Gloucester Street (now Seán MacDermott Street) – supposedly a 'safe-house'. McKee and Clancy had been delayed leaving the meeting in Gardiner Street as they had to issue fresh instructions to one of the Bloody Sunday raiding parties: two of the British agents had changed residences and new orders were required. This delay caused them to be out just after curfew and they went directly to the Fitzpatrick house where they were captured on the Saturday night of 20–21 November. The Fitzpatrick family delayed the raiders long enough for McKee and Clancy to burn their papers, and Fitzpatrick was arrested with McKee and Clancy.[39] They were taken to Dublin Castle where McKee and Clancy were killed by a squad led by Captains William Lorraine King and Jocelyn Lee (Hoppy) Hardy.[40] (John [Shankers] Ryan, the tout who turned them in, was later killed in Hyne's Pub in Gloucester Place). Also on Saturday night, Conor Clune, a Gaelic Leaguer from County Clare, was taken in Vaughan's Hotel. Clune had nothing to do with the Volunteers and only came to Dublin to confer with journalist Piaras Béaslaí. Clune was staying in Vaughan's, which was a noted IRA meeting place, and he was taken to Dublin Castle where he was killed with McKee and Clancy late Sunday.

McKee and Clancy had been instrumental in the planning of the operation and when he heard of their capture, Collins screamed 'Good God. We're finished now. It's all up.' Collins then ordered his police agent James McNamara to find where they were being held, and he thought it was at the Bridewell. Collins sent McNamara and Neligan to search for them at the Bridewell, but they found that McKee and Clancy were held in Dublin Castle. Mulcahy realised what McKee's and Clancy's deaths meant to Collins, particularly, and to their operations.[41]

> In McKee and Clancy he [Collins] had two men who fully
> understood the inside of Collins's work and who were ready and
> able to link up the Dublin resources of the Dublin Brigade to any

work that Collins had in hand and to do so promptly, effectively and sympathetically.[42]

Though IRA legend has it that the men were tortured, there is no evidence that the three men were mutilated; but they were beaten. Writing in *Dublin's Fighting Story*, Ernie O'Malley wrote:

> At night Collins and some of the intelligence squad brought doctors who examined the bodies so that the minds of their comrades could be satisfied for they had not been tortured, as their imaginations had led them to think.[43]

Edward McLysaght, Clune's employer from County Clare, collected Clune's body from the King George V Hospital and examined those of McKee and Clancy as well. He wrote:

> the claim that their faces were so battered about as to be unrecognisable and horrible to look at is quite untrue. I remember those pale dead faces as if I had looked at them yesterday. They were not disfigured.[44]

Further, David Neligan wrote:

> I have read that McNamara and I reported to Collins that these men had been bayoneted and otherwise mutilated; this is not true. We never saw the bodies and certainly made no such statements; the truth was bad enough without embroidery.[45]

Nonetheless, stories that they were savagely bayoneted have persisted.[46] Of the killings in the Castle, General Crozier wrote:

> The evidence before the military inquiry, which enquired into these deaths, was faked from beginning to end, evidence being given by the police that the unarmed and closely guarded men attempted to 'overpower' the guard (in a guard room inside 'The Castle' which was itself closely guarded) in an attempt to 'escape'.

Anything 'did' for a paper acquittal then because Parliament accepted anything willingly as an explanation.[47]

Prime Minister David Lloyd George said of the British killed: 'They got what they deserved – beaten by counter-jumpers!' 'Ask Griffith for God's sake to keep his head and not to break off the slender link that has been established. Tragic as the events in Dublin were, they were of no importance. These men were soldiers, and took a soldier's risk.'[48]

Collins said:

> My one intention was the destruction of the undesirables who continued to make miserable the lives of ordinary decent citizens. I have proof enough to assure myself of the atrocities which this gang of spies and informers have committed. Perjury and torture are words too easily known to them. If I had a second motive it was no more than a feeling I would have for a dangerous reptile. By their destruction the very air is made sweeter. For myself, my conscience is clear. There is no crime in detecting and destroying, in wartime, the spy and the informer. They have destroyed without trial. I have paid them back in their own coin.[49]

It was Bloody Sunday, more than any other, that gained Collins the reputation in the British press as a gunman and a 'murderer'. The British 'Record of the rebellion', prepared after the war, indicated: 'if the rebels had perpetrated no other outrage, [Bloody Sunday] would have marked them as the most cold-blooded and cowardly of murderers'.[50] The British press made much of the fact that the men were British spies in civilian clothes, and under assumed names, playing a game of 'kill or be killed'. That same press, for the most part, ignored the terror reprisal of the Black and Tans and Auxiliaries later that day at Croke Park.

Following the morning raids, a combined group of British Army, Black and Tans and Auxiliaries raided Croke Park.[51] According to the police, the 'official plan' was that fifteen minutes before the final whistle there would be an announcement by megaphone. Instead of the usual 'stewards to end-of-match positions', the crowd would hear someone telling them to leave by official exits and that all men would be searched for weapons. But in the event, no sooner had the police, Black and Tans and the Auxiliaries arrived at the Park than they started shooting. The exact events that led to the shooting have never been proven, with each side contradicting the other. The only public and official statement was one by Dublin Castle blaming the IRA for starting the shooting.[52] Fourteen innocent people attending the match were killed, sixty-two people were injured inside Croke Park during the raid, and another twelve were injured in the stampede out.

The following were killed in Croke Park that afternoon:

Jane Boyle (26); 12 Lennox Street, Dublin;
James Burke (44); Greenland Terrace, Dundrum, Dublin;
Daniel Carroll (30); Ballincara House, Templederry, Co. Tipperary;
Michael Feery (40); Smith's Cottages, Gardiner Place, Dublin;
Michael Hogan (24); Grangemockler, Co. Tipperary;
Tom Hogan (19); 24 St James' Terrace, Dublin;
James Mathews (38); 42 North Cumberland Street, Dublin;
Patrick O'Dowd (57); Buckingham Street, Dublin;
Jeremiah (Jerome) O'Leary (10); 69 Blessington Street, Dublin;
William Robinson (11); 15 Little Britain Street, Dublin;
Thomas Ryan (27); Viking Road, Dublin;
John William Scott (14); 15 Fitzroy Avenue, Drumcondra, Dublin;
James Teehan (26); Green Street, Dublin;
Joe Traynor (21); Clondalkin, Dublin.

Because of the fear of a British reprisal, the Volunteers were told to avoid Croke Park that afternoon; several, however, attended the GAA match. Johnny McDonnell, who had been on the raid at 38 Upper Mount Street played in goal for the Dublin side. Tom Keogh, one of the men at 22 Lower Mount Street, would stand on what became known as Hill 16. Bill Stapleton, one of the raiders at 92 Baggot Street Lower, said 'I was beside a man who was shot and I was splashed with his blood'.[53]

Edward 'Ned' Corcoran, a Volunteer from the 5th Battalion and a spectator at Croke Park, wrote he was told not to go to the match because there might be trouble, but he went anyway. He wrote he:

thought that the British would not fire on a gathering of women
and children, but I got a lesson that day that I never forgot ...
People ran in all directions, and firing seemed to come from all
directions. I thought it was time to take cover ... A [British
soldier] shouted 'hey you, with the black soft hat, put up your
hands'. [But] black soft hat refused saying 'I can't, I'm carrying a
wounded man'. 'Put up your hands or you'll be wounded, too'. So
he had to put the wounded man down in the mud ... I saw a girl
kneeling besides the body of Tipp player Hogan, her beads in her
hands. All were bloodstained. Someone asked her how he was. She
said he died instantly ... We were brought in batches to the gate,
searched & scrutinised and then let go ... Now when I go to the
matches and see such a large, carefree crowd, the Flag flying, the
bands playing the Nat. Anthem, and if a plane is heard, you know
it's a friendly one. Such a change.[54]

Central to all inquiries regarding the shooting at Croke Park, and still
in dispute, is: who fired first? All that is agreed upon is that the firing started
at the south-west corner of the pitch, where Jones's Road crosses the Royal
Canal. Some witnesses at the inquiries said the firing started within the
Park, presumably by armed spectators, before the British troops had entered
the grounds. Whoever fired first, 'of all the bloody days of the War of Independence, this was the bloodiest of them all – at least in terms of its impact
on the public psyche'.[55] Terror is imagined as well as experienced.

Some of the police later claimed that they were fired on first by IRA
sentries, but this has never been proven. Correspondents for the *Manchester
Guardian* interviewed eyewitnesses, and concluded that the 'IRA sentries'
were actually ticket-sellers:

It is the custom at this football ground for tickets to be sold
outside the gates by recognised ticket-sellers, who would probably
present the appearance of pickets and would naturally run inside at
the approach of a dozen military lorries. No man exposes himself
needlessly in Ireland when a military lorry passes by.[56]

The *Freeman's Journal* reported that:

The spectators were startled by a volley of shots fired from inside the turnstile entrances. Armed and uniformed men were seen entering the field, and immediately after the firing broke out scenes of the wildest confusion took place. The spectators made a rush for the far side of Croke Park and shots were fired over their heads and into the crowd.[57]

Major E.L. Mills commanded the British Army back-up troops and re-ported adversely on the actions of the Black and Tans, Auxiliaries and RIC. He blamed the 'excited and out of control RIC constables for the deaths'. He went on: 'I did not see any need for any firing at all and the indiscrim-inate firing absolutely spoilt any chance of getting hold of people with arms'.[58]

General Crozier, O/C of the Black and Tans and Auxiliaries and who would shortly resign in protest over the British administration condoning the misconduct by his troops, publicly stated that one of his officers told him the Auxiliaries started the shooting. 'It was the most disgraceful show I have ever seen,' the officer said. 'Black and Tans fired into the crowd with-out any provocation whatever.'[59]

Crozier interviewed Major Mills, who was furious. 'A rotten bloody show ... the worst I've ever seen,' Mills said.

The military surrounded the hurley ground according to plan and were to warn the crowd by megaphone to file out of the gates where they were to be searched for arms. A rotten idea anyhow, as, of course, if anyone had a gun on him he'd drop it like a hot poker! Well, would you believe it, suddenly the Regular R.I.C from Phoenix Park – Black and Tans from England, arrived up in lorries, opened fire into the crowd, over the fence, without reason and killed about a dozen and wounded many more! I eventually stopped the firing. What do you think of it?

'Rotten' I [Crozier] replied 'sit down here now, write a report to me and I'll forward it to the Castle at once'.[60]

Mills's report, though incomplete and with some inaccuracies, was damning:

At 1.30 pm 21st inst. I was detailed to take charge of a mixed force of RIC and Auxiliary Division to hold up and search people at CROKE PARK.

I arranged with Major Dudley, DSO, MC, who was in charge of a party of 100 RIC, to split up the two forces so that there would be an equal number posted on the 4 gates of the ground to search people as they came out.

... I was in a car in a rear of the RIC leading the Auxiliaries. As we approached the railway bridge ... I saw men in the tender in front of me trying to get out of their car and heard some of them shouting about an ambush ... At this moment I heard a considerable amount of rifle fire. As no shots were coming from the football field and all along the RIC constables seemed excited and out of hand, I rushed and stopped the firing with the assistance of Major Fillery. There was still firing going on in the football ground. I ran down into the ground and shouted to all the armed men to stop firing at once and eventually the firing ceased.

The crowd by this time was in a state of panic.

... I went round the ground and found two children being carried out apparently dead. I found one female who had been trampled to death, also a man who had apparently died the same way. I saw a few wounded men and I got some sense into the crowd. I got the DMP to get ambulances for the wounded. We found no arms on any of the people attending the match.

... I did not see any need for any firing at all and all the indiscriminate firing absolutely spoilt any chance of getting hold of any people in possession of arms.

The men of the Auxiliary Division did not fire. [sic]

The casualties I personally saw were 6 dead, and 4 wounded, 2 of the dead were apparently trampled to death.

The RIC, including Black and Tans and Auxiliaries, fired a total of 238 rounds of small arms ammunition, in addition to a single drum of fifty rounds fired from the Lewis machine gun in the armoured car.

The *Freeman's Journal* had graphic stories of the events at Croke Park, comparing the British shootings to the massacre in Amritsar, India, in the previous year, where British soldiers shot and killed hundreds of Indian nationalists.[61] The paper's lead paragraphs proclaimed:

> Scenes of bloodshed on a football field, unparalled in the history of the country were enacted yesterday at Croke Park by armed forces of the Crown.
>
> ... The armed forces, according to many onlookers, gave no warning to the spectators to disperse, beyond a preliminary volley of shots in the air.
>
> ... Then the bullets came in thick as hail, dealing out death in their swift passage; a wild scene of panic ensued, and women and children were knocked down and walked on.[62]

There was a secret court of inquiry that found the shooting was unauthorised and excessive, even if some members of the crowd fired on the Auxiliaries. Major General G.F. Boyd, O/C of the British soldiers in Dublin, concluded that the firing on the crowd, which began without orders, was both indiscriminate and unjustifiable.

That court of inquiry was convened at Dublin Castle and at Jervis Street Hospital. (Some reports indicated that part of the inquiry was held at British Army HQ in Parkgate Street.) The inquiry was held 'in lieu of an inquest', and in camera, under the Defence of the Realm Act. The personnel of the three-man inquiry were Major R. Bunbury, president, Lieutenant S.H. Winterbottom of the 1st Lancashire Fusiliers and Lieutenant B.J. Key of the 2nd Worcester Regiment. There are two different versions of the proceedings—one is handwritten and one is typed—but the contents are practically identical.[63]

In addition to the main inquiry, there was also a separate one, again 'in lieu of an inquest' (under the Restoration of Order in Ireland Act), into the deaths of fourteen civilians at Croke Park.[64] On 8 December 1920 the verdict of that court of inquiry was issued. The court concluded that during a raid on Croke Park on 21 November 1920 by a 'mixed force of RIC, auxiliary police and military, firing was started by unknown civilians, either as a warning of the raid or else to create a panic, and that the injuries to dead civilians were inflicted by rifle or revolver fire from the canal bridge by the

RIC, some of whom fired over the crowd's heads, others of whom fired into the crowd at persons believed to be trying to evade arrest'. It also found that the RIC firing was carried out without orders and in excess of what was required but that 'no firing came from the auxiliary police or the military, except that soldiers in an armoured car (at the St James's Avenue exit) fired a burst into the air to stop the crowd from breaking through and out of the ground'.

Though the inquiries were held in camera, the medical reports make grim reading. In the inquest on the death of Thomas Hogan of St James Terrace in Dublin, Dr Patrick Moran of the Mater Hospital testified:

> Thomas Hogan was admitted to this hospital at 4pm on November 21st. There was a small round wound 3/8 inch in diameter under the spine of the right scapula. There was a large round wound one inch in diameter just beneath the acromion process in front. This was apparently an exit wound. There were two other small wounds a quarter inch in diameter one inch above acromion process, and about an inch apart. These might have been caused by bone splinters. On admission the patient was bleeding profusely, and was in a state of severe collapse. The right arm was amputated on Monday, 22nd November. The shoulder joint was found to be completely disorganised. The head of the humerus was completely severed from the shaft and about 2 inches of the shaft was shattered. The auxiliary border of the scapula was also shattered. A small piece of nickel casing was found in the region of the shoulder joint. Gas gangrene set in after the operation and the patient died at 12.30 on November 26th. Death was in my opinion due to toxaemia following gas gangrene following gunshot wounds.[65]

Appended to the inquiry report is a copy (marked 'Secret and V. Urgent!') dated 21 November 1920 of the (unsigned) order given by a brigade major, Infantry Brigade, to the RIC and containing details of the operation planned to take place that day at Croke Park. The ground was to be surrounded and pickets placed at specified points, e.g. on the railway and at the three known exits. One infantry platoon was to be kept in reserve and at 3.15 p.m. two (army) armoured cars would meet the mixed RIC and Auxiliary police at Fitzroy Avenue (opposite the main entrance). A quarter of an hour before the end of the match a special intelligence officer would warn the crowd by megaphone that anybody trying to leave other than by the exits would be shot, and that all males would be stopped and searched.

The opinion of the competent military authority that convened the court of inquiry on 11 December 1920, was:

(i) that it agreed with the court findings [summarised above];

(ii) that the first shots were fired by the crowd and led to the panic;

(iii) that the firing on the crowd was carried out without orders and was indiscriminate and unjustifiable, with the exception of any shooting which took place inside the enclosure.

Major General G.F. Boyd, commanding officer, Dublin, certified this opinion.[66] The findings of all the inquiries could be classified as being as much propagandistic as informative.

Whatever the finding of the inquiries, the attack on Croke Park was clearly a terror attack, a reprisal for the morning attacks. International law holds that reprisals should be resorted to only on the authority of the government or the commander after the truth of the enemy's guilt has been established, and after the enemy has been called upon to put a stop to his misconduct. They should not be applied merely in a spirit of vindictiveness, for their purpose is to obtain redress or ensure compliance with established rules. They ought not to be widely disproportionate to the offences committed. And, in general, they should not be incompatible with the conceptions of justice and humanity.[67] The British forces met none of these conditions that afternoon. In fairness, it must be noted that some commentators have declared that this was not a reprisal, and, insofar as their perspective of reprisals being pre-determined acts of savagery, they are correct.[68] Nevertheless, while some commentators have denied that this action was actually a reprisal by the Auxiliaries, the Auxiliaries' commander, General Crozier, had no doubt that it was, recording in his diary: 'Croke Park massacre. Many murder'd [sic] by R.I.C.'[69] The Croke Park attack was an intimidatory terror reprisal for the morning's attacks.

What is not clear is what caused the British to fire in the first place.

What set them off? The British claimed the first shots came from the spectators inside Croke Park before the troops entered the grounds. Republicans claimed that this was a case of the British forces simply gunning people down as they had at Amritsar. Neither of these claims is completely satisfactory. If one accepts the republican propaganda, one would have to believe that the troops deliberately tried to kill innocent people, including women and children, which is unlikely. It is more probable that a noise startled the troops causing them to open fire. Any loud noise could be mistaken for gunfire, especially with train tracks at the north and south ends of the field, or the backfire of a passing motorcar. But, whatever the reason for the first British shot, once the firing started, it was out of control, and there was no return fire from the Irish.

The brutal reprisal and terror operations carried out by the British beginning in the spring of 1920 brought uniform international condemnation of the policy. The story of reprisals does not need retelling, but only discussion insofar as they pertain to the change in the police. The concept behind reprisals was simple: harsh retaliation for a specific act would make the costs of further acts too much to bear for the Irish.[70] Eventually, the rebels would have to stop, or be stopped by the population–the terror and intimidation would do the stopping.

Contrary to popular legend, violent British reprisals were relatively rare in Ireland prior to 1920.[71] Originally, reprisals and atrocities committed by the British were simply the frustrations of a few soldiers or constables. Achieving no satisfaction from the courts that had been thoroughly intimidated by the IRA, they resorted to extra-legal measures. That is not to say that British forces did not appreciate the effects behind such actions; in those instances noted in the RIC Monthly Confidential Reports, such as the burnings of Volunteer or Sinn Féin property, the tone of the reporting was sometimes almost triumphal. Terrible as these activities were, they were usually in retaliation for IRA attacks. As always in irregular wars, the militarily weaker side is critically dependent for strategic leverage upon the errors committed by its regular enemy. So it was in Ireland. In fact, the British policy of reprisal played right into the IRA's message: the IRA deliberately invited reprisals, which the RIC duly provided, ultimately at fatal political cost. The republican-controlled press excoriated the reign of terror that the British were imposing on Ireland. The *Irish Bulletin*, an unabashedly republican journal, published weekly a 'List of the Acts of Aggression committed in Ireland by the Police and Military of the Usurping English Government'. While the frustrated acts of a few soldiers might be understandable given the tension of the situation, the approval, and in some cases the direction by the British military and government, to commit such reprisals and other acts of terror was inexcusable and counterproductive.

In 1920, with the arrival of the Black and Tans and the Auxiliaries, violent reprisals and terror increased.[72] The greatest difference between the newcomers was that the Black and Tans were inserted into the existing organisation of the RIC, whilst the Auxiliaries were a separate unit, under their own command. The Black and Tans might have had the help of a restraining effect of the remaining and more experienced Irish constables.[73] The plight of those serving with the RIC in this period was defined pessimistically by the military command in Ireland in the following terms:

> The R.I.C. were at this time distributed in small detachments throughout the country, quartered in 'barracks', which consisted, in the vast majority of cases, of small houses adjoining other buildings, quite indefensible and entirely at the mercy of disloyal inhabitants. The ranks of the force had already been depleted by murders, and many men, through intimidation of themselves or more often of their families, had been induced to resign. Although, in the main, a loyal body of men their moral[e] had diminished, and only two courses were open to their detachments; to adopt a policy of *laisser [sic] faire* and live, or actively to enforce law and order and be in hourly danger of murder.[74]

The British authorities responded to this situation in an extraordinary fashion by advertising in England for British ex-servicemen firstly, and then later for ex-officers, to join the RIC and bring their recent experience of weapons and warfare to what had formerly been a distinctly Irish police force. Known respectively as the 'Black and Tans' and the 'Auxiliaries', these two elements of the RIC became infamous for utilising their experience of war to terrorise the civilian population of Ireland.[75]

Both the Black and Tans and Auxiliaries seemed for the most part to behave in a patently undisciplined manner. According to one Irish observer:

They had neither religion nor morals, they used foul language,
they had the old soldier's talent for dodging and scrounging, they
spoke in strange accents, called the Irish 'natives', associated with
low company, stole from each other, sneered at the customs of the
country, drank to excess and put sugar on their porridge. Even
worse, though, was their tendency to engage in the wanton
destruction of property, indiscriminate shooting and violence and,
on occasions, even deliberate murder, in their apparent quest 'to
administer random terror'.[76]

The lasting image of the Black and Tans as brutes derives from this kind of
outrageous behaviour on their part that was anything but conducive to the
restoration of law and order in Ireland.

This military mindset, combined with military weapons and tactics, but
without the disciplinary controls of a military force, such as the Articles of
War or courts martial, hampered command and control from the outset.
Furthermore, many of them were imbued with a sense of mission, which
contributed to unrestrained violence against civilians and military foes alike.
While they were often in response to IRA actions, the British reprisals were
more aggressive, long drawn out and indiscriminate than the actions to
which they were responding. British terror, savage as it was, has been argued
to have been shaped by the IRA's violence, by the nature of Ireland's guerrilla warfare, and by the imagined dangers as much as the real threats. In
that view, it was inspired and driven by the demands of British politics and
by Ireland's place in its midst; it was an answer to a domestic problem before
it became a colonial phenomenon.[77] In Britain, however, the war-weary
public was sickened and disgusted by reports of the actions of the Black
and Tans and Auxiliaries, whom they viewed as immoral mercenaries.
David Fitzpatrick has correctly written 'the reprisal [was] always more
vicious than the incident provoking it'.[78] In fact, the Black and Tans'
first O/C, General F.P. Crozier, resigned in February 1921 and later described the Auxiliaries as 'soldiers in disguise, under no army and no
RIC code'.[79] He claimed that they were being employed to 'murder,
rob, loot and burn up the innocent because they could not catch the
few guilty on-the-run'.[80] When he resigned, he said 'I resigned because

the combat was being carried out on foul lines, by selected and foul men, for a grossly foul purpose, based on the most Satanic of all rules that "the end justifies the means'". Crozier summarised the dark stain on the reputation of British Forces:

> Had I been told, in 1918, after four and a half years of blood-
> letting, that in our own British Isles I should be witnessing acts of
> atrocity, by men in the King's uniform, which far exceeded in
> violence and brutality those acts I lived to condemn in the
> seething Baltic, I – well, I would have laughed out loud. I am
> concerned here with the conduct of Englishmen in the uniform
> of the Crown, because I greatly respect the Crown and have no
> wish to see it dragged in the mud.[81]

In another book, Crozier was even more damning:

> It must be remembered that while all revolution carries with it,
> liked or disliked, wanted or unwanted, revolver rule, largely carried
> on sub rosa, there is no justification for similar methods on the
> part of the Crown.[82]

By the end of the war, within the British military establishment two of the most vocal critics of the British policy of reprisals and its terror were General Nevil Macready and Field Marshal Henry Wilson. At first, Macready tolerated reprisals, if not actively encouraging them. According to Mark Sturgis, Macready was:

> on very delicate ground over this reprisal business; he sees clearly
> that to wink at organised reprisals is the end of discipline. On the
> other hand he said frankly that a regiment that did not try to break
> out when a story – however untrue was told them e.g. that one of
> their comrades had been chucked into the Liffey and shot at in the
> water – was not worth a damn.[83]

Macready even thought that reprisals might be useful and gave specific orders to the British Army because he was concerned about the effects of uncontrolled actions on discipline.

> Punishments, including confiscation, or, if necessary, destruction of houses and property, may be carried out against any person or persons who may be considered to be implicated in or cognizant of outrages against Crown forces. Such outrages to include ambushes, attacks on barracks, &c.
> Punishments will only be carried out on the authority of the Infantry Brigade Commander, who, before taking action, will satisfy himself that the people concerned were, owing to their proximity to the outrage, or their known political tendencies, implicated in the occurrence, and will give specific instructions in writing or by telegram to the officer detailed to carry out the operation. The punishment will be carried out as a military operation, and the reason why it is being done will be publicly proclaimed.[84]

As the war escalated, however, both Macready and Wilson were concerned that these undisciplined paramilitaries would have an adverse effect on the morale of regular British Army troops.[85] Macready wrote to the cabinet:

> Lately the Royal Irish Constabulary has been reinforced by recruits from England, usually ex-soldiers known by the sobriquet of 'Black & Tans' – who on account of their Uniform are often mistaken by the populace for soldiers. It is not for me to criticize the methods employed by the Police for keeping order, but in certain parts of the country this is attained by promiscuous firing, with the object, presumably, of keeping the people off the streets, and I am informed that such methods are necessary and effective. Retaliatory measures are often indulged in, especially by the 'Black & Tan' contingent, when incensed by the murders of their comrades. I mention these facts merely to illustrate the atmosphere in which the young soldiers who compose the Army to-day are called upon to serve.[86]

Wilson had a conversation with Lloyd George and Andrew Bonar Law
on 29 September 1920:

> I told them what I thought of reprisals by the Black and Tans, and
> how this must lead to chaos and ruin. Lloyd George danced about
> and was angry, but I never budged. I pointed out that these
> reprisals were being carried out without anyone being responsible;
> men were being murdered, houses burnt, villages wrecked ... It
> was the business of the Government to govern. *If these men ought to
> be murdered, then the Government ought to murder them.* I got some
> sense into their heads and Lloyd George went for Hamar
> Greenwood, Macready, Tudor, and others to come over tomorrow
> night ...[87] [Emphasis added.]

Clearly, Wilson did not object to the reprisals, *per se*. He, however, wanted
them taken out of the hands of the Black and Tans and directly overseen
by the British military and government.

Macready wrote to Sir John Anderson in February 1921 that the
Auxiliaries 'treat the Martial Law areas as a special game preserve for
their amusement'.[88] (Some few of the Auxiliaries were arrested and tried
for crimes, including three murders, but few were imprisoned for any
period and most were granted probation and returned to their units.[89])
While noting that reprisals were not officially sanctioned, in his memoirs
Macready described the British reprisals as 'terrorism':

> Although these unauthorised reprisals at that time had a marked
> effect in curbing the activities of the IRA in the immediate
> localities, and on these grounds were justified, or at all events
> winked at, by those in control of the police, I saw that they could
> only result in the police taking the law into their own hands. And
> lost no time in protesting to the Chief Secretary [Hamar
> Greenwood] on the subject, urging him to carry out reprisals as
> authorised and controlled operations, or to stop them at all costs.
> Unfortunately at that time certain persons in London were
> convinced that *terrorism in any description* was the best method with
> which to oppose the gunmen, not realising that apart from all

other reasons the gunmen could always 'go one better'.[90]
[Emphasis added.]

One of his officers reported to Macready: 'We are importing crowds of undisciplined men who are just terrorising the country'.

British General Sir Hubert Gough went still further in condemning their actions:

Law and order have given way to a bloody and brutal anarchy. ...
England has departed further from the standards even of any
nation in the world, not excepting the Turk and the Zulu, than has
ever been known in history before![91]

Further, *The Times* editorialised:

Methods, inexcusable even under the loose code of
revolutionaries, are certainly not fit methods which the
Government of Great Britain can tolerate on the part of its
servants.[92]

By October 1920, even the RIC newsletter from Dublin Castle, *The Weekly Summary*, warned:

reprisals are wrong ... They are bad for the discipline of the force.
... But they are condoned as the result of the brutal, cowardly
murder of police officers by assassins who take shelter behind the
screen of terrorism and intimidation which they have created.[93]

But on top of everything, the harsh and 'terror' methods of the Black and Tans did not work, and certainly did not defeat the IRA. Professor Roy Foster wrote of the Tans: 'They behaved more like independent mercenaries; their brutal regime followed the IRA's policy of killing policemen, and was taken by many to vindicate it'. Peter Hart agreed: 'It was astoundingly counter-productive. The militarised police formed their own death squads and regularly engaged in reprisals against civilians. IRA violence only in- creased.'[94] Because of the battering that all this inflicted on the image of

Britain at home and abroad, the continuing IRA campaign eventually led Lloyd George to seek talks with the republicans, which led to the British withdrawal.[95]

Collins viewed the Black and Tans, the Auxiliaries, and the terror that followed them, as a sort of mixed blessing. Clearly the terror instilled by the Black and Tans and the Auxiliaries drove many doubting nationalists into the arms of Sinn Féin, and Collins took full advantage of that: 'Apart from the loss which these attacks entail, good is done as it makes clear and clearer to people what both sides stand for'.[96] But it must be noted that Collins and the Irish did not hesitate to use terror when they felt it necessary for their aims.

He later wrote in more detail about why the British officers were selected for assassination and the means used to kill them.

> Let it be remembered that we did not initiate the war, nor were we allowed to choose the lines along which the war developed. Our only way to carry on the fight was by organised and bold guerrilla warfare. However successful our ambushers, however many 'murders' we committed – England could always reinforce her army. To paralyse the British machine it was necessary to strike at individuals outside the ranks of the military. Without their criminal agents in the capitol it would be hopeless to affect the removal of those leaders marked down for murder. It was these men we had to put out of the way.[97]

Notes

[1] T. Carey and M. de Burca, 'Bloody Sunday 1920: new evidence', *History Ireland* 11 (2) (2003).

[2] M.C. Hartline and M.M. Kaulbach, 'Michael Collins and Bloody Sunday: the intelligence war between the British and Irish intelligence services', *CIA Historical Review Program*, 2 July 1996, approved for release 1994.

[3] D. Lloyd George in *The Times*, 10 November 1920.

[4] See T. Bowden, 'Bloody Sunday, a reappraisal', *European Studies Review* 2 (1) (1972), 'The Irish underground and the War of Independence 1919–1921', *Journal of Contemporary History* 8 (2) (1973); A. Dolan, 'Killing and Bloody Sunday, November 1920', *Historical Journal* 49 (3) (2006); Gen. F.P. Crozier, *The Men I Killed, A Selection from the Writings of General F.P. Crozier, including selections from* Ireland Forever, A Brass Hat in No Man's Land *and* The Men I Killed (Belfast, n.d.), p. 95 *et seq.*; M. O'Meara, *Bloody Sunday, 1920–1995, A Commemorative Booklet* (Dublin, 1995); C. Townshend, 'Bloody Sunday: Michael Collins speaks', *European Studies Review* 9 (1979).

5   Carey and de Burca, 'Bloody Sunday 1920: new evidence'.

6   There is no mention of a 'Cairo Gang' in the reports and records of 1919–22. The first appearance of the term is in Rex Taylor's *Michael Collins* (London, 1958), pp 125–34: 'In Cairo sixteen officers were chosen for a special task … The Cairo group travelled under assumed names and arrived in Dublin singly on different dates. They were in plain clothes and posing as commercial travellers … rented flats in Pembroke Street and Mount Street.' The agents frequented the Cairo Café (59 Grafton Street, five doors from the corner of South King St.) and Kidd's Buffet (Kidd's was where the Berni Inn was until the 1980s in Nassau St, later it was where Lillie's Bordello is now at the bottom of Grafton Street) or the Porterhouse pub at 46 Nassau Street. The Squad called them the Cairo Gang, but the origin of the name is unclear.

7   Robert Jeune Papers, PRO 76/172/1; M. Smith, *The Spying Game* (London, 2003), p. 370.

8   Robert Jeune Memoirs, Imperial War Museum; M. Foy, *Michael Collins's Intelligence War* (Stroud, 2006), p. 153.

9   Mark Sturgis Diary, 1 September 1920, PRO 30/59; David Neligan, however, described him as 'a decent old fellow'.

10   Hartline and Kaulbach, 'Michael Collins and Bloody Sunday'.

11   David Neligan: Witness Statement 380.

12   Frank Thornton: Witness Statement 510.

13   M. Ryan, *Michael Collins and the Women in His Life* (Dublin, 1996), p. 70.

14   Lily Mernin: Witness Statement 441.

15   P. Béaslaí, *Michael Collins and the Making of a New Ireland*, Vol. 1 (London, 1926), p. 448.

16   R. Mulcahy, Béaslaí critique, Vol. 2, p. 51 (see explanatory note in Bibliography).

17   Frank Thornton: Witness Statement 510.

18   J. Gleeson, *Bloody Sunday* (London, 1962), pp 101–23.

19   Dolan, 'Killing and Bloody Sunday'.

20   J. Leonard, '"English Dogs" or "Poor Devils"? The dead of Bloody Sunday morning', in D. Fitzpatrick (ed.), *Terror in Ireland* (Dublin, 2012). Leonard gives pen-pictures of the British killed on Bloody Sunday and contends that 'most of them appeared to be officially employed in other posts, both military and non-military. It is unclear if those were just "aliases" and "cover" jobs or if the men were not actually intelligence agents.' In contrast, see J.B.E. Hittle, *Michael Collins and the Anglo-Irish War: Britain's Counter-insurgency Failure* (Chicago, 2007), pp 162–89, in which he argues that all but two of the men were connected with British intelligence.

21   R. Taylor, *Michael Collins* (London, 1958), p. 104.

22   Gen. Paddy Daly: Witness Statement 387. See M. Moran, *Executed for Ireland. The Patrick Moran Story* (Cork, 2010).

23   H. de Montmorency, *Sword and Stirrup* (London, 1936), p. 348.

24   M. Forester, *Michael Collins, The Lost Leader* (Dublin, 1989), p. 170.

25   Proceedings of a court of inquiry in lieu of inquest on Temp Cadet F. Garniss and Temp Cadet C.A. Morris, London NA WO 35/159B.

26   Caroline Woodcock, wife of Colonel Woodcock, wrote prolifically about her period as a British army wife in Dublin in her diary. Her diaries were published as a book in 1921: C. Woodcock, *Experiences of an Officer's Wife in Ireland* (London, 1921).

27   W. Sugg, 'British intelligence wiped out', *An Phoblacht*, 20 November 1997, 'Bloody Sunday', *An Phoblacht*, 27 November 1997.

28   Patrick Kennedy: Witness Statement 499.

[29] T. Ryle Dwyer, *The Squad,* pp 176 and 211-12. See Moran, *Executed for Ireland.*.

[30] James Doyle: Witness Statement 771.

[31] Collins letter to Mulcahy, 7 April 1922, Irish Military History Archives, Cathal Brugha Barracks.

[32] Daniel McDonnell: Witness Statement 486.

[33] De Montmorency, *Sword and Stirrup*, p. 184.

[34] Joe Dolan: Witness Statements 663, 900.

[35] 'Bloody Sunday', account of Mrs B.C.H. Keenlyside, 21 November 1920, CO 904/168.

[36] David Neligan: Witness Statement 380.

[37] *Ibid*. Auxiliary H.E. Spenle hanged himself.

[38] 'Record of the rebellion in Ireland in 1920–1921 and the part played by the army in dealing with it', Imperial War Museum, Box 78/82/2, Volume 2, Intelligence; File WO 35/88, Public Record Office, Kew, London; B.P. Murphy, *The Origin and Organisation of British Propaganda in Ireland, 1920* (Dublin, 2006), p. 54; Hittle, *Michael Collins and the Anglo-Irish War,* pp 160–77.

[39] Author's correspondence with Terry Fagan of the North Dublin Inner City Folklore Project.

[40] S. Cronin, *Three Murders in Dublin Castle* (Dublin, 2002).

[41] S. MacAodh, 'Murder in the Castle', *An Phoblacht*, 22 November 2001; S. O'Mahony, 'Three murders in Dublin Castle' (pamphlet, Dublin, 2000).

[42] Mulcahy, Béaslaí critique, Vol. II, p. 51.

[43] E. O'Malley, 'Bloody Sunday', in B. Ó Conchubhair (ed.), *Dublin's Fighting Story, 1916–1921* (Cork, 2009), p. 293.

[44] Edward McLysaght deposition at the official inquiry, National Library of Ireland, MS 5369.

[45] D. Neligan, *The Spy in the Castle* (London, 1999), p. 125.

[46] See Cronin, *Three Murders in Dublin Castle*: 'McKee was bayoneted in the liver, suffered from broken ribs, abrasions to the face and many bullet wounds' (p. 8). Clancy was 'captured, tortured and murdered in exactly the same circumstances as McKee' (p. 10). 'The general belief was that they were tortured in order to extract from them the names of Volunteers who had earlier shot the Cairo Gang …When this information was not forthcoming they were killed. The condition of the bodies when delivered to their families supported this belief' (p. 12). See also 'The First Bloody Sunday', *Irish Republican News,* 25 February 2007: 'William Pearson, an ex-colonel in the British army and doctor, went along with Ed McLysaght to King George V Hospital [now St Bricin's Hospital] to identify Clune's body. On examination of the 13 wounds inflicted on Clune, Pearson believed that these wounds would not have been inflicted if Clune had been trying to escape. The bodies of McKee and Clancy were returned to their families and laid out in their coffins in full Volunteer uniform, but because their faces were so badly beaten it was decided to close the coffins.' Molly O'Reilly identified their bodies in the hospital, and she swore that they both had bayonet wounds (author's correspondence and documents from Clare Cowley, granddaughter of Molly O'Reilly, http://mspcsearch.militaryarchives.ie/docs/files//PDF_Pensions/R2/MSP34REF20325MaryTCorcoran/W34E4055MaryTCorcoran.pdf). See Molly O'Reilly, in T. Fagan (ed.), *Rebels and Heroes. Hidden Stories from Dublin's Northside* (Dublin, 2016), p. 54 *et seq.* Tim Pat Coogan wrote, 'Battered faces certainly, and bayonet thrusts, and bullet wounds, but not the mutilations expected' (*Michael Collins, The Man Who Made Ireland* (London, 1992), p. 161).

[47] Crozier, *The Men I Killed*, p. 84.

[48] Gleeson, *Bloody Sunday*, p. 181.

[49] Gleeson, *Bloody Sunday*, p. 191; Taylor, *Michael Collins*, p. 106.

[50] 'Record of the rebellion in Ireland in 1920–1921 and the part played by the army in dealing with it, a new campaign, September 1920'.

[51] M. Foley, *The Bloodied Field* (Dublin, 2014) is the best and most comprehensive account of all the events at Croke Park that afternoon. See also D. Leeson, 'Death in the afternoon: the Croke Park Massacre, 21 November 1920', *Canadian Journal of History* (April 2003).

[52] Carey and de Burca, 'Bloody Sunday 1920'.

[53] William Stapleton: Witness Statement 822.

[54] Statement of Edward 'Ned' Corcoran. Author's correspondence and documents from Clare Cowley, granddaughter of Ned Corcoran.

[55] M. Cronin, M. Duncan and P. Rouse, *The GAA: A People's History* (Cork, 2009), p. 154.

[56] *Manchester Guardian*, 16 December 1920.

[57] *Freeman's Journal,* 1 December 1920.

[58] Major E.L. Mills, ADRIC, letter to Adjutant ADRIC, 22 November 1920, 'Mater Hospital Inquiry', 8 December 1920, NAUK WO 35/88B.

[59] Dwyer, *The Squad*, p. 190.

[60] Crozier, *The Men I Killed*, p. 78.

[61] On 10 April 1919 Satya Pal and Saifuddin Kitchlew, two popular proponents of the Satyagraha movement led by Gandhi, were called to the deputy commissioner's residence, arrested and sent off by car to Dharamsetla, a hill town, now in Himachal Pradesh. This led to a general strike in Amritsar. Excited groups of citizens soon merged into a crowd of about 50,000, marching on to protest to the deputy commissioner against the arrest of the two leaders. The crowd, however, was stopped and fired upon near the railway footbridge. According to the official version, the number of those killed was twelve and of those wounded between twenty and thirty. Evidence before an inquiry of the Indian National Congress put the number of the dead between twenty and thirty. Three days later, on 13 April, the traditional festival of Baisakhi, thousands of Sikhs, Muslims and Hindus gathered in the Jallianwala Bagh. An hour after the meeting began as scheduled at 16.30, British General Reginald Dyer arrived with a group of sixty-five Gurkha and twenty-five Baluchi soldiers. Without warning the crowd to disperse, Dyer blocked the main exits and ordered his troops to begin shooting toward the densest sections of the crowd. The Indian National Congress determined that approximately 1,000 people were killed.

[62] *Freeman's Journal*, 22 November 1920.

[63] File WO 35/88, PRO, Kew, London.

[64] Carey and de Burca, 'Bloody Sunday 1920'.

[65] File WO 35/88, PRO, Kew, London.

[66] *Ibid*.

[67] B.M. Leiser, 'Terrorism, guerrilla warfare, and international morality', *Stanford Journal of International Studies* 12 (1977); C.R. King, 'Revolutionary war, guerrilla warfare, and international law', *Case Western Reserve Journal of International Law* 4 (2) (1972).

[68] R. Bennett, *The Black and Tans: The British Special Police in Ireland* (New York, 1959), p. 117.

[69] Gen. F.P. Crozier, *Impressions and Recollections* (London, 1930), p. 258 *et seq*.

[70] RIC I-G Reports generally in 1919, PRO CO 904/108-10; S. Tery (trans. M.G. Rose), 'Raids and reprisals: Ireland: eye-witness (1923)', *Éire-Ireland* 20 (2) (1985); M. Seedorf,

'Defending reprisals: Sir Hamar Greenwood and the "Troubles", 1920–1921', *Éire-Ireland* **25** (4) (1990); J.S. Donnelly Jnr, '"Unofficial" British reprisals and IRA provocation, 1919–1920: the cases of three Cork towns', *Éire-Ireland* **45** (1) (2010).

[71] A. Silke, 'Ferocious times: the IRA, the RIC, and Britain's failure in 1919–1921', *Terrorism and Political Violence* **27** (3) (2016).

[72] J.A. Simon, 'Irish reprisals: Auxiliary Division's record', *The London Times*, 25 April 1921.

[73] C. Townshend, *The British Campaign in Ireland 1919–1921: The Development of Political and Military Policies* (Oxford, 1975), pp 95, 112.

[74] General Headquarters, the Forces in Ireland, 'Record of the rebellion in Ireland in 1920–1921 and the part played by the army in dealing with it, Vol. 1: Operations'; Lt Gen. Sir Hugh Jeudwine Papers, Imperial War Museum, Box 78/82/2.

[75] J. Ainsworth, 'The Black & Tans and Auxiliaries in Ireland, 1920–1921: their origins, roles and legacy', paper presented to the Queensland History Teachers' Association, Brisbane, Queensland (12 May 2001).

[76] P. O'Shea, 'Voices and the sound of drums', in P. Somerville-Large, *Irish Voices: An Informal History 1916–1966* (London, 2000), pp 38–9.

[77] A. Dolan, 'The British culture of paramilitary violence', in R. Gerwarth and J. Horne (eds), *War in Peace: Paramilitary Violence in Europe after World War I* (Oxford, 2012).

[78] D. Fitzpatrick, 'Ireland since 1870', in R.F. Foster (ed.), *The Oxford Illustrated History of Ireland* (Oxford, 1989).

[79] General F. Crozier, *Ireland Forever* (London, 1932), p. 133.

[80] D. Macardle, *The Irish Republic* (New York, 1937), p. 373.

[81] Crozier, *The Men I Killed*, p. 119.

[82] Crozier, *Ireland Forever*, p. 148.

[83] Mark Sturgis Diaries, 19.8.1920, Vol. 1, p. 45.

[84] 'Record of the rebellion', Vol. 1, p. 31; General Officer, Commanding-in-Chief, Ireland, Weekly Situation Report, 1.1.1921, S.I.C. (PRO CAB 27/108).

[85] J. Ainsworth, 'British security policy in Ireland, 1920–1921: a desperate attempt by the Crown to maintain Anglo-Irish unity by force', Queensland University of Technology, School of Humanities and Social Science, 11th Irish–Australian Conference (25–30 April 2000).

[86] P. Hart, *British Intelligence in Ireland, 1920–21: The Final Reports* (Cork, 2002), p. 19.

[87] Diary of Sir Henry Wilson, 29 September 1920.

[88] K. Griffith and T. O'Grady, *Ireland's Unfinished Revolution, An Oral History* (London, 1982), p. 193.

[89] www.theauxiliaries.com/index.html.

[90] N. Macready, *Annals of an Active Life,* Vol. 2 (New York, 1925), p. 498.

[91] General Sir Hubert Gough Papers, Imperial War Museum.

[92] *The Times,* 28 September 1920.

[93] 'What causes reprisals?', *The Weekly Standard*, No. 9, Friday, 8 October 1920, PRO, CO 904/38.

[94] P. Hart, *Mick* (London, 2006), pp 267–8.

[95] Some of the Black and Tans and Auxiliaries were recruited to the police forces in Palestine where, under much stricter discipline, their performance was judged a success. See the discussion in Chapter 4.

[96] Collins's letter to Donal Hales, 13 August 1920.

[97] H. Talbot, *Michael Collins' Own Story* (London, 1923), p. 93.

3. The effect of Bloody Sunday on intelligence

… though Republican propaganda made a brilliant job of portraying the operation as a body blow against the government, this did not alter the reality of the situation.

Charles Townshend

Oscar Traynor claimed that the effect of Bloody Sunday was 'to paralyse completely the British military intelligence system in Dublin'.[1] Frank Thornton elaborated: 'The British Secret Service was wiped out on Bloody Sunday'.[2] Both statements are exaggerations, but Bloody Sunday demonstrated not only the horrific logic of terror and reprisal tactics, but also the importance of the intelligence network. In fact, Bloody Sunday did not decisively affect the intelligence war for either side, and many British agents were more effectively on their guard thereafter, making a repeat of the attacks impossible. Further, Collins knew the day had fallen far short of his expectations and, when balanced against the tragedy at Croke Park and the loss of McKee and Clancy, it was perhaps as great a blow to the Irish as to the British.

For all the trauma of the day, when the Irish intelligence department met on the morning of 22 November for a debriefing on the events, they were 'disappointed with the result'.[3] They expressed dismay at the discrepancy between the department's original projections and the number of British agents finally killed. Though some British had not been home and some changed lodgings, there was regret expressed that some Volunteers were not enthusiastic about the operation and killing in cold blood and did not carry out their orders. GHQ was particularly dissatisfied with the 4th Battalion and its failure to attack many homes on the North Circular Road, and this led to Collins quickly dismissing its O/C, Christy Byrne.[4]

Another planned attack was controversially called off on Saturday night. John V. Joyce was a former medical student and 1916 veteran of the South

Dublin Union, and was the captain of C Company, 4th battalion. Joyce cancelled the operation at the Standard Hotel. Colonel Dan Bryan, a member of C Company, who was to take part in the action, said the decision to call it off was taken by Joyce only after consultation with other officers, because the job was considered 'too big'.[5] Others, however, felt that Joyce called the attack off on his own, and Ernie O'Malley later pilloried him in his book, *On Another Man's Wound*, although O'Malley did not name Joyce.[6] As would be expected, accounts of the cancellation presented a confused picture in the Bureau of Military History witness statements. There is enough contradictory detail in files and witness statements from other anti-Treaty men who had actually taken part in the abortive Standard Hotel attack to suggest that much of what O'Malley implied should be treated with caution. Joe Byrne told the pension board someone else had demobilised his company on Bloody Sunday.[7] Patrick Mullen said Joyce was in charge, but that the job was cancelled because the two British targets had left the hotel.[8]

C.S. (Todd) Andrews echoed a note of scepticism regarding the raids, but made clear that their ultimate effect was meaningful. He wrote:

> The fact is that the majority of the IRA raids were abortive
> because, as in our case, the man sought was not at home or, in
> several cases the Companies concerned bungled the job. In our
> Fourth Battalion there were at least four abortive raids ...
> ... Nevertheless the success of the operation, followed as it was a
> few weeks later by the success of Tom Barry in wiping out a unit
> of the 'invincible' Auxiliaries at Kilmichael, convinced the British
> that they could not win at a cost they could afford to pay ...[9]

Despite the disappointment expressed by some Irish in their discussion, the British reports on the effects of the morning's killings made clear the havoc rendered on both the civilian administration at Dublin Castle and on the military and police command.[10] Following Bloody Sunday the concentration of British agents in the Castle and the Central Hotel located at 1–5 Exchequer Street, just a stone's throw from Dublin Castle, prevented them from collecting intelligence, and had an adverse effect on their morale as well as their intelligence operations. Macready wrote that 'they were reduced to a state of nerves that it was pitiable to behold'. The morning's slayings had the desired intimidating result – the shootings had an immediate chilling effect on the British ability to continue their operations.[11] Intimidation is one of the major goals of terrorism. The scale of the effectiveness of the IRA's action induced intense alarm within the Castle administration, and Mark Sturgis wrote in his diary that 'it was a day of black murder. What they hope to gain by it, no one knows.'[12]

In his report to the British cabinet, Chief Secretary Hamar Greenwood minimised the events, and one wonders just how well the cabinet was kept abreast of events in Dublin.

> The motive for these terrible crimes ... is hard to explain, but the fact that several of the murdered officers were engaged on work connected with the preparation of cases for courts martial suggests an endeavour on the part of desperate criminals to strike back at men who were thought to be specially concerned in bringing them to justice.[13]

The afternoon's events in Croke Park were passed off by Greenwood as a search operation, intended to capture Volunteers:

> Men belonging to the Tipperary units of the Irish Republican Army ... most desperate characters in that organisation. The police were fired upon by armed Sinn Féin pickets at the entrance to the field. The police returned the fire. There is no doubt that some of the most desperate criminals in Ireland were amongst the spectators. The responsibility for the loss of innocent lives must rest with those men, and not with the police or military who were forced to fire in self-defence and used no unnecessary violence. A civilian and a boy of ten ... were shot in the streets of Dublin, and three prisoners who were being detained in Dublin Castle were shot while trying to escape.[14]

For further British opinion, one turns to that of Captain Robert Juene, a British intelligence officer who finished his tour in Dublin just a few months later. 'As a result of all this, those of us who had survived were shut up under guard in a hotel from where it was impractical to do any work.

In fact our job had to all intents and purposes been done, and the organisation was breaking up.' He also noted, however, that while British intelligence on the IRA was hampered by Bloody Sunday making many agents take shelter in Dublin Castle or the Central Hotel, the IRA was being ground down by General Nevil Macready's intensified campaign of massive searches and widespread arrests.[15]

After Bloody Sunday, the IRA still regarded Ormonde Winter and his Raid Bureau as serious opponents, and sent him warning letters to desist his attacks on Irish intelligence operations. In April 1921 Winter was severely wounded in the hand in an unsuccessful assassination attempt in Dublin, but he recovered to carry on and continued to exhort the RIC operatives to campaign against Irish intelligence.[16] In fact, the British were able to rebuild an effective intelligence organisation very quickly. Peter Hart wrote:

> Rather than bringing relief, the shootings actually precipitated the
> worst setback yet for the rebels at the hands of British intelligence.
> Military and police intelligence officers had now identified most
> of their opponents. Raiding parties were unleashed all over Ireland
> to round up known IRA officers and activists and detention camps
> were hurriedly established to receive the large numbers of men
> caught in the net. Informers sprang up once again and arms were
> found in unprecedented numbers.[17]

David Neligan recounted that the damage done to the British intelligence effort did not stop their raids:

> Following on Bloody Sunday, as it came to be called, British
> raiding went on non-stop. Those arrested were paraded before
> masked spotters, and in other cases prisoners were observed
> through slits in doors and fences … Failing identification, suspects
> were generally interned. These camps held thousands of prisoners,
> notably one at Ballykinlar, Co Down. Numbers of these were held
> on the flimsiest of suspicions.
>   … After this body-blow on Bloody Sunday, there was an interval
> while the British sought to reorganise their network. Their star

operators were gone and those now coming on the scene were not as good.

But Neligan also noted the effect on Irish intelligence:

Things were very bad at this time and even the Squad was very much circumscribed in their activities. One night I was waiting at a street corner for one of the Squad. None of them turned up, but Collins came instead. There was a real reign of terror in Dublin at the time.[18]

It is likely that the Volunteers had no plan to deal with the aftermath of the attacks in Dublin. While Irish intelligence and military activities were curtailed shortly afterward in Dublin, there was no slowing down in the rest of the country.

Bloody Sunday was made to be as spectacular as possible, and intended to coincide with attacks on property in Britain, as much to demonstrate Irish resolve as to tackle the specific problem of dedicated British agents in Ireland. Terrorism necessarily involves spectacle – this is what grants it the power to terrorise, to assault relations between individuals and the wider world.[19] In sum, Collins's 21 November attack was intended as a temporary measure to eliminate some agents, scare off some others, achieve maximum propaganda impact with simultaneous killings, buy time, intimidate any Irish who were wavering in their support of the IRA, and pre-empt British intelligence from capturing him. All these goals had been achieved, but the cost, especially considering the attacks at Croke Park, had been terribly high. Charles Townshend comments: 'though Republican propaganda made a brilliant job of portraying the operation as a body blow against the government, this did not alter the reality of the situation'.[20] The British had about 160 intelligence officers deployed in Ireland, so it is hard to see how losing six to ten officers could have dealt a mortal blow to their intelligence operations. Moreover, the papers seized during the raids by the IRA do not appear to have yielded a significant amount of hard information. The British proved their resilience by their response: a wave of arrests, internment without trial and martial law.

The terrorist shock effect on the British authorities was considerable, but the operation failed to restore the Irish intelligence organisation to its previous mastery.[21] A considerable improvement in British intelligence gathering was apparent in early 1921, and was noticed throughout the country. The fact was that beneath the brilliant structure of Collins's department in Dublin, the Irish intelligence system outside of Dublin was seriously defective. Local units simply failed to grasp the necessity of intelligence gathering and the analysis of the gathered information to plan operations.[22]

At least in the short term, the IRA's action had the intended effect on British intelligence. In Townshend's elegant phrase, 'Victory is achieved not so much by knocking the enemy's sword from his hand as by paralysing his arm'.[23]

Its political effect was also dramatic. As noted by C.S. Andrews, when combined with the news of the Kilmichael ambush in County Cork one week later, the British press made Lloyd George's boast to have 'murder by the throat' seem like a fantasy statement in the British public opinion. Until Bloody Sunday, the British maintained their thinking that the Irish were incapable of conducting co-ordinated attacks. One fact is indisputable: the scale and speed of the operation was a shock to the British. Further, the British were publicly appalled at the ruthlessness of the operation. It was staged at multiple addresses at precisely the same time, with officers shot at point blank range while mostly unarmed, in some cases still in their pyjamas, and in some cases in front of their wives. The British would have understood that this could not have been carried out by a mere gang of assassins. Over a hundred men of varying reliability had to have been assembled, assigned, armed and briefed by the IRA leadership, without a single detail leaking to the enemy. Bloody Sunday was a shocking and pivotal moment in the Irish War of Independence, a war that forever changed the relationship between Ireland and Britain. After that, the British opinion of Irish capabilities changed, as did their outlook and approach. Diarmuid Ferriter wrote:

> It was unquestionably a turning point, and it probably heightened
> the sense of urgency and speeded up the momentum and
> negotiations which led to the truce. We know now that Michael
> Collins would have settled for a truce as early as December, 1920.
> The assassinations carried out that morning and the shootings in
> Croke Park – which even the *Daily Mail* described as a 'reprisal' in

all its negative connotations, led to the declaration of martial law.

And it was not a total imposition, but it was still recognition of the fact that things had become out of control in Ireland. And even at the very worst point, there was always some form of negotiations going on.[24]

The key fact the British had to accept was that the IRA knew where to find them and that their intelligence network had been compromised. How many other agents and intelligence officers would be exposed? Men with secret agendas who needed to live quietly among the civilian population could no longer do so. They had to withdraw inside the security cordon around Dublin Castle and nearby hotels.

History has seemed more concerned with the afternoon's events. Shooting unarmed football supporters is the stuff nationalist mythology is made of, particularly when the British authorities disputed who fired first in Croke Park. The morning's events have been left to those concerned with spies and spying, to those who consider the killings largely in terms of their effects on British intelligence. It has been established that the Irish made mistakes, that some of the British killed were not the spies they were purported to be, and the accusation is made more pointed by killing of civilians and at least one that Collins admitted was 'the wrong man' (Patrick McCormack in the Gresham Hotel). But it should be noted that General Crozier was particularly critical of the British cabinet to sanction activities like those of the British officers killed on Bloody Sunday. He wrote:

> Captains A and B and many others at the War Office (backed up secretly by the CIGS [Commander of the Imperial General Staff], Sir Henry Wilson) set out in the name of 'law and order' on a similar mission before Michael Collins with this difference – Collins never denied what he did … The reader may not remember the solemn pomp and circumstance which accompanied the cavalcade of death through the streets of London when coffins or gun carriages draped with the Union Jack, containing the remains of murdered officers and ex-officers, were solemnly paraded before the populace followed by Ministers of the Crown and attended by the King's representative and guards of honour. I do. Either those Ministers knew they were

following the mortal remains of men who had died in the service of the Crown while engaged in a 'murder stunt' or they did not. Sir Henry Wilson knew and went to his own death within two years under very similar circumstances. If they did not they should have. It was their duty to know.[25]

Since the Bloody Sunday raids, historians have debated whether the results created a larger effect on Irish and British intelligence operations, or had greater effects on politics and propaganda owing to their longer lasting traumatic consequences. The executions of the British agents had a shattering effect on the morale of the British in Ireland, as well as in Britain. The British public and government were shocked and could not believe that with all their mighty resources they could be so humiliated. Though Lloyd George fumed about 'murderers' in public, it was this event as much as any other that led him to begin sending emissaries to Ireland seeking peace.

There was little chance from that point on that the British would win. Collins and his guerrilla army had grasped the principle enunciated by the Narodnaya Volya in Russia that 'the terrorists cannot overthrow the government, cannot drive it from St Petersburg and Russia; but having compelled it for so many years running to do nothing but struggle with them, by forcing it to do so still for years and years, they will render its position untenable'.[26] Like for the Irish, for the Narodniks, selective assassination was one of their principal techniques, with the chief targets being police officials, policymakers, and government officials who were known for their brutality or their advocacy of repressive policies. They argued they had no alternative, since the regime had closed all possible avenues of peaceful reform. In Collins's words,

> Ireland's story from 1918 to 1921 may be summed up as the story of a struggle between our determination to govern ourselves and to get rid of British government and the British determination to prevent us from doing either. It was a struggle between two rival Governments, the one an Irish Government resting on the will of the people and the other an alien Government depending for its existence upon military force – the one gathering more and more authority, the other steadily losing ground.

It could be said that if one were scoring, the British would have lost the intelligence war, tactically, but they were more successful strategically in determining just how far Collins and the Irish would go in Treaty negotiations. After Bloody Sunday, Collins's goal was to get to those negotiations.

Two aspects of Bloody Sunday had long-ranging ramifications. The first is that, immediately after the day, the British intelligence operation was in disarray and it would take many months to partially and finally rebuild it, a situation with which the government could not live. The British consequently started to negotiate with the Irish about greater concessions. Secondly, several groups of men at a precise hour, and in widespread locations carried out the complex operation. The skilful co-ordination for such an operation was impressive, making it obvious that the IRA was not a small-time 'hit-and-run' operation. The successful execution of such a complex operation finally forced Lloyd George and the other British leaders to reassess their opponents. Until Bloody Sunday, the British had not altered their opinion of the capabilities of the Irish. After that, their outlook and approach changed.

What is most interesting was Lloyd George's private reaction to Bloody Sunday. With eleven officers dead in Dublin, fourteen civilians killed at Croke Park, and armed police patrolling Whitehall and Westminster for fear of IRA actions in London, he might have been forgiven, or at least understood, for breaking off contacts that had begun in September and continued through the autumn. Instead, what message did he send to Arthur Griffith?

To Patrick Moylett, Irish businessman and a Volunteer who had been talking with British cabinet member Herbert Fisher, he said: 'Ask Griffith for God's sake to keep his head and not to break off the slender thread that had been established'. Moylett met C.J. Phillips in Downing Street each day of the week after Bloody Sunday, to discuss every angle of a possible settlement. From the location of the meetings alone, it's clear the Prime Minister approved. Lloyd George felt that if there was to be a settlement between the British government and Sinn Féin, it had to happen while the Liberal and Tory Parties were in a coalition government, otherwise each would take an opposing line to the other, were one of the parties to be in government and one in opposition. According to Dáil Minister Ernest Blythe years later, Éamon de Valera, upon his return from America in December, had exactly the same view as Lloyd George, at exactly the same time. How much co-ordination there was between Downing Street and the military command in Dublin could be questioned, because on 26 November Arthur Griffith was arrested, against the wishes of the Prime Minister.

The nascent talks continued, however, and – further illustrating how Bloody Sunday irrevocably changed the course of the war – a mere two weeks afterward, on 7 December 1920, Collins met Archbishop Patrick Joseph Clune of Perth, Western Australia, at Prime Minister David Lloyd George's behest, to discuss peace feelers. One goal of the British was to determine with whom they could negotiate.[27] (Archbishop Clune was an uncle of Conor Clune, who had just been killed on Bloody Sunday.) How much store to set by his intervention is hard to decide, but what is not in doubt is his access to the people who mattered on both sides, and that makes his experience in those few weeks of December worth exploring. It was at this time that the British were showing the ongoing signs of negotiation in earnest. Lloyd George sent out feelers for additional talks, but he did so in a fashion calculated to produce the maximum of distrust and obstinance on the part of the Irish.

Archbishop Clune, born on 6 January 1864 in Ruan, Co. Clare, was first asked to mediate on behalf of his native land by the Honorable Lord Morris, T.P. O'Connor MP and Joe Devlin MP at a luncheon in London on 30 November. That night there were severe Black and Tan reprisals at Lahinch, Co. Clare, with several people killed and many homes burned. Lloyd George condemned all reprisals, and asked the archbishop to go to Dublin, interview the Sinn Féin leaders, arrange a temporary truce, and prepare an atmosphere for negotiations. Lloyd George, however, could not guarantee the safety of the archbishop, and would not consent to a safe conduct for the Sinn Féin leaders to meet the archbishop. In order to remain incognito, Archbishop Clune travelled to Ireland on the mailboat as 'Revd Dr Walsh'.

Joe O'Reilly, Collin's prime messenger, was assigned to bring the archbishop to Collins:

My [O'Reilly's] next meeting with Dr. Clune was the evening of the next day, Monday, 6th December, 1920, when about eight in the evening I called at the Gresham Hotel in O'Connell Street, met Dr. Clune, and told him of the time and place where he would meet Michael Collins the next day. I again warned him to be very careful on leaving for the appointment, and to show no surprise if the driver of the car that I would send took a roundabout way. His Grace took me aside and expressed his uneasiness at the prospect of being followed by Dublin Castle. He then said to me: 'I will go to Dublin Castle and see if my movements have been watched. It were better drop the negotiations than risk the capture of Michael Collins'.

On 7 December, accompanied by Dr Michael Fogarty, Bishop of Killaloe, Clune was driven to meet Collins.

The next day, Tuesday, 7th December, Dr. Clune, accompanied by Dr. Fogarty, Bishop of Killaloe, set out from All Hallows College, Drumcondra, for the first interview with Michael Collins. They were driving quite a time, not noticing where they were, too interested in their chat, when Dr. Clune looked out as the car drew up before one of the fine residences in Merrion Square, a most unlikely hide-out for a man with a price on his head. The driver knocked at the hall-door and the two bishops were shown into the consulting room of Dr. Robert Farnan, one of Dublin's leading gynaecologists. I called upon Dr. Farnan in October 1935, and he told me that Dr. Clune and 'Mick' Collins met in his house regularly during the negotiations. Mick usually came on a bike which he left at a tobacconist in Merrion Row, just round the corner. At that time, December 1920, Dr. Farnan was attending the wives of two of the auxiliaries, and consequently his house was never suspected. He remembered the horrible feeling he had on one occasion as a lorry full of auxiliaries pulled up before the door while Mick and Archbishop Clune were upstairs. The doctor had a few bad minutes until the husband of one of the two patients handed him a message from his wife. Another day Mick came down the stairs arm-in-arm with the Archbishop. Both were laughing at some story as Mick opened the hall door, and stood behind it until Dr. Farnan hailed a cab from across the street. As the Archbishop got into the cab a lorry full of 'Black-and-Tans' moved slowly past the house. Perhaps some one had recognised Mick on one of his many visits. Mick closed the door, drew his revolver and watched the lorry from a corner of the curtain. The lorry continued its beat up and down the street, so Mick decided to get out through the back garden. That his house was never once searched or suspected throughout the negotiations Dr. Farnan attributes to his professional interest in the wives of the auxiliaries he was attending. Suspicion there undoubtedly was, probably through some policeman glimpsing Michael Collins on one of his visits, but, fortunately, the house escaped a search, luckily for all concerned.[28]

Following his meeting with Collins, Archbishop Clune assured the British cabinet that Collins 'was the one with whom effective business could be done'.[29] Collins was 'on the run' but Arthur Griffith was in Mountjoy Prison at this time, and on 8 December, Dr Fogarty and Archbishop Clune met with Alfred W. Cope, the Assistant Undersecretary for Ireland, at Mountjoy, and then with Griffith. Cope had been appointed to his position with a brief to open covert lines of communication with the nationalist movement. Griffith enthusiastically welcomed the prospect of a truce. Then they met with Eoin MacNeill, who was not so enthusiastic but accepted it. Cope was told to present a draft of a truce agreement to Dublin Castle authorities, but this received a hostile reception by Chief Secretary for Ireland Sir Hamar Greenwood and the British military.[30]

These negotiations were opposed by General Sir Nevil Macready, but favoured by most of the British cabinet and government.[31] General Macready provided a less than generous judgement of Cope: 'He was *persona grata* with the leaders of the rebellion, in whom he had a belief that was pathetic as, in my opinion, it was misplaced'.[32] Curiously, Macready was more complimentary in another description of Cope, who he described as 'a tireless worker, highly strung, a firm believer in self-government for Ireland … and feverishly anxious to do all in his power, even at the risk of his life, to ensure the success of Mr Lloyd George's policy'.[33] Macready's unflattering view of Cope was shared by many in Dublin Castle and by other members of the military. One member of Winter's staff remarked Cope was universally detested by everyone in the Castle, it being generally supposed that 'he was going to sell us to the rebels'.[34]

I do not know if anything can be done to restrain persons like Mr
Cope from preaching rebel doctrines in this Brigade Area. The
area administered by the Essex Regiment is a bad one, and the
rebels were only kept from over-running the whole area by the
good military spirit shown by this regiment.[35]

A key challenge Cope faced was one of trust, compounded by a British
modus operandi that attempted to impute onto Sinn Féin what were the
British negotiating positions. This would deflect any accusation that they
were acceding to Sinn Féin's demand of an independent Irish Republic.
Predictably, back came the counter-demand from the British for a surrender
of arms before any talk of a truce. There was even a deadline set for such a
surrender – 27 December. The problem, as Cope saw it, was that the cabinet
was heavily influenced by the conviction of the military leaders in Dublin,
Macready and French, that the war was turning in their favour, and that
talk of a truce would only take the pressure off the IRA. Frank Gallagher
cited a communication written by Collins on 14 December 1920 to Arthur
Griffith and a number of republican prisoners, Michael Staines, Eamonn
Duggan and Eoin MacNeill: 'We have clearly demonstrated our willingness
to have peace on honourable terms. Lloyd George insists on capitulation.
Between these there is no mean.'[36]

Events in Ireland seemed to confirm the British conviction of imminent
victory, and stiffened Lloyd George's resolve to take a hard line with the republican leadership. Two events in particular are believed to have caused
Lloyd George to hold back in any peace feelers towards the Dáil government. To the disbelief of the Dáil government and the IRA, a minority of
councillors on Galway County Council, notwithstanding their previous
pledge of allegiance to the republican government, and the fact that most
of their colleagues were in prison or on the run, passed a resolution calling
on Dáil Eireann and the British government to send delegates to negotiate
a truce. Then, Father Michael O'Flanagan sent a telegram directly to Lloyd
George, asking him what steps he would take to start peace talks within
days. The problem was that Father O'Flanagan happened to be Sinn Féin
Vice-President, and his telegram was taken by the British press as an official
Sinn Féin communication.

Archbishop Clune returned to London and met Lloyd George on 10

December, had another meeting with him on 11 December, and returned to Dublin that night. Dr Clune gave Cabinet Secretary Phillip Kerr one final set of proposals: 1) a one-month cessation of hostilities to create a peaceful atmosphere, and 2) Dáil Eireann would be allowed to meet 'to discuss among themselves, or with plenipotentiaries of the government the final settlement of the Irish question'. The British authorities in Dublin Castle agreed to meet with the Dáil, but Collins and Richard Mulcahy could not attend. Moreover, the proposed truce would still require the IRA/Volunteers to surrender all their arms, and the Dáil could not meet publicly. Clune again returned to London on 18 December, and though meetings continued until 28 December, his negotiations were at an end.

Further attempts at negotiations continued following these failures, and Andy Cope (from Dublin Castle) and Collins (from GHQ) met several times in complete secrecy. Collins remained sceptical, but he knew that the IRA's military position was beginning to unravel. British military intelligence still expressed confidence the military could crush the revolt. David Boyle of British intelligence wrote a report predicting military victory in six weeks. This was a great influence on the British cabinet to shut down peace initiatives.[37] But the Clune negotiations indicated a willingness to continue to negotiate and that Collins was a 'major player', and from this time forward the British began to accept that a negotiated settlement was possible. As with the military actions, however, negotiations had to proceed at a pace that could be acceptable to both sides – ideologues and militarists on both sides had to be cajoled to the table. Georges Clemenceau was right: 'War is much too important to be left to soldiers'.

Cope addressed the problems he was having, and his letters to his boss, Sir Warren Fisher, the head of the British Civil Service, illustrated them. Cope wrote he was 'taking his career in his hands, and abandoned the traditional methods of the Castle peace parleyings and got into direct and personal contact with the leaders of the Irish people'. He 'had to first convince the powers of Sinn Féin that he meant to play straight with them, and then persuade the powers residing in Dublin Castle and elsewhere that the leaders of the "murder gang" desired an honourable settlement'. Finally, in a letter to Fisher, he wrote, 'I have met quite a number of prominent Sinn Féiners – two were sentenced to death in the rebellion and reprieved – and I feel that I have the temper of the present situation'.[38]

Many were to look back on Clune's failed efforts with dismay, and former Prime Minister H.H. Asquith called them the 'big missed opportunity'.[39] When the Truce was finally declared in July 1921, de Valera noted that as long as the British government would do the same, he was willing to abide by the terms negotiated by Clune in the previous December. These early negotiations having failed, the parties would have to fight through another bloody six months until the Truce of July 1921. When welcoming the Treaty several months later, Sir Warren Fisher wrote: 'Better late than never, but I can't get out of my mind the unnecessary number of graves'.[40]

Notes

[1] Oscar Traynor: Witness Statement 340.

[2] Frank Thornton: Witness Statement 510.

[3] Daniel McDonnell: Witness Statement 486.

[4] Christopher Byrne: Witness Statement 642.

[5] Dan Bryan quoted in C. Townshend, *The Republic: The Fight for Irish Independence, 1918–1923* (London, 2013), p. 207.

[6] E. O'Malley, *On Another Man's Wound* (Dublin, 1979), p. 269.

[7] Sworn statement made by Joseph Byrne, 3 July 1936 and J.V. Joyce to Sec, MSP Board, 17 April 1936, MSP34REF18108, MSPC, MAI.

[8] Patrick Mullen: Witness Statement 621.

[9] T.R. Dwyer, *The Squad and the Intelligence Operations of Michael Collins* (Cork, 2005), p. 190.

[10] Report of Dublin Metropolitan Police, 21 November 1920, CO 904/168.

[11] C.S. Andrews, *Dublin Made Me* (Cork, 1979), p. 165

[12] Mark Sturgis Diaries, PRO 30.59, 1–5.

[13] Chief Secretary's Report, CAB 27/108, POR, London.

[14] *Ibid.*

[15] Captain Robert Jeune Memoirs, Imperial War Museum.

[16] Correspondence from Winter to Chief Secretary Hamar Greenwood and General Hugh Tudor, PRO, CO 904/1772 (2).

[17] Hart, P. (ed.), *British Intelligence in Ireland, 1920–21: The Final Reports* (Cork, 2002), p. 12.

[18] David Neligan: Witness Statement 380.

[19] M. Richardson, 'Terrorism: trauma in the excess of affect,' in J.R. Kurtz (ed.), *Cambridge Critical Concepts: Trauma and Literature* (Cambridge, 2018), p. 329.

[20] C. Townshend, 'The IRA and development of guerrilla war', *English Historical Review* 93 (371) (April 1979).

[21] C. Townshend, *Political Violence in Ireland. Government and Resistance since 1848* (Oxford, 1983), p. 338.

[22] GHQ IRA memorandum, 'Serious Deficiencies in Country Units, March 1921, Mulcahy papers, MSS P.7/A/II/17.

[23] Townshend, 'The IRA and development of guerrilla war. See V.N. Giáp, *People's War, People's Army, The Military Art of People's War* (New York, 1971).

24 Diarmuid Ferriter, quoted in K. Duggan, 'Remembering a dark and murderous day in the capital', *The Irish Times* 19 November 2005.
25 General F.P. Crozier, *Ireland Forever* (London, 1932), p. 148.
26 Stepniak, *Underground Russia* (New York, 1892), p. 32.
27 Townshend, *Political Violence*, p. 274.
28 Revd J.T. McMahon: Witness Statement 362. See also Most Revd Dr Michael Fogarty: Witness Statement 271.
29 Cabinet conclusion 77 (20)6, of App. III, Conference of Ministers, 24 December 1920.
30 Alfred William (Andy) Cope was born in 1877 and entered government service as a boy clerk. He joined the detective branch of the Department of Customs and Excise in 1896, and was made a preventative inspector in 1908. His energy and intelligence soon made him head of the branch in London and he spent ten adventurous years pursuing smugglers and illicit distillers, especially in the docklands (M.R.D. Foot, *Dictionary of National Biography 1951–1960* (Oxford, 1971), p. 251). Cope was involved in many discussions of the time, and was often in contact with Collins. He was asked to submit a witness statement of his role and how the negotiations evolved. He refused to outline his role or the negotiations but submitted the following letter as his statement: 'It is not possible for this history to be truthful … The IRA must be shown as national heroes, and the British Forces as brutal oppressors. Accordingly the Truce and Treaty will have been brought about by the defeat of the British by the valour of small and ill-equipped groups of irregulars. And so on. What a travesty it will and must be. Read by future generations of Irish children, it will simply perpetuate the long standing hatred of England and continue the miserable work of self-seeking politicians, who, for their own aggrandizement, have not permitted the Christian virtues of forgiveness and brotherhood to take its place … Ireland has too many histories; she deserves a rest' (Sir Alfred Cope: Witness Statement 469).
31 C. Younger, *Ireland's Civil War* (New York, 1979), p. 128 *et seq.*
32 Macready, *Annals of an Active Life, 2 vols* (New York, 1925), p. 493.
33 *Ibid.*
34 H. de Montmorency, *Sword and Stirrup* (London, 1936), p. 356.
35 Memo by Colonel Commandant, 17th Infantry Brigade to Headquarters 6th Division, Ireland, 15 September 1921, Strickland Papers, Imperial War Museum, p. 363.
36 F. Gallagher, *The Anglo-Irish Treaty* (London, 1965), p. 23. Frank Gallagher was editor of the Irish republican newspaper, *The Irish Bulletin.*
37 Letter from David Boyle to Cabinet, 11 December 1920.
38 M. Smith, *The Spying Game* (London, 2003), p. 371.
39 M. Sturgis (ed. M. Hopkinson), *The Last Days of Dublin Castle: The Mark Sturgis Diaries* (Dublin, 1999), p. 193.
40 Sir Warren Fisher letter to Mark Sturgis, 17 December 1921.

4. Terror is just around the corner

I didn't like myself in Ireland. I don't think anybody else did either.
Lieutenant Frederick A.S. Clarke, Essex Regiment

Terrorism is often used to conduct armed conflict against a militarily stronger enemy when the organisation launching the armed struggle is not yet at a stage where guerrilla warfare is viable. Terrorism can also be used to supplement insurgency warfare, as it was on Bloody Sunday and throughout Ireland. In such cases, it is employed to keep the enemy off balance and distracted, principally by conducting strikes against vulnerable targets at the enemy's rear. The mode of struggle adopted by insurgents is dictated by circumstances rather than by choice, and whenever possible, insurgents concurrently use a variety of strategies in the struggle. Terrorism, which is the easiest form of insurgency, is practically always one of these modes. In the war, the British used terror to implant fear into the Irish who were helping the IRA, and the Irish were the ones using terrorism to keep the British off balance and to intimidate the local population.[1] It was seen as one of the modes of warfare that the Irish required to achieve their political objectives.[2]

In general terms, terror has been a thread in human experience that has existed in political life and wartime since ancient times and is certainly a constituent element of many wars and insurrections in the last 100 years. What was earlier known as shock or a moral crisis became more psychological and intimate in the language of Freud: trauma. Trauma is as much about rupturing or damaging how a body experiences the world at a relational level as it is a function of individual psychology. Etymologically, 'terrorism' derives from the Latin *terrere*, meaning 'frighten' or 'extreme anxiety and fear'. The nineteenth-century slogan 'propaganda by the deed' still applies today: terrorism is primarily a psychological weapon.[3] But trauma, in short, needs to be recognised as affective and not simply psychological. It has particular resonance with the public, with the ordinary person living in the times, because the trauma is linked to the core issues of human risk, safety and survival, and it is driven by fear and apprehension heightened by the apparent unpredictability of the violence. It is a collocation of material and ideational factors that create its coming together as intimidating events of terror that evoke dismay, fear and anger. There is a range of acts that can be considered terror, ranging from those that constitute a public nuisance to massacres that include a significant loss of life. Terrorism has a disproportionate political impact with its acts of violence.

There is also a deterrent intent to terror: it resonates throughout the country, thereby preventing any further resistance. It is deliberately aimed at intimidating, humiliating or eliminating individuals who are deemed as actively or potentially hostile. This inhibitory intent is particularly important in the context of defining terror, which even while killing or injuring individuals is more concerned with wounding the social and political fabric of the community. Lenin has been credited with saying 'terror is meant to terrify'. Whether he said it or not, the statement is correct. That has to be the ultimate goal – to terrify the opponent into capitulation or concession. Even the rhetoric of terror is a political weapon. Charles Townshend wrote that 'the greatest accomplice to terrorism is collective alarmism'.[4] How many are terrified by the possibility of a 'replicable act', in modern anti-terror parlance? Its very status as trauma is defined by its refusal to be known, especially as terror is directed against people who do not expect to be the targets of an attack.

But beyond the acts themselves, there also exists the genuinely legal and philosophical problem of *how* or *if* violent acts are to be judged as terror. To do so, it is incumbent to define as precisely as possible the concept of 'terror' in war. Terrorism is as old as insurgency – in fact, most modern political and military authors consider terror a strategy, rather than an ideology. Questions abound regarding terrorism, including: What is terrorism or how should it be defined? When is violence 'just' violence and when does it become terrorism? Can terrorism ever be justified? Some have argued that terrorism is not necessarily morally wrong and not morally worse than war and that if war can be justified, then so can terrorism.[5] Ethicists ask if a country can go to war, and send thousands to kill others, can it also send one person to kill one particular person? Isn't assassination just a smaller act of war? Machiavelli's main assertion was that ethical and religious notions have no place in politics:

> It must be understood that a prince cannot observe all of those virtues for which men are reputed good, because it is often necessary to act against mercy, against faith, against humanity, against frankness, against religion, in order to preserve the state.[6]

Violence by itself is not identical to terror, and violent acts may not be terror. Not all acts of war are terrorist acts, but terrorism frequently forms an integral part of war.

It has been suggested that terror is one of the tactics common to all guerrilla wars, but on closer analysis it is clear that the terrorism to which reference is made often consists of assassinations of military and political leaders, and other attacks designed to weaken and destroy the morale of the enemy.[7] The victimisation of defenceless, innocent persons is quite a different matter from the assassination of political and military leaders, but they can also be considered terror.[8] This is unlike the indiscriminate killing of civilians that is the current hallmark of terrorism. Acts of terror regularly are found in 'conventional war', as well as in guerrilla actions; it is, however, often harder to distinguish between acts of terrorism and guerrilla warfare. This distinction cannot always be rigidly maintained in practice – some guerrillas may slip over into terrorist activities, and some terrorists may engage in more 'conventional' guerrilla operations. A soldier or group selects terrorism as a course of action from a range of perceived alternatives.

It is difficult to establish boundaries between terrorism and other forms of political violence. The primary aim of war, morality apart, is to win. Whether one lies in wait for the enemy to ambush him under cover of darkness or scrub or outcrops of rock is quite immaterial. Guerrilla warfare is like terrorism in that both are actual evidence of comparative weakness: the insurgent lacks the manpower, equipment or support to defeat a conventional army, and turns to an asymmetrical strategy.[9] Guerrilla warfare is characterised by small-scale, unconventional, limited actions carried out by irregular forces against regular military forces and personnel, their supply lines and communications. Though terrorism and guerrilla tactics are two distinct phenomena, there is an overlap between the two. The most impor-

tant distinction between them is that unlike terrorism, guerrillas try to establish physical control over an area. Insurgency and terrorism are always
brutal – both involving:

- fear,
- force,
- torture and executions, and
- forcible conversion of the civil population.

Historically, the approach to dealing with an insurrection was to crush it as
quickly as possible. When guerrilla tactics were used, regular armies would
resort to destruction of crops, livestock and property. Such a policy of military power and some State terror was effective and the rebels were soon
crushed – but the historic tactics proved futile when both the insurrection-
ists and the State were willing to use terrorism as a political tactic.[10] The
nature of guerrilla wars of longer duration is inextricably linked with the
terrorism of retaliation and reprisal.

Some have defined 'terror' as 'apart from a state of mind, a conscious attempt to create an acute fear of violence against the person or property,
which may affect individuals, groups or the population at large'.[11] Any definition of terrorism returns to the concept of *fear*. There is an ancient Chi-
nese proverb of war: victory is gained not by the number killed – but by
the number frightened. A simple definition is that terror is the deliberate
use of violence, or threat of its use, against people – against their life and
limb, or against their property – with the aim of intimidating some other
people into a course of action they would not usually take. The US State
Department and NATO define terrorism as 'premeditated, motivated violence perpetrated against non-combatant groups by sub-national or clandestine agents, acting as individuals or in groups, intended to influence an
audience wider than the immediate victim or victims'.[12] These definitions
seem to eliminate actions by or against state agents, and a definition of terror
must include actions by and against state as well as non-state agents. In fact,
as Brian Hanley points out, any definition should be 'agent neutral'.[13] A
more inclusive definition of terrorism is: terrorism is an indirect strategy of
using fear or terror induced by violent attacks or force (or the threat of its
use) against one group of people (direct target) or their property as a means

to intimidate and coerce another group of people (indirect target) and influence their actions in order to reach further political objectives. Terrorism is a type of violence calculated to alter the attitudes and behaviour of multiple audiences. The violent acts that form part of such a strategy should be called terrorist acts.[14] One of the goals of terrorism is to disturb the normal lives and liberties that people have, which is against human rights. The UN stresses that this one of the most important ways in which terrorism should be defined.[15] It targets few in a way that affects many.[16]

Richard English, who has written several books on Irish uses of terror (especially in 'the Troubles' of the late twentieth century), defines terrorism as:

> Terrorism involves heterogeneous violence used or threatened
> with a political aim; it can involve a variety of acts, of targets, and
> of actors; it possesses an important psychological dimension,
> producing terror or fear among a directly threatened group and
> also a wider implied audience in the hope of maximizing political
> communication and achievement; it represents a subspecies of
> warfare, and as such it can form part of a wider campaign of
> violent and non-violent attempts at political leverage.[17]

Terrorism is intentionally used for political effect, even more than military effect. Whenever terrorism is used, one must ask if it is possible to successfully deal with it without resorting to coercion or equal acts of terrorism? Governments must balance a perceived need to control the direct consequences of terrorism, by maintaining order and security, with the realisation that any coercive response to terrorism reduces democratic freedoms. When the British instituted – and accepted – a policy of reprisals, they lost their chance to win the 'hearts and minds' of the Irish population.

Current discussions regarding 'what constitutes terrorism' may seem to be more concerned with recent events, especially since the World Trade Center attacks on 11 September 2001 ('9/11') in New York City or the subway bombings in London on 7 July 2005 ('7/7'). These discussions, however, and difficulties defining terrorism were apparent even in the late nineteenth and early twentieth centuries. Many definitions make a distinction between violence aimed at property and violence aimed at persons. For example, a spokesperson for the International Workers of the World in 1912 took pains to distinguish between 'anti-social direct actions', such as the 1910 bombing of the *Los Angeles Times* building, which resulted in murder, and 'sabotage', which destroys buildings, rails, tools and machinery. A critical issue was the worker's relationship to property as the means of production. Such distinctions had been made earlier by the Fenians in their 'dynamite campaign' in Britain in the 1880s.[18]

Achieving a consensus on the meaning of the term 'terrorism' is not an important end in itself except, perhaps, for linguists. Given all the definitions of terror, it remains a highly manipulative term mainly used to condemn certain incidents or actors, with blurriness and negative connotation being its crucial characteristics. To take this further, clearly the imprecise use of the term 'terror' in the public sphere is not entirely accidental: rather it often reflects a political calculus.[19] That is why in some instances the term 'terrorism' seems to have become separated from its denotative content or military/political intent and is merely used to express one's moral disaffirmation. No matter what characteristics a special incident displays, labeling it 'terrorist' occasionally expresses nothing more than the speaker's rejection of the incident or the desire to convince others of its moral abjection. For the purposes of this book, there are three common elements to a terrorist attack:

- the use or threat of violence,
- political objectives, and
- the intention of sowing fear in a target population.

Creation of fear is the key. While Collins said that 'the organisation [the Irish and the IRA] conducted the conflict, as far as possible, in accordance with the rules of war. Only the armed forces and the spies and criminal agents of the British government were attacked', he also wrote: 'careful application of terrorism is also an excellent form of total communication'. Certainly, terror takes advantage of the publicity inherent in it to be used as a political transmission. Terrorism and brutality were at the very roots of the Irish independence campaign. The nationalist newspaper *An t'Óglach* published an editorial on the eve of the War of Independence in late 1918, which called on the Irish forces to:

acknowledge no limit and no scruple in resistance to the British ... we must recognise that anyone, civilian or soldier, who assists directly or by connivance in this crime against us, merits no more consideration than a wild beast, and should be killed without mercy or hesitation as opportunity offers ... the man who voluntarily surrenders when called for ... the man who drives a police car or assists in the transport of army supplies, all these having assisted the enemy must be shot or otherwise destroyed with the least possible delay.[20]

Not all Irish accepted the direction of the editorial at the time. C.S. Andrews wrote:

This was a comprehensive blueprint for the 'terror', but the Volunteers of 1918 who may have read it would not have taken it as anything but rhetoric. At that time they were certainly not psychologically attuned to killing except in pitched battle.[21]

Both the British and Irish actions and policies transformed as the war went on.

An t'Óglach continued publication throughout the war, and addressed the 'official' response to British announcements. For example, in September 1918 Lord Lieutenant Sir John French indicated that the English 'Government's policy toward Conscription for Ireland remains unchanged'. *An t'Óglach* strongly opposed conscription and in response to the Lord French statement, it editorialised:

It is desired that we should eliminate all talk and all thought of passive resistance, [against conscription] because passive resistance means, in effect, no resistance at all.
  We must fight with ruthlessness and ferocity ...[22]

The article went on to quote George Bernard Shaw: 'Nothing is ever done in the world unless men are willing to kill each other if it is not done'. Collins liked the article, had many copies distributed, and asked its author, Ernest Blythe, for more of the same.

At the start of 1919 IRA leaders writing in *An tÓglach* sketched the outline of a strategy in only broad strokes, but giving warning of the hazards to follow:

> We will strike in our own way, in our own time. If we cannot, by force of arms, drive the enemy out of our country at the present moment, we can help to make his position impossible and his military activities futile.
>
> ... England must be given the choice between evacuating this country and holding it by a foreign garrison with a perpetual state of war in existence. She must be made to realise that that state of war is not healthy for her. The agents of England in this country must be made to realise that their occupation is not a healthy one. All those engaged in carrying on the English administration in this country must be made to realise that it is not safe for them to try to 'carry on' in opposition to the Irish Republican Government and the declared wishes of the people. In particular, any policeman, soldier, judge, warder, or official, from the English Lord Lieutenant downwards, must be made to understand that it is not wise for him to distinguish himself by undue 'zeal' in the service of England in Ireland, nor in his opposition to the Irish Republic.[23]

The result in practice would largely boil down to a guerrilla war of movement in the country as well as terrorism in the cities and large towns. It is important to remember that the IRA had distinct goals in mind that (in their view) justified the use of violence. The function of the rebels' armed struggle was:

> not to destroy the enemy, for that is utopian, but it is indeed to force him, through prolonged war of psychological and physical attrition, to abandon our territory due to exhaustion and isolation.[24]

As the British learned to their dismay, counterinsurgency is by its very nature a cruel and nasty war. Insurgents feel free to take whatever steps they feel are necessary to secure victory, justifying their actions by the fact that they are fighting for their freedom from an oppressive power. When facing a totalitarian state, these measures are matched by an equally unrestrained policy on the part of the state, acting unchecked by either domestic or international opinion. When a politically free and democratic government is fighting an insurgency, however, it cannot act or respond in such an uninhibited manner. The effects of a democratic state's use of terror are seen by the outside world as atrocities by the established order and call into question the legitimacy of that established order. This effect was amplified in Ireland when the Irish declared that the true government was Dáil Éireann, and that the Dáil represented the 'oppressed' population. As a basis for insurrectionary tactics, the alternative administration of the Dáil, both as a political conception and as a political fact, was extremely important. It gave the Irish a national standing after January 1919 that it otherwise could not have claimed at that stage. The Irish Volunteers became the Irish Republican Army, the accredited force of a nation that was fighting for its life.[25] The Irish leaders were then able to apply the concept of a nation at war, an idea that enabled them to justify the war and the killings that were to become an essential part of the campaign for undermining the British political hold on Ireland, but which otherwise might have been seen solely as futile acts of terrorism. *An t'Oglach* made the point:

> The state of war which is thus declared to exist, renders the
> national army the most important national service of the moment.
> It justifies Irish Volunteers in treating the armed forces of the
> enemy, whether soldiers or policemen, exactly as a national army
> would treat the members of an invading army. Every Volunteer is
> entitled morally and legally, when in the execution of his duty, to
> use all legitimate methods of warfare.[26]

By definition and intent, most individuals in the Irish war generally encountered terror vicariously rather than directly. Terror's affectivity, however, makes it inseparable not simply from the violence of the terrorist act but also from the trauma that the event instils. When considering events in the Irish war, we should accept that both sides had a strategy of influencing the behaviour of others than the immediate victims by using terror. Terrorism is an indirect, twofold strategy. At the first level, terrorism seeks to provoke fear through the employment of violence. At the second level, it seeks to provoke certain reactions to the threat or fear spread by the violent acts. Wouldn't reprisals by the Black and Tans or a sign on an individual executed by the IRA indicating a 'spy or informer' qualify under this view? Whether an act was directed at a particular person or group of the public or not becomes irrelevant – terror is imagined as much as experienced. Should we call any act that generated fear in order to exploit it for further objectives 'terror'?

The British forces in Ireland – specifically the Black and Tans and Auxiliaries – used terrorism to crush nationalist sentiment. The 'Tans' and 'Auxies' were fearful of the fact that any civilian could be a guerrilla fighter, so they unleashed a campaign of terror against the entire civilian population, as well as the IRA. The sole purpose of their terrorist actions was to 'make an appropriate hell for rebels' in an effort to reduce support for Sinn Féin and the IRA. Men would be dragged outside, stripped, beaten and often brought back to RIC headquarters for questioning and further torture. One recorded incident details how a raiding party captured six IRA members in Kerry Pike (near Cork) and proceeded to cut out the tongue of one, the nose of another, the heart of another and bashed in the skull of a fourth.[27] Episodes of terror were meant to strike fear in the hearts of Irishmen and make them give up their quest for a free Ireland. Civilians who had no part in the Irish independence movement also became victims to British terror at the hands of the Black and Tans and Auxiliaries. The 'Tans' and the 'Auxies' acted as if *no* law applied to them, as if they were above the law. Any form of behavior, however atrocious it might be in the eyes of civilised men and women, seemed to be justified in their minds if it succeeded in achieving the limited goal for which it was designed.

The newspaper of Dublin Castle, *The Weekly Summary*, really a British propaganda news organ, succinctly and directly stated:

> When a war has begun the soldier has only one point of view, and a single duty, which is to defeat the enemy. Leaving political, and to a great extent ethical, considerations to others, he has to devise means for achieving his aim swiftly and effectively. He must study the hostile methods of warfare and contrive plans to counteract them. In so doing he may sometimes find it necessary to adopt or imitate practices he condemns.[28]

In fairness, Canadian historian David Leeson posited that historians have undervalued the importance of situational factors when analysing Ireland's policing in 1919–21.[29] In his view, the brutality that the Black and Tans and Auxiliaries frequently displayed mainly derived from the challenges of the situation into which they were thrust – a vicious guerrilla insurgency against which they formed an inadequate frontline. One recruit who was subsequently to resign recalled 'we were mercenary soldiers fighting for our pay, not patriots willing and anxious to die for our country … Our job was to earn our pay by suppressing armed rebellion, not die in some foolish … forlorn hope'. Leeson submits that since little can be determined about the nature of the Black and Tans' service in the First World War, that it should not be presumed many suffered from 'shell shock' or PTSD. While this book makes no claim regarding the number of Black and Tans who were so suffering, their actions, and recent research into the actions of those who have been diagnosed with PTSD, suggest that many of the Black and Tans and other participants in the war could be considered to be suffering the effects of it.

Further, the men operated in a very different environment during their time with the British Gendarmerie in Palestine, and there was little so-called 'BlackandTannery' there.[30] Historian Michael Hopkinson saw the Black and Tans as 'effect rather than cause; however appalling their deeds, they were the product of Lloyd George's policies' and he quotes from an article in May 1921 by Violet Asquith, a Liberal activist and daughter of the former prime minister, Herbert: 'We have to feel sorry for the Black and Tans … losing their souls in carrying out duties which no Englishman should have been asked to perform'.[31] Further to Leeson's position and to illustrate the confusion that was apparent throughout Irish history as to which side was the 'terrorist' and which was the 'counter-terrorist', is demonstrated in Chapter 18, *Terror and Counter-Terror*, of Edgar Holt's book, *Protest in Arms*.[32] While it is commonly thought, and written, that the first terror came from the British, and especially the Black and Tans and Auxiliaries, Holt presents the Irish as the first to use terror, and the Black and Tans being the 'counter-terror' forces. Holt lists various Irish actions which he deems to be terrorist in nature: the events that followed 20 May 1920 when Irish dockers embargoed British 'war materials' and railway workers followed suit; the killing of Colonel Gerald Smyth in the Cork County Club for his speech at Listowel addressing RIC members at their barracks in Listowel on 19 June: 'Sinn Féin has had all the sport up to the present, and we are going to have the sport now'; the killing of policemen in Cork in July. Holt indicated these led to *counter*-reprisals by the British. As a further example, Frank Brooke was the chairman of the Dublin and South-eastern Railway. On 30 July Collins intervened in the embargo by making 'non-combatant' supporters of the British war effort in Ireland legitimate targets and Brooke knew he was in danger. That day, Brooke chaired a meeting at Westland Row Railway Station and Collins sent Jim Slattery to lead Squad members to kill him.[33] The same could be said of Alan Bell's killing on the road in front of Elm Park Golf Club. Bell was taken off a tram opposite there and shot on 27 March 1920 when Bell was getting too close in his investigation of the funds for the Dáil Loan funds. (While most comments on Bell's activities restrict themselves to his activities investigating the Dáil Loan, it is clear from his personal papers that he was involved in a small, secretive committee that was directing intelligence work, particularly in regard to the William C. Forbes Redmond assassination on 30 July 1919. With the demise of the DMP in Dublin, the British authorities decided to bring down Redmond from Belfast to reorganise the detective force, and he was getting too close to Collins.) Holt points out that at these events the witnesses and observers raised no outcry because the IRA and its terror had so intimidated them, and that it was clear that the British administration and law were no longer respected. Confusion reigned in Ireland – and in the historiography since.

Intimidation was bi-lateral when the policies of terror were instituted in Ireland, and that was another form of terror for the entire community. As always, the simple thought of 'them' versus 'us' is incorrect when recounting the times. It must be emphasised that both the British and the Irish used terror.[34] When Voltaire wrote *pour encourager les autres* in the French Revolution of 1789, he could have been thinking of the Irish War of Independence 130 years in the future, and one must continually ask: who are the 'others' the terror was to 'encourage'?[35] The trauma of the terrorist and the terrified have much the same results – both lives are changed decisively and irrevocably. The tension that this bred was clear in the actions of many: both British and Irish would sleep with weapons under their pillows or on a bedside table, always fearing the sound of a door opening would signal their murder. Such precautions only heightened the fear further.

In so many cases, the intimidation was directly or indirectly aimed at the Irish civilian population itself, and is much more complex and nuanced than often thought. As the war progressed, the line between combatant and non-combatant became more and more difficult to draw. It is impossible to understand what must have been the inescapable part of life – the uncertainty of living in a community where no one was immune to the daily possibility of violence. Men and women lived and worked in an atmosphere of unbroken tension and fear that never relaxed – an atmosphere of horror that is almost unimaginable. It necessitated that people went about their lives with closed lips and open eyes. It is said: 'people don't live history, they live their lives'. They faced the dangers and humiliations of hold-ups, searches, raids, arrests, confinement to their homes, and the ever-present risk of being caught by rifle or revolver fire. Waiting for the terror – the trauma, either real or imagined – was a choking sensation that could be neither lessened nor supported. All of Ireland lived in the shadow of apprehension. Imaginations that had been stunned by the fearful casualty lists and reports of the front in the First World War could more easily recognise the face of terror when it was brought down to the small scale of their daily lives. In recounting myriad stories of reprisals one can lose sight of the nature of the terror suffered – 'what happened' is not always superior to determining 'what people thought happened'.

Kathleen McKenna Napoli, who worked on *The Irish Bulletin*, wrote of what a Sunday morning in Dublin looked like. Instead of empty streets with only Mass-goers about,

> citizens were thronging to hear Mass through the streets filled with British Regulars carrying rifles with fixed bayonets, Auxiliary Cadets, Black and Tans and here and there, broad-shouldered plainclothesmen distinguishable as members of the 'G' Division of the Dublin Metropolitan Police engaged in political espionage. A tank was ambling along Bachelor's Walk, military lorries, filled with armed-to-the-teeth troops, their rifles at the ready, were racing through O'Connell St, and military cordons were drawn with barbed wire around entrances from Grafton St from Nassau St and College Green.[36]

There was no joy in the people anymore – a hunted people listening for the rumble of lorries or the distant clatter of shots.

Frank Wearen, who joined the *Fianna* in 1915 as a 14-year-old boy and went on to become a Volunteer after the Rising, remembered:

> But, oh, everyone then was afraid of the Black and Tans. Because if you were walking along the path and you sort of looked at them they'd come and give you a boxing. Give you a box across the back of the neck or on the side of the head and tell you to keep going – for *nothing*. For only *looking*! That was the sort they were. No, you couldn't get worse … That was *life!*[37] [Emphasis in original.]

Nellie McCann was born on City Quay and lived there all her life. She knew the terror of the Black and Tans well:

> there were twelve of us children. My father was a sea captain and drowned in London. He used to say to me mother 'Susan, when I die, I'll come back as a seagull'. And after he died, for years after, this seagull used to come and knock on the window and she used to say to me 'That's your father knocking'.
>
> … Oh, and I remember the Black and Tans. They had little hats to the side of their head. Oh, we were terrified of Tans. The Tans, they were definitely villains. When the Tans were going into public houses and they were supposed to be going in to search but they were taking the drink themselves, the beer and everything. We used to see that from the window … And then we'd be peeping out. And me mother'd say 'get *away* from that window! 'cause there'd be sniping. Oh, they used to shoot people down and we had a curfew and everyone had to be in … I remember one man, Gerry Farrell, and he went over to see the quay wall and they *riddled* him with bullets. And me mother and a man named Corrigan went across to the wall and brought him over to put in our hall. And me mother was a woman who never cursed, she was a very polite woman, but she said 'Those *bastards!*' I remember that as a young one now. Oh, it was dreadful. We had terrible times.[38] [Emphasis in original.]

A British Army private, J.P Swindlehurst, stationed in Dublin from January to February 1921, concurred:

> Dublin seems to be a rotten place to be … people hurry along the streets, armoured cars dash up and down, bristling with machine guns … The men who style themselves as Black and Tans walk about like miniature arsenals … They dash about in cars with wire netting covering at all hours of the day bent on some raid reprisal or capture of some Sinn Féiners … One can sense the undercurrent of alarm and anxiety in the faces of the passers-by.[39]

Douglas Duff, a Black and Tan, noted 'the real sufferer in this fratricidal war was the non-combatant', as civilians were targeted by both sides.[40]

Some of the British in Ireland had a different view of the Auxiliaries. Caroline Woodcock was the wife of Colonel Wilfred James Woodcock, who was wounded in a raid on Bloody Sunday. She spent most of 1920–1 in Dublin and her diaries were later published as a book, which was more sanguine. She viewed the Auxiliaries on the streets of Dublin and the street scene as:

> Soldiers piqueted every corner, and a house-to-house search was made and usually numerous streets affected. Throughout tanks waddled slowly up and down the street…
>
> … During these raids ever the most awe-inspiring sight for me was the car loads of Auxiliaries: eight or ten splendid-looking men in a Crossley Tender, armed to the teeth…
>
> … I know little of what the Auxiliaries have done or left undone but I do know that they have put the fear of God into the Irish rebels. When criticising them, it should be never forgotten that these men are the survivors of the glorious company of those who fought and died for England.[41]

In a similar vein, Mark Sturgis wrote a left-handed compliment in his diary: 'The Black and Tans have done fine work and could have been ideal for the job if some of them hadn't taken a completely wrong view of their functions'.[42] The Auxiliaries and the Black and Tans were always on their best behaviour with their compatriots and very careful to hide their excesses from the British people. If the British, however, could not control the streets of Dublin without resorting to such methods, how could they convince international opinion that they could control Ireland in the face of opposition?

At the time, most of those in Ireland just wanted to live their lives in tranquillity. Ernest Dowdell quoted an anonymous Auxiliary who observed:

> Over the whole of Ireland there hangs a shadow of great fear. Whilst Sinn Féin carries on its guerrilla warfare against the Crown Forces, and the Crown Forces conduct their policy of reprisals against Sinn Féin, ordinary citizens, whose only wish is to be allowed to live in peace and attend to their own affairs, walk in terror of their lives. No man knows how soon he may be called upon to give an account of his movements or a statement of his politics to secret agents of Sinn Féin or the Crown ... Everyone suffers from nerves, and the women of Ireland, after the manner of womankind, suffer untold agonies of apprehension for the safety of their men.[43]

Just as the military phase of the guerrilla war changed as it went on:

> over the revolutionary period, the practice of terrorism was radically altered, as all protagonists discarded their initial inhibitions, devised new tactics to cope with increasingly difficult opposition, and expressed their growing frustration in ever more ruthless brutality.[44]

Collins's Squad, the IRA intelligence unit, began the assassination of detectives and informers in 1919, and by 1920 the state forces resorted to a policy of lethal reprisals throughout Ireland. British forces employed terrorism in order to maintain the conquest of Ireland and subdue the Irish nationalist movement during the war.[45] Once the War of Independence began, however, the IRA embarked upon its own campaign of terrorism. In time, IRA terror was so effective that many of the British representatives in the courts, police, magistrates and local authorities eventually ceded the authority of their positions to their Irish counterparts, who, with the support of Dáil Éireann, were already running large portions of Ireland.[46] The commission of British reprisals was exacerbated when the Irish propaganda machine successfully capitalised on them, despite the fact that the Irish themselves were carrying out their own reprisals.[47] The British did not understand the will of the Irish, and often overreacted. Mao Zedong later had as one of his principles of guerrilla warfare to let the state 'overreact with human rights abuses'.[48] In fact, it was clear that the Irish provoked British reprisals in order to generate propaganda. Michael Hopkinson wrote:

> a central, if unstated, aim of the IRA was to provoke a harsh
> response and hence to court publicity and international
> sympathy.[49]

British 'reprisals and counter-reprisals' proved to be counterproductive time and time again. Reprisals must certainly be counted as terror, and they must be used discriminately to minimise the risk of alienating the population. The Irish needed the British to overreact, and when they did so they were able to manipulate that overreaction to mobilise Irish and international opinion to win the all-important political and psychological war. Collins's intelligence and the IRA's strategy followed one of Sun Tsu's dicta: 'To secure ourselves against defeat lies in our own hands – but the opportunity of defeating the enemy is provided by the enemy itself'. When the British responded to Irish provocation, they defeated themselves.[50] Collins and the Irish continually attacked the British in ways calculated to provoke their blind reactions. This handed the propaganda initiative to the Irish internationally and extended the movement's control over the population, although that was at least partially due to the fact that the Irish were engaging in terrorism as well to intimidate the population.

The traditional view that a symbiotic relationship uniformly existed between the IRA and the community at large has been successfully challenged since the mid-1990s.[51] The claim of united Irish opposition to British government without coercion should be re-examined. Earlier historians took more or less at face value the republican claim that the Irish people substantially backed the rebel forces. Their co-operation, whether a result of national enthusiasm or fear of the IRA's reputation for omniscient and ruthless punishment of 'spies and informers', created an unbridgeable 'intelli-gence gap' between rebels and government, ensuring that the former worked in the light of comprehensive information, the latter in the dark. While the Irish people were firmly on the side of self-governance, and it is acknowledged that there was widespread support for Irish nationalism, it must be stressed that the IRA often had to resort to intimidation in order to enforce Irish allegiance to their cause and to its alternative government.[52] Attempts by Sinn Féin supporters to garner support were enforced by in-timidation as early as the winter of 1916. In Wexford, letters were sent to people accusing them of sneering at Sinn Féin and threatening that they 'would be made to pay at the next rising'. In Dublin, the 'separation women' (so called because they were given a 'separation allowance' as the wives of British soldiers serving in World War I) were targets of abuse, and threats were made to employers urging them to reinstate the male Irish prisoners taken after the Rising, and terminate the women's employment.[53]

It is apparent that important differences existed between parts of the country, and often the amount of acceptance for the republican cause was in proportion to the success of the IRA, as well as to the numbers of Protes-tants and loyalists in the area.[54] It must be noted that only a small percentage of local loyalists assisted the British, which is not surprising given the risk to life and property if locals were suspected.[55] At times, the IRA turned to terror against those of the Irish population who they thought were helping the British, as well as against British or loyalist targets. In January 1921 Cork Brigade No. 2 reported that they were experiencing a great deal of hostility from local farmers, and that they were finding it hard to billet in their area. 'What is to be done with such people?'[56] The Irish resorted to terrorism to keep the people 'in line' and Tom Barry admitted that exe-cutions were necessary in 1921. In May 1921 his column reported that an ambush had to be abandoned and Barry blamed an informer who 'he was unable to trace'.[57] As another example of local units acting without GHQ authorisation (or 'claimed knowledge'), Richard Mulcahy insisted no civilian should be liable for IRA punishment 'unless they were active enemies of the national cause'. On 14 May 1921 he wrote to Cathal Brugha (Minister for Defence) that 'no-one shall be regarded as an enemy of the state, whether they be described locally as a Unionist, Orangeman, except that they are actively anti-Irish in their outlook and in their actions'.[58] Yet Barry admitted that he never sought sanction for any execution.[59] He went further in his dismissive opinion of GHQ: 'right through to the end our General Headquarters didn't know what a flying column was doing until they read about it in the paper'.[60]

Barry identified the three groups liable to be executed as 'spies and informers':

- Irishmen who 'sold out for gold',
- ex-servicemen who still owed allegiance to Britain, and
- wealthy land-owners with a vested interest in maintaining the British government.[61]

Michael Hopkinson has expressed another view in that the increased British effectiveness in Cork in 1921 'emphasised the need to root out informers and led to a big rise in the execution of so-called spies leading to something of a "vendetta"'.[62] The British report after the war indicated that there were many in the area who were giving information to the British, and the IRA killed those they thought were doing so. The report continued that Protestant loyalists in West Cork had actively assisted the British:

in the Bandon area where there were many Protestant farmers who gave information. Although the Intelligence Officer of the area [A.E. Percival] was exceptionally experienced and although the troops were most active it proved almost impossible to protect those brave men, many of whom were murdered while almost all the remainder suffered grave material harm ...[63]

In recent years, Peter Hart has written that 'many suspects were guilty only by association. Almost all victims were officially described as "spies or informers", but in practice this could mean anything.' Hart found that though some were genuine 'spies and informers', many were just those who did not assist the IRA.[64] 'They were killed not for what they did but for who they were: Protestants, ex-soldiers, tramps and so on down the communal blacklist'.[65] Hart contended:

It might be suggested that Protestants and ex-soldiers were
naturally hostile to the IRA, and more likely to be working with
the police and military, and to be shot. This was not so. The
authorities obtained little information from either group and in
fact by far the greatest damage was done by people within the
organisation, or their relatives.[66]

While there were certainly some killed to settle personal scores, or in a
'vendetta', there were clearly some in Cork who were assisting the British.[67]
The West Cork County Inspector reported in January 1921 that 'information
is being freely given and I believe it will still be given'.[68] Further, the records
of Major A.E. Percival, compiled after the war, give evidence that information
was forthcoming from loyalists in Cork. His post-war lectures given to the
British Staff College were definitive on the point:

> The most profitable methods [of obtaining information] were as
> follows:
> (i) Most important of all, an I.O. [Intelligence Officer] must move
> about the country and hunt for information. It will not come to
> him if he sits in his office all day.
> (ii) He must keep in close touch with the Loyalists – especially
> those who are not afraid to tell them what they know.
> This is not always an easy thing to do, as if the IRA suspected a
> Loyalist of giving information or being too friendly with the
> Crown Forces, it meant certain death for him. It was our usual
> practice therefore to approach their houses after dark and very
> long night journeys had to be made in order to do this.[69]

The British records after the war indicated that information was forthcoming from loyalists in the area, and that many suffered the consequences
of talking to the British forces. British intelligence officers were constantly
on the lookout for such information and, while it proved invaluable, it
also dried up as the war progressed. The officers had:

> been considerably developed and better able to deal with any
> information which came to hand and that at the same time the

proclamation of Martial Law had undoubtedly frightened a large number of civilians and made them more willing to give information to the Crown forces. This fact, apparently, was realised by the rebel leaders as, commencing in February, a regular murder campaign was instituted against Protestant Loyalists and anybody who might be suspected of being an 'informer', quite irrespective of whether he really was or not. This campaign was intensified as time went on, and it had the result of making information very hard to obtain.[70]

General Macready also indicated that information on the IRA was being given to British forces, and he reported to the cabinet that the IRA was brutal in its attempts to halt the flow:

Information continues to come in more freely and the murder lately of several men believed by the IRA to be informants points to the feeling of insecurity existing amongst them.[71]

Tom Barry noted instances in which he put on an Auxiliary uniform and talked to individuals in Cork, leading them to give information regarding IRA activities that would be of interest to the British. Barry did so with Thomas Bradfield in February 1921. Bradfield had been accused of arranging 'to give further information [to the Auxiliaries] later on through his local clergyman and pressed very hard for the immediate capture and execution of certain local boys who were members of the IRA'.[72] Barry met with Bradfield in uniform and when Bradfield was deceived into giving information leading to Barry's column, Barry had him killed that night.[73] Barry and the other Irish leaders determined that they would make it 'unhealthy' for Irishmen to betray their fellows, and to make it deadly for the British to exploit them.

Debate has raged since the mid-1990s whether much of the Irish killing of 'informers' was really sectarian, specifically targeting Protestants, ex-soldiers, tramps and others for violence and killing, but it is important to note that British civil servant and political polemicist Lionel Curtis wrote at the time that:

loyalists were not especially victimised.

... Protestants in the South do not complain of persecution on sectarian grounds. If Protestant farmers are murdered, it is not by reason of their religion, but rather because they are under suspicion as loyalists. The distinction is a fine, but a real one.[74]

In addition, the British *Report on the Situation in Ireland* issued after the Truce stated:

The gradual development of [the Military Intelligence Section] gave excellent results which were soon evident. The raids on houses, which had previously been carried out on the information supplied by the police, now came to be conducted as the result of evidence pieced together from captured documents, and from the reports of law-abiding people who at this time occasionally came forward.[75]

Between January 1919 and December 1921, the IRA killed at least 277 civilians and, of those, 186 (or 65 per cent) were executed as 'spies'. In absolute terms, this is a small figure in the context of other cases of twentieth-century irregular conflict and is dwarfed by thousands of recorded and unrecorded incidents of non-violent intimidation or unpunished civilian defiance. But even if most of those who fell foul of the IRA did not experience physical violence, the influence of killing was felt beyond its direct victims, and fatal violence remains critical to an understanding of the nature of coercion during the Irish War of Independence. Historian Sathis Kalyvas has highlighted two key motivations for the use of lethal violence against civilians and non-civilians in irregular warfare. The first is tactical: targeting an individual or group to remove a specific risk. The second is strategic: 'to deter others from engaging in similar behaviour'.[76] Resorting to lethal violence was both an act of intimidation and a tacit admission that in some places warnings had become ineffective and sterner measures were needed.

The placing of the bodies of executed civilians in public areas where they would be easily found and the labelling of corpses with cards identifying them as 'spies and informers' (the 'performance' of killing) was strategic. Both the body and the label pinned to it aimed to 'communicate a message to the relatives, friends, and local community of the deceased'.[77] This violence works most effectively as intimidation when those it targets with terror can quickly recognise and interpret it as such – on all who saw a body so designated – but also on those who didn't actually see the body but heard the story. The sharp increase of labelled bodies in the months before the Truce in July 1921 is indicative of both the increased brutality of the conflict and the confirmed status of civilians as legitimate targets for punishment.[78] The trauma remained long after the death of an accused spy as clearly as if the label on the body was tied around each of their own necks, isolated by a community that had no wish to be visited by the same fate.[79]

Those who were deemed 'spies and informers' were not just executed in County Cork or the south-west and Munster.[80] Moreover, some of the witness statements taken by the Bureau of Military History in the 1940s–50s demonstrate that the Irish also committed barbarous acts throughout Ireland but these are seldom glamorised in more romantic accounts. One of the most grisly executions happened in County Kilkenny, for example. William Kenny, an ex-British soldier who had reported the IRA's activities to the RIC was executed in August 1920. When John Walsh, the O/C in Kilkenny, determined the British might hear the gunfire if Kenny were shot, the IRA chose another method for his execution.

> We gagged and blindfolded him, and having bound his arms and legs, we dropped him into the River Barrow just a few yards from [Blanchfield's] eel house. The water at this point would be 8 or 10 feet deep and, as an additional precaution, we tied a 56 lb weight to his body before dropping him into the river. As far as I can now recollect, the date of Kenny's execution was 31 August 1920. About two months later, his decomposed body was washed ashore about three miles down the river and, with two other volunteers, I had the gruesome task of again tying weights and heavy stones to the body and dropping it into the river for a second time.[81]

Some who were deemed 'spies and informers' were not 'labelled', but it is also worth considering the potentially powerful cumulative effect of ru-mours and gossip surrounding the disappearance of individuals within a community. Rumours of terror generate further terror.

Whether it was the only way open to them, or can be justified, the reality was that the Irish chose terror on this scale in order to discourage the passing of information to the British, as well as to settle local scores, and to exact revenge on people considered pro-British in retaliation for the sufferings of northern nationalists. Sometimes plain robbery, the settling of local land disputes by resort to the gun, or the protection of an illegal racket was the motive for violence. But to read the disorder of the period primarily in terms of banditry, local vendettas and general mayhem is misguided. Charles Townshend has pointed out that it is 'impossible at this remove to assess the assertion (or admission) that spies represented a major threat to the IRA's survival' or, indeed, to judge the overall effectiveness of the IRA's attempts to detect and punish informers.[82] Of a later war in Ireland, a member of the Provisional IRA stated clearly of violence: 'At one time, that was all we *could* do, that was the only avenue open to us, was to engage in armed struggle'.[83] Did those later members of the IRA learn it from those who fought in the Irish War of Independence?

Throughout the war, in all of its theatres, it is clear that great efforts by the Irish insurgents were needed to overcome inertia, ineptitude and fear on the part of the Irish population. It was necessary to ensure that the fear behind was greater than the fear in front. A battalion commander in Derry later wrote that:

> In the beginning of 1920, I had a company of about fifty men, and was the only functioning unit in the city, twenty-five per cent of these I held together by means of threats etc., the remainder were particularly unenthusiastic.[84]

Testimony during trials and after the war attests to instances when the threat of violence was used to fill out the Irish ranks. Volunteer Jim Croke became involved in Cork since 'I had to do it or I would be shot. The men made me go'.[85] Similarly, James Denby of Wexford said he 'knew what I was doing [was] wrong but I was afraid not to go.'[86] In Cavan, Michael Mc-Cearty was court-martialled in 1920 for participating in an attack on a police patrol. When he pleaded guilty, he said 'I had to do it, as I would be shot in my bed if I had not'.[87] British reports, too, noted 'practically every male of fighting age has willingly or *unwillingly* become a member of the IRA [emphasis added]'.[88]

Coercion was a necessary component of the Volunteers in the Irish war. Coercion, collaboration or persuasion can take different forms. T.E. Lawrence noted the insurgents must have:

> a friendly population, not actively friendly, but sympathetic to the point of not betraying rebel movements to the enemy. Rebellions can be made by two percent active in a striking force, and ninety-eight sympathetic.[89]

Further to that, Stathis Kalyvas argued that political actors invariably seek the exclusive collaboration of the whole population. Active collaboration – such as sharing information, carrying or hiding arms and providing supplies or accommodation – is only required from a minority but compliance from the rest of the population should be exclusive. Collaboration with the opposition must also be prevented. Armed actors, therefore, 'prefer exclusive but incomplete collaboration to nonexclusive collaboration (such as neutrality or hedging) … they prefer a low level of collaboration to no collaboration at all'. Allowing defiance or defection to go unchecked can result in it increasing and becoming overwhelming.[90] While some of Kalyvas's assumptions regarding the use of violence in guerrilla wars are controversial, the Irish knew that intimidation was as important as military action and used coercion, threats and ostracism to control the political and propaganda narrative. Kalyvas confirms points well attested by studies of other conflicts: that most informers are never suspected or discovered; that family ties are common features of insurgent groups and that insurgency creates new generational conflicts between 'newly empowered youth and the dispossessed elders'.[91]

Coercion of the Irish by the Irish took many forms. Ernie O'Malley's notes on his interview with Frank Busteed indicated: 'In the [Civil War], we shot 4 or 5 locals – *then we could move anywhere* [emphasis added]'.[92] In many instances, however, the vast majority of civilian defiance can be considered minor or everyday. Many Irish were not informers or enemy agents but instead guilty of 'non-co-operation' and 'nonconformity'. In both cases the act of non-co-operation was essentially financial: selling or purchasing prohibited goods in violation of a boycott or refusing to contribute money.

For example, the West Cork Brigade realised that as its columns increased in size, they had an obligation to protect and care for the men, 'reducing as far as possible the hardship that was their lot'. The generosity of the local population in providing for the men's needs created a heavy burden that the Brigade wished to lessen. As a result, it was decided in September 1920 to launch a drive to raise funds to support the men in the columns, to provide them 'with clothing and the ordinary amenities of life'. A levy was placed on all the 'farmers and professional and business people', and a sum of £7,000 was raised.

> In some cases, it is true, the levy was refused, and *where this refusal was found to arise from lack of sympathy with the national cause* the Volunteers seized cattle and sold them publicly at fairs in quiet areas to recoup the refused levy.[93] [Emphasis added.]

Rather than continue to attempt to persuade obstinate individuals, the IRA often punished them for their refusal through boycotting, raids and destruction of property. Intimidation like this had a chilling effect on neighbouring farmers and business owners.

Intimidation of another sort was to be found making reluctant or talkative Irish conform to the wishes of the IRA. In Tralee, John O'Riordan spoke years later of a Volunteer who had a habit of discussing IRA matters in the presence of strangers and was ordered to carry out the execution of a 'spy' named O'Mahony: 'having carried out the execution he would have to remain silent about it'.[94]

All revolutionaries must strike that balance between controlling a population and harming it in the process. To do too much damage to the local infrastructure would harm the local economy, which would backfire on the Irish. Controlling too much of a community's affairs would make the IRA appear overbearing, and not too different from the British. While the Irish did engage in actions causing trauma among the people, they also exhibited a concern for local citizens and avoidance of harm to them that was well-placed – their movement depended greatly on the support of the local populace to survive. Jim Power, a member of the West Wicklow flying column, wrote of the care those men took with regard to locals coming into the way of an ambush:

three military lorries full of British soldiers came into view. At the very moment the lorries appeared, there happened to be three or four carts with civilians driving to the creamery also on the road. We decided not to open fire as if we did it was almost certain that the civilians would either be caught accidentally in the crossfire, or most likely they would be shot afterwards by the British military when the [firing] was over. We left the ambush position shortly afterwards ...[95]

Intimidation came in many forms, and one that created terror in many men, and especially their families, was the ostracising of the RIC.[96] Beginning in 1917, and then officially in April 1919, the Irish were told to avoid the RIC members and their families throughout Ireland. In January 1919 the Dublin County Inspector wrote:

There is no boycotting but intimidation in a great way exists owing to the malign influences of Sinn Féin. People are afraid to offend the extremists and comply with their wishes [avoiding contact with the RIC or their families] fearing injury if they did not do so. Also there is no doubt a general scheme on the part of Sinn Féin to intimidate and cow the police to prevent them from doing their duty and to deter young men from joining the police.[97]

'Fearing injury by extremists' is a not-so-subtle form of terrorism.

The intimidating effect of ostracising is more complex than apparent at first glance, and many Irish in the community felt the results along with the RIC and their families. The majority of constables in rural areas were drawn from the same social class, religion and general background as their neighbours. The constables enjoyed a prestigious position and were well regarded despite being armed – a singular requirement in the UK. While measures were taken, not always successfully, to maintain an arms-length relationship between police and public, most of the constables and their families became an integral part of their communities. Constables in charge of police stations were required to make regular reports to their superiors, and from time to time would be moved around the district to prevent ac-

quaintanceships from developing too closely, but this policy was not followed assiduously. A constable was not permitted to marry until he had
been in the force for some years, and was not supposed to serve in his home
county, nor in that of his wife, but after marriage their families mingled into
schools, churches and community life.

Despite their status as an armed force, RIC constables seldom carried
guns, only waist belt, handcuffs and baton. Enforcement of eviction orders
in rural Ireland caused the RIC to be widely distrusted by the poor Catholic
population as the mid-nineteenth century approached, but later policing
generally became a routine of controlling petty misdemeanours such as
moonshine distilling (poitín), public drunkenness, minor theft, and vandal-
ism against property crimes.[98] And when violence was involved, it was usually fuelled by passion, alcohol or a combination of the two. Often, along
with the priest, the constables would have an informal leadership role in
the community, and people needing help with forms and letters would appeal to local constables who were literate. A majority of RIC men were
Catholics like their fellow countrymen and they probably had the same
range of political opinions by 1919–20. The constables were in the unen-
viable position of being expected to enforce repressive measures against
their own people. Some of them had family members in the IRA but those
who had long service were not prepared to forego their pensions. Many
RIC men generally conducted themselves with forbearance and dignity in
the face of a ruthless terror campaign directed at them – their primary loyalty was to their job of keeping the peace and serving the community rather
than any political party or ideology.

Recruiting for the RIC had been suspended on the outbreak of World
War I in 1914, as had resignations on pension. As many of the younger
members went off to the War the force was no longer at full strength. The
RIC was trained for police work, not war, and was woefully ill-prepared to
take on the counter-insurgency duties that were required in 1919.

How, and to what extent, the change in feeling came about in the
RIC has always been a matter of speculation … They rather
suddenly found themselves 'between the devil and the deep blue
sea'. They were Irish and knew it. The army of occupation was a
foreign army acting according to the policies of a foreign

government ... The job of the police was to keep law and order. That it happened to be the law stipulated by an outside power ... was not germane to the issue. It was still de facto the legal system which obtained throughout the land and which they had sworn, and were being paid, to maintain ... Of those who turned a blind eye to the times, and stayed on with the RIC, many tried to pursue a policy of passivity. They rolled with the punch, doing reluctantly what they were ordered to do ... Some acted as informants for the IRA, and justified themselves somehow. At first resignations came as a wavering trickle. The trickle became a stream, the stream a flood by mid-summer of 1920. Weighing rather heavily on the other side of the scales were those who decided against and went over lock, stock and barrel, to the enemy.[99]

Over time, the effort to soften up the RIC by turning it into a pariah force proved highly effective, fatally compromising its function as an intelligence service for Dublin Castle. In the view of many of the RIC constables they were executing their duty enforcing the law of the regular government – but 'duty' can become seen as treason in a time of revolution. (While the 'regular' RIC was also guilty of atrocities and of pointing the Black and Tans and Auxiliaries in the direction of their targets, it was the unwillingness of many RIC men to respond in kind that prompted the British govern- ment to import the Black and Tans and Auxiliaries to wage a counter-terror campaign.)

On 10 April 1919 Éamon de Valera officially called for all the police forces to be socially ostracised. De Valera stated:

The people of Ireland ought not to fraternise, as they often do, with the forces that are the main instruments in keeping them in subjugation ...

Given the composition of these forces, boycott meant accentuating divisions among Irish people, including family members and community residents. De Valera said that he was reluctant to move against the RIC and DMP be- cause they were Irish as well. In the course of the speech he called the constabulary 'England's janissaries', and said that they were:

> no ordinary civil force, as police are in other countries … The
> RIC, unlike any other police force in the world, is a military body
> … They are given full licence by their superiors to work their will
> upon an unarmed populace. The more brutal the commands given
> them by their superiors the more they seem to revel in carrying
> them out—against their own flesh and blood, be it remembered!
> … a full boycott will give them vividly to understand how
> utterly the people of Ireland loathe both themselves and their
> calling.[100]

It is notable that this speech was given almost a full year before the appearance of the Black and Tans in Ireland.

Diarmuid O'Hegarty, the director of communications for the IRA, left no room for ambiguity when he composed a memorandum early in 1919 on what the targeting of the RIC should amount to:

> The police should be treated as persons who having been
> adjudged guilty of treason to their country are regarded as
> unworthy to enjoy any of the privileges or comforts which arise
> from cordial relations with the public.

The policy had its effect on the constables, as the DMP report stated 'these murders and intimidation must destroy the morale of any police force no matter how good it may be'.[101] A telling example of what the police endured came from an August 1920 RIC Inspector General's report and summarised the entire campaign against them at the time:

> Resignations from the force are becoming very numerous and no
> body of men can be expected to support indefinitely the
> conditions under which the police in many places are forced to
> live, boycotted, ostracised, forced to commandeer their food,
> crowded in many instances into cramped quarters without proper
> light or air, every man's hand against them, in danger of their lives
> and subjected to the appeals of their parents and their families to

induce them to leave the force and so put an end to the danger
and annoyance to which continued service exposes them all.[102]

Even though friendships developed between the RIC and their families
and the Irish, by 1920 the RIC as an organisation was reviled as the most
obvious instrument of British rule in Ireland.[103] In October the County
Inspector for Clare reported that:

> The people appear to regard the police as their enemies and have
> ceased all friendly intercourse with them. Shops continue to
> supply provisions, but they would rather that the police did not
> come to them.[104]

The initiation of the boycott was not without problems for the IRA:
'The mere fact that these men were rather decent men in peaceful times
made them all the more a menace when the national resurgence burst forth,
and it took some time and some exhortation to convince local people that
the RIC were really enemies'.[105]

The RIC became virtually helpless and useless. A plea from the Balli-
nasloe police to the *de facto* Chief Secretary, Sir John Anderson, illustrates
their plight:

> We consider it is almost an impossibility to carry out our functions
> as a civil police force under the present circumstances. The strain
> on the force is so great, by the daily assassination of our comrades
> who are ruthlessly butchered and murdered by the roadside ... and
> the boycotting and threats arraigned [sic] against us, against our
> families, our relations and our homes, that the agonies of a
> suffering force cannot be much further prolonged ... The men are
> resigning in large numbers ... we are now useless as a civil police
> force ... We as a body are not able to restore law and order in this
> country today nor is there any hope on the horizon for a changed
> order of things when we could do so — we consider the best thing
> to be done is to wind up the force.[106]

Assassination of RIC men was a real possibility and between January 1919 and October 1920 over 100 RIC were killed, and a total of 410 were killed before the Truce in July 1921.[107] 'Join the RAF and See The World. Join the RIC and See the Next' proclaimed graffiti daubed on street walls.[108]

It is clear that there was a 'double-edged' intimidation to the ostracising of the RIC and their families. When the Irish were admonished not to have any social or economic congress with them – not to share a pew in church, or to meet and talk with the families, or to drink a pint in the pub with the men, or to sell goods or provisions to them in shops – there was an expressed or implied 'or else' to the Irish as well. The Irish were warned not to have any dealings with the men and their families, and if they did then they ran the risk of being ostracised too, or worse. Locals who worked in any capacity to support the police were harassed and threatened. All such intimidation contributed to the trauma of the time.

The administration in Ireland thus failed to provide for a modicum of internal law and order. Once a government can no longer guarantee public security, it has abdicated its mandate. It can be argued that the failure of the British administration to enforce its position in Ireland in 1918 was a major blow to its authority, resulting in the victory of Sinn Féin in the 1918 election and establishment of Dáil Eireann. When the Dáil assumed the role of an elected native Irish government, the British administration was thus doubly illegitimate. Certainly one of the better examples of this defeat of British authority was the necessity to recruit non-Irishmen into the RIC as Black and Tans and Auxiliaries.

It must be recognised that both the British and the Irish used terror – murder, reprisals and shearing women's hair – to intimidate and punish the population.[109] Terror and violence can be one and the same, and fear and forcible actions often are not classified as 'terror' when they should be. Forcibly cutting women's hair, a widespread practice in Ireland and in many other wars, was a form of serious violence that singled out and marked women as enemies, sexual transgressors and traitors. It often involved humiliating, terrorising or hurting women in a manner that had long-term consequences for their physical and mental health.

Professor Marie Coleman has suggested that informally defined ideas on morality and acceptable violence, the considerations of a national and international propaganda war, and the prominence of female activists in the republican movement, may all have restrained violence (both lethal and sex-

ual) against women, and ensured that those who defied the IRA were usually treated differently to men.[110] Almost certainly even more so than today's
low reporting of sexual violence, most such incidents on both sides went
unrecorded a hundred years ago and will be impossible to ever be numbered. However often these incidents occurred, all such terror actions are
to be condemned.

Both sides in the War of Independence extensively deployed 'hair taking'. There was an official RIC memorandum that 'women must invariably
be respected [… and just] because the cowardly blackguards of the IRA cut
women's hair, it is no reason why the RIC should retaliate by similar action'.
On the Irish side, some of the Irish press suggested that this gender-based
violence was exclusively linked to British forces:

> If the 'Black and Tans' or their agents indulge in the practice of
> 'Reprisals' by cutting off the hair of girl Sinn Féiners we trust that
> there will be no counter-cutting of loyalist hair. The practice of
> cutting off the hair of terrified girls is not one to commend itself
> to any decent citizen of the Republic; it is base and cowardly as
> well as futile and degrading … Even a state of guerrilla warfare
> enjoins decencies at least upon those fighting in the righteous
> fight.[111]

While *The Irish Citizen* condemned all violence, and urged republicans not
to retaliate, it is clear that neither side had a monopoly on such gender-
based violence, and that 'hair cutting' was a weapon of war. The RIC memorandum and *The Irish Citizen* editorial illustrate a common thread of the
war – a binary construct: 'we don't, but they do' or 'they don't, but we do'.
As with most binary constructs, this one was wrong. They both did.

Elizabeth Bloxam of Cumann na mBan wrote, 'These were the days
when girls were roughly searched and had their hair cut off by British soldiers'.[112] (In her statement, Bloxam pointed to the composure of women
that was vital during stressful times: she recalled that after receiving a message regarding the illness of a young relation, 'the tears sprang to my eyes. I
quickly remembered that I dare not cry'.) The Irish sexual justification for
'bobbing' women was described by Leo Buckley, of the Cork No. 1 Brigade
of the IRA:

> I remember at the time, young girls from Cork going out to
> Ballincollig to meet the British soldiers. We curbed this by
> bobbing the hair of persistent offenders. Short hair was completely
> out of fashion at the period and the appearance of a girl with
> 'bobbed' hair clearly denoted her way of life.[113]

Irish women suspected of espionage or informing were frequently punished in such a way that was physically punitive, segregated them from their community but also rendered them undesirable women, arguably in the hopes of making them physically unattractive to their British suitors, and thus unable to undermine the Irish state through fraternising with the enemy. According to Michael Walsh's witness statement, the RIC 'displayed annoyance when their girl friends had their hair bobbed' by the IRA.[114] In other words, while killing a woman was not an acceptable form of punishment, the Irish considered rendering her appearance 'unfeminine' an entirely appropriate punitive measure.

The cropping of hair offered a grimly visual reminder of transgression for the victim and an immediate warning to others. Some public announcements made it explicitly clear that the women who interacted with the Crown forces would have their hair cropped. In Mallow, County Cork, a notice posted on the chapel gate warned that 'Any girls speaking to the police from this day forward are liable to the penalty of hair cut'. A Galway notice threatened that women found in company with the police would have 'their hair cut and their ears amputated'.[115] In Wicklow, 'young girls' were warned against keeping company with Crown forces and any who disobeyed would 'have her hair cut off so that she will be held in contempt by all loyal citizens of the "Irish Republic"'.[116] One should, however, question whether those women who had their hair shorn by the Irish were always correctly targeted. An IRA intelligence report from May 1920, captured by British forces, noted: 'Our information about girls walking with "Peelers" (which are few) is that they give no information because they are not in a position to get any'.[117]

Both the British and the Irish used hair cutting and other forms of shaming, and the effects would last far longer than it took the hair to grow out. The humiliations garnered through hair shaving were seen as 'humane' punishments, but hair shearing was a deliberate violation of the victim's femininity. While the cutting itself was painful, the aftermath could be worse, as the shaved woman became a symbol of betrayal and a warning to others. In fairness, Major General Henry Hugh Tudor, who was appointed 'police advisor' to the Viceroy on 16 May 1920 and was the O/C of the Auxiliaries, recommended flogging of the British for hair cutting and other 'outrages against women'.[118] (Tudor's recommendation was ignored by the Black and Tans and the Auxiliaries, and the chief of the Imperial General Staff, Sir Henry Wilson, denounced Tudor's plan for the force as 'truly a desperate and hopeless expedient ... bound to fail'. Further, Wilson's prediction that the force would inevitably have 'no discipline, no *esprit de corps*, no cohesion, no training' proved prescient. The Auxiliaries went on to commit some of the most infamous crimes of the entire revolutionary period.[119]) The guerrilla aspect of the war was reflected in the widely reported, coercive practice of gangs of masked men typically assailing and cutting women's hair in isolated, unseen or domestic settings rather than as a public spectacle in front of large crowds, more common in France after World War II, for instance.

Hair cutting was not limited to women, as most Irish men had their hair cut when they were imprisoned. During the War of Independence, a republican having his hair shorn in prison could serve as a badge of honour. Seán Kennedy recalled, 'we all, of course, underwent the ordeal of having our hair cut to the scalp by the prison barber'. Kennedy stated later on the prison haircut was looked upon as 'the martyr's badge and the prison barber's time was kept fully occupied cropping the heads of the various prisoners'.[120]

Female hair shearing by the British or the IRA was deliberate in its victimisation, and it was rarely reported to be accompanied by further acts of sexual violence, though a lack of reporting or treatment cannot be seen as an indication of its lack of occurrence. Physical and sexual violence was waged against both men and women during the War of Independence, and historians are just now addressing that against women. More research is required before a definitive conclusion regarding the true comparative scale of sexual violence in the war can be determined.

Rape and sexual assault can certainly be considered forms of terror, and in wartime they are used to punish women, as well as to intimidate a population. There are few reports of rape or sexual violence against women and, notwithstanding the understandable reticence in reporting such crime, it seems to have remained relatively rare during the Irish war.[121] Sarah Benton argues that while there is no doubt that 'forces of the crown' subjected women to 'acts of sexual humiliation', there is no evidence of mass rape being carried out by British troops.[122] In his witness statement, Volunteer George F.H. Berkeley observed, 'it would be very difficult to prove cases of sexual assault on Irish women. Firstly, because the Irishwoman would rather die than appear in court. Secondly, because, although assaults on women undoubtedly existed, they were few in number'.[123] A British Labour Party commission that visited Ireland in 1920 explained that it was 'difficult to obtain direct evidence of incidents affecting females, for the women of Ireland are reticent on such subjects', but clearly suspected a sexual assault, and perhaps even a rape, had taken place in a case where 'a young woman who was sleeping alone in premises which were raided by the crown forces was compelled to get out of bed and her nightdress was ripped open from top to bottom'.[124]

In Ulster, for instance, the absence of recorded allegations of the rape of Protestant women by the IRA suggests that cases were infrequent as any such propaganda opportunities offered by the allegations were unlikely to be spurned. Gemma Clark has shown that in Munster, 'besides a few shocking cases', there is similarly little evidence of rape during the Civil War.[125] There is, however, the case of Cumann na mBan member Margaret Doherty, who died in December 1928 in Castlebar Mental Hospital from pulmonary TB. Doherty's family testified that the decline in her health stemmed from an incident in May 1922 when three Free State Army officers 'pulled her out of her bed ... brought [her] a short distant from home and rape[d] [her] in succession'.[126]

While sexual assaults and the targeted killing of females apparently were rare in the records and newspapers of the time, actions do not have to descend to that degree to terrorise the female population. Moreover, rape is always under-reported and it was certainly even more so during that period. Women were not going to come forward for fear of rejection by their husbands, their families and their communities. It is generally understood that while trauma is unrepresentable and essentially defies language, it can only be mitigated when the seemingly unspeakable traumatic experience is brought to articulation and the survivors can begin to recreate their shattered identity.[127] The shame and stigma surrounding sexual trauma in conservative Ireland was certainly not conducive to 'working through' such experiences. Further, there is no doubt that the trauma of the times was affecting many all over Ireland. Suffragist Meg Connery reported to the Irish White Cross in 1921 that across Munster:

> Women and children were in a constant state of depression and nervous breakdown, and in the case of expectant mothers, it produces grave results for mothers and children. ... Women know that it is during curfew hours attempts of a sexual character have been made, it is difficult to appreciate the effects this continued strain is producing upon the health of women.[128]

Connery thought that this problem was not confined to a small number of areas, but was an issue throughout the country. Most of the women she interviewed, however, refused to allow their stories to be told publicly.

Just as there were few studies on killing and its effects on young men acting as guerrillas in the Irish war, in recent years the issue of how to interpret and contextualise conflict-related violence and trauma has elicited more research into the effects of stress, and asks whether rape and other crimes were covered up and occurred clandestinely. While Gavin Foster was writing about the Irish Civil War, his reasoning could apply equally to the earlier time period:

> rape was not a common form of violence in the Civil War, but given social taboos and the notorious problem of under-reporting of sexual assault, one wonders if the compensation files are an adequate basis for drawing conclusions about the prevalence of rape in the Civil War or in other phases of the revolution.[129]

Further, as Gemma Clark notes, sole reliance on official state compensation files proves problematic, as 'the mental trauma engendered by Ireland's revolutionary period did not emerge in the neat, linear fashion conducive to the operation of government compensation committees with strict terms and dates of reference'.[130] Moreover, when the first Military Service Pensions Act was introduced in August 1924, neutral and anti-Treaty veterans were excluded.[131] Cumann na mBan was only legislatively recognised as an organisation eligible for military service pensions in the Pension Act of 1934 after an appeal through the Senate.[132]

Physical abuse was particularly known to occur during British raids, and women in their nightdresses were especially vulnerable to dehumanising actions when their homes were raided and they were forcibly thrown out of their beds. While much of the terrorising of women by the British occurred during raids, the majority of violence against women perpetrated by the IRA was the 'victimisation of policemen's wives and barrack servants'. This included eviction from and destruction of their homes, verbal and written threats, enforced resignation from employment in police barracks, ostracising and exile. The overall absence of reported sexual violence by both sides might indicate there was a relatively high level of discipline among the Crown forces and the IRA, but research must continue in that vein. Some British reports argued that, far from being a lawless mob, the violence of the Tans and Auxiliaries was somewhat orchestrated – a certain level of venting of frustration and retaliation was permitted but this was controlled and curtailed.[133] Any such argument should not minimise the degrading treatment nor excuse it in any way. Purely and simply, they were criminal acts of the most abhorrent kind.

Women were not the only ones terrorised by night-time raids. The emergence of 'anti-murder gangs' – police who undertook retaliatory midnight raids, taking men from their beds and shooting them – terrified much of Munster. Although the numbers of such incidents were small, the terror they evoked was very real and many Volunteers took to sleeping away from their homes at night as a survival strategy.[134]

There are examples of gender mitigating violence, as men accused of the same action would most likely have been executed. IRA GHQ issued a directive on the subject of 'Women Spies', outlining that the punishment of death for a man guilty of informing was to be mitigated for female spies on account of their gender.[135] Moreover, IRA orders were that 'a formal public statement of the fact of the conviction shall be issued in poster or leaflet form or both according to local circumstances, as a warning and a preventative' in order to 'neutralise' female spies.[136] There were only three recorded intentional killings of Irish women by Irish men in the war:

1. Maria Georgina (Mary) Lindsay, a loyalist in County Cork who had given the British information about an upcoming ambush near her home near Dipsey. Her butler/driver, James Clarke, was executed with her.

2. Kate (Kitty) Carroll, a poitín-maker in County Monaghan who wrote to the police. Some claim she was intellectually challenged and wrote not about IRA activity, but to turn in rival poitín makers; there are, however, notes from Thomas Brennan, an IRA leader, that she told of IRA arms dump locations and hiding places.

3. Bridget Noble, of Castletownbere in County Cork, who was shot as a spy because she had named Liam Dwyer and Patrick Crowley as the men who had shot Volunteer William Lahane [alias William Lyons]. Previously she had had her hair 'bobbed' for giving that information to the RIC, and she returned to the RIC with information about the IRA men who had cut her hair. When another raid on her house found a letter from the RIC telling her to meet the head constable that night, she was intercepted and executed.

The IRA executed each of the women as a 'spy or informer'.[137] All three executions were in violation of a GHQ order setting out the procedure for dealing with such cases. General Order No. 13 on 'Women Spies', issued in November 1920, instructed that:

> Where there is evidence that a woman is a spy or is doing petty spy work, the Brigade Commandant whose area is involved will get up a Court of Enquiry to examine the evidence against her. If the Court finds her guilty of the charge, she shall then be advised accordingly and, except in the case of an Irishwoman, be ordered to leave the country within seven days. It shall be intimated to her that only consideration of her sex prevents the infliction of the statutory punishment of death. A formal public statement of the conviction shall be issued in poster or leaflet form, or both, according to the local circumstances, as a warning and a preventative.[138]

There are no recorded cases of women being executed by the British – in many cases where women died during the war it was as a result of non-targeted or random acts of violence.[139]

In the winter of 1920 the following request came to Collins and Mulcahy from an IRA Brigade in the west of Ireland:

> Have you decided whether capital punishment should be inflicted on women spies? A number of us through the work of women spies had a miraculous escape in a hail of bullets. Had we fallen the whole Brigade organisation was gone.[140]

In 'dangerous and insistent cases' commanders were ordered to seek instructions from GHQ. In July 1921 Ernie O'Malley wrote to Richard Mulcahy arguing that 'women spies' should be shot, adding bitterly that some 'are only hiding behind their skirts', but there remained a general aversion to sanctioning the execution of women. Seán Healy recalled orders to deal with a female informer in Cork, a 'fiend' who 'hated the army of the people, and openly boasted that she would get all the IRA men she knew hanged or shot by her English masters'. Healy was clear on her crimes, but recalled that this was a 'more delicate problem'; the 'shooting of women being abhorrent to soldiers generally, we decided to take her prisoner in the first instance.' In terms of lethal violence, Healy's belief that shooting women was 'abhorrent to soldiers' may suggest an additional explanation linked to contemporary morality and perceptions about women's roles in combat. When Michael Brennan wrote to Mulcahy asking what action to take regarding 'one notoriously bad case in which the girl concerned has defied the Volunteers when she was warned & another of a girl who has applied for a job as a woman searcher', Mulcahy suggested that Brennan consider 'the various ways in which from your knowledge of their circumstances, you consider they can be punished'.[141]

The consequences of psychological violence were also gendered. According to the 1920 republican pamphlet *'Women and Children Under the Terror'*:

> owing to the merciless pressure exerted unceasingly over the
> people by the Army of Occupation, there [were] numerous cases

of premature births, haemorrhage, still-born children and grave complications at birth resulting in the terrible nervous strain and loss of sleep which is the common lot of women in the Martial Law Areas.[142]

These serious complications are distinctly women's health issues, further displaying how sex was implicated in the long-lasting consequences of this terror.[143]

A recent study of the traumatic effects on the women of the period is damning in recounting how the women were treated medically, or found it difficult or impossible to obtain treatment, and especially in contrast to how the men were treated.

Women suffered from diverse emotional, physical and sexual traumas during the Irish Revolution. Oftentimes, medical diagnoses and treatment were strongly informed by gender ideologies, resulting in medical treatment that emphasized domestication and re-feminization, in contrast to men's treatment, which aimed to be swift and return the patient to the conflict zone or workforce. The available files in the MSPC give some insight into often-questionable analeptic drug and electrical treatments prescribed to female revolutionaries and highlight how, throughout the 1930s, women's mental welfare continued to be connected to the female reproductive system. While various 'rest' therapies were most commonly prescribed to those women with the financial resources to benefit from private treatment, the particularly destitute could find themselves committed to the country's overcrowded mental institutions or may have emigrated in an effort to combat their nervous conditions. However, state administrative files may only scratch the surface, meaning that cultural forms of remembrance are as essential as medical files in attempting to further uncover this aspect of Ireland's past. This medicalization of revolutionary women in the post-independence period speaks to the shaming, marginalization and institutionalization of transgressive women which characterizes much of twentieth-century Ireland.[144]

One of the largest and most infamous British terror reprisals followed shortly after Bloody Sunday in Dublin and the Kilmichael ambush in County Cork. On 10 December 1920, at Dillon's Cross, the IRA ambushed a regular convoy of Auxiliaries, who had just left Cork's Victoria Barracks (now Collins Barracks). The ambush killed one Auxiliary and wounded twelve, and it especially angered the Auxiliaries because it happened so close to the barracks. On the night of 11/12 December, groups of Auxiliaries, Black and Tans, and even regular troops went into Cork city centre and began to mine and burn premises on Patrick Street, especially the three major department stores of Roche's, Cash's and Grant's. The troops also burned down City Hall, as well as the Carnegie Library next door. The British threatened and shot at the fire brigade as the tenders tried to dowse the flames – and cut the fire hoses to prevent the firemen bringing any fires under control. Some five acres of the city centre were burned and over forty businesses and some 300 residential properties were destroyed. Many people were left homeless and 2,000 people were left unemployed, just weeks before Christmas. Many of the city's trams had also been damaged or destroyed. The loss of stock was never properly quantified but the loss of property was calculated at £3 million – a huge sum at the time (roughly £150 million today). Fortunately, few lives were lost – despite houses being torched while the inhabitants were still inside. Two IRA volunteers were shot dead and a woman had a fatal heart attack when the Auxiliaries burst into her home, and the whole of Cork city was terrorised by the night's events.[145]

The terror appeared to be carefully co-ordinated, as Alan Ellis reported in the *Cork Examiner* that 'some of the attackers, while not hiding their uniforms, wore scarves over their faces'. Ellis saw Fred Huston, Chief of the Cork Fire Brigade, who 'told me bluntly that all the fires were being deliberately started by incendiary bombs, and in several cases he had seen soldiers pouring cans of petrol into buildings and setting them alight'.[146] Sir Hamar Greenwood, Chief Secretary for Ireland, denied that any Crown forces were involved, and blamed the IRA. In January 1921, however, the Irish Labour Party and Trade Union Congress published a report to refute this. It was written by Alfred O'Rahilly, the President of University College Cork, and drew on hundreds of eyewitness testimonies that showed clearly that Crown forces had indeed committed the crime.

Evidence bristles with statements which in themselves constitute most serious charges against portions of the armed forces of the Crown. Residents of some of the burned buildings, and members of the Fire Brigade all gave testimony under oath ... As far as possible the witnesses sought were men and women of independence and standing and without bias in favour Sinn Féin – ex-officers, ex-service men, Americans, Englishmen, Unionists, substantial business men, and professional gentlemen.[147]

Shortly afterwards, an Auxiliary who participated in the burnings wrote to his mother:

I contracted a chill on Saturday night during the burning and looting of Cork in all of which I perforce took a reluctant part. We did it all right no matter how much the well-intentioned Hamar Greenwood would excuse us. In all my life ... and in all the tales of fiction I have read I have never experienced such orgies of murder, arson and looting as I have witnessed during the last 16 days with the RIC Auxiliaries. It baffles description. And we are supposed to be ex-officers and gentlemen.[148]

Terror and violence were not limited to the southern counties of Ireland. Between 1920–2, Belfast endured the most intense terror experienced in Ireland. Republican activity in Londonderry and Belfast, which were rocked by sectarian riots throughout the conflict, took on an organised nature.[149] Police and military posts were simultaneously attacked in Londonderry on 1 April 1920, and British propagandist C.J.C. Street pronounced that attacks on Belfast police became routine.[150] Between 21 July 1920 and the end of the year, seventy-four people were killed in Belfast, of whom thirty-six were Catholics.[151] Sectarian tensions, and the possibility of partition, contributed to the trauma in the North. Michael Hopkinson wrote 'what would today be called ethnic cleansing occurred in large parts of the city ... From then on up to the Truce, regular bouts of sectarian violence took place'.[152]

These actions in Northern Ireland were alarming, but attacks in Britain itself threatened public panic.[153] Immediately after Bloody Sunday there was a realisation of just what the IRA could potentially do in this war out-side of Ireland. Armed police cordons went up that Sunday evening in Lon-don – far away from the conflict – around Downing Street, Westminster and Whitehall, because the British government now feared that such attacks could also be mounted in Britain. Those killings totally undermined Lloyd George's claim that the authorities in Ireland 'had murder by the throat'. In 1920 the IRA extended their attacks to the British mainland,[154] and John Pinkman wrote:

> The ordinary English people couldn't have cared less about what was happening in Ireland, being unconcerned about these reports of murder and destruction there. IRA headquarters in Dublin wanted to impress upon the English people that a war of terror was being waged in their name against the Irish people, and reluctantly ordered massive reprisals to be carried out in England to show the English the kind of havoc that was being wrought in Ireland.[155]

Rory O'Connor, O/C of the IRA in Britain at the time, co-ordinated the attacks in Britain. GHQ instructed O'Connor to confine the attacks to England – there were to be no attacks in Scotland or Wales. He was also told to minimise civilian casualties as much as possible. Finally, he was told to avoid attacks on businesses, factories or farms that employed many Irish so as not to displace them from employment.

The November 1920 burnings of seventeen warehouses in Liverpool were just the first of a series of republican sabotage missions. The IRA ter-rorism in Britain was motivated at least partly by revenge. When Ernie O'-Malley reported to Dublin in July 1920, he told GHQ that the country officers 'pressed hard for a campaign in Britain to counteract the destruction of creameries by the military and RIC'.[156] When Collins sent men to Britain he told them that their attacks were 'by way of reprisals that were being carried out by Black and Tans'.[157] In his witness statement, Paddy O'-Donohue said Collins's aim was 'to bring home to the British people the sufferings and conditions to which the Irish were being subjected'.[158] Liv-erpool IRA officer Edward M. Brady said the arson and sabotage efforts were in retaliation for the destruction wrought by police in Ireland.[159]

Cathal Brugha pushed GHQ staff to emphasise operations in Britain, and by March 1921 this evolved into a sustained campaign as he led squads of Volunteers to London on aborted assassination missions. Nationalism blossomed in all the 'Little Irelands' in British cities, and by 1921 there were more than 2,500 Volunteers in Britain.

The first attacks were on warehouses on the Liverpool docks on 27 November 1920. On 9 March 1921 a series of fires began to break out at farms in Cheshire, Lancashire and Liverpool.[160] Three days later, *The Times* reported that republicans had specifically targeted property near Liverpool owned by an Auxiliary Section Leader serving in Ireland.[161] One of Collins's agents was John Harrington, a young doctor at Richmond Hospital in North Brunswick Street. As a member of the staff, he had access to the medical records of the British treated at the hospital and at the North Dublin Union, and he was able to pass along to intelligence their home addresses in Britain. This resulted in many Auxiliary or Black and Tan's relatives' homes being fire-bombed in retaliation for reprisals. On 2 April fires broke out in various hotels in Manchester.[162] Also in April, armed IRA men raided Lyons' Cafe in Manchester, firing shots in the air to disperse customers and staff, and dousing the premises in paraffin. Before setting the building alight, one Volunteer explained their actions: 'We are doing what you are doing in Ireland'.[163] In May a London timber yard went up in flames, and republicans raided and burned the homes of Auxiliaries and Black and Tans in the capital, St Alban's and Liverpool.[164] During the night of 16 June, armed and masked men raided railway stations all around London. They assaulted railway employees, burned signal huts, cut telegraph and signal wires, and fired on police when they tried to interfere.[165] The campaign had the desired effect of altering the normal course of life in Britain. Between 1 and 3 July, London police searched carts, examined drivers' licences and noted vehicles moving in and out of the city. The *New York Times* correspondent wrote that there 'was practically a complete cordon' around the capital.[166]

One of the most famous terror attacks in Britain was an assassination that took place after the Treaty, and was one of the immediate precipitating factors leading to the start of the Civil War in June 1922. Following Bloody Sunday, Field Marshal Sir Henry Wilson pleaded with Churchill for the imposition of martial law in Ireland, and that was finally done on 10 December 1920. After retiring from the army in December

1921, Wilson served briefly as a Member of Parliament, and also as security advisor to the Northern Ireland (Unionist) government. Wilson was an unrepentant imperialist and unionist, and thought the Truce and Treaty irresponsible. At the time he was acting as military advisor to the Northern Ireland government, and was a particularly close confident to James Craig. The Treaty of 6 December 1921 split the republican movement in Britain as thoroughly as in Ireland, with pro- and anti-Treaty camps rapidly being established on either side of an uncertain middle ground.

Thus was precipitated the assassination of Wilson on 22 June 1922 by Reggie Dunne, O/C of the London IRA, and another London veteran of the British Army, Joseph O'Sullivan.[167] Dunne and O'Sullivan trailed Wilson on a journey to unveil a war memorial at Liverpool Street Station, London. Following this ceremony, Wilson returned home where O'Sullivan and Dunne shot him as he was walking between the taxi from which he had just alighted and the door of his residence in Eaton Square.[168]

> Joe went in a straight line while I determined to intercept him [Wilson] from entering the door. Joe deliberately levelled his weapon at four yards range and fired twice. Wilson made for the door as best he could and actually reached the doorway when I encountered him at a range of seven or eight feet. I fired three shots rapidly, the last one from the hip, as I took a step forward. Wilson was now uttering short cries and in a doubled up position staggered towards the edge of the pavement. At this point Joe fired again and the last I saw of him he [Wilson] had collapsed.[169]

In addition to Wilson, two policemen and a civilian were wounded whilst both men tried to escape; O'Sullivan and Dunne were, however, quickly caught and arrested. O'Sullivan lost a leg in World War I, so an escape by foot seems incomprehensible. Moreover, their lack of planning was apparent: Dunne and O'Sullivan had no escape system set up, had to find and buy their own weapons only a week before the shooting, and O'Sullivan had gone to work that day and the assassination was carried out on his lunch break.[170]

The motives for Wilson's killing are not difficult to theorise. Seán Moylan recalled that Collins often stated that Wilson was a thorn in his side and repeatedly made the procurement of arms in Britain much more difficult. Dunne, like most Irish nationalists, was growing more and more outraged by the continuing attacks on Catholics in Northern Ireland and blamed Wilson, in his capacity as military advisor to the Northern Ireland government, for those attacks.[171] While the motives may be suggested, however, who was ultimately responsible remains more elusive.

It has become accepted (although it was not publicly known at the time) that Collins ordered Wilson's assassination some months previously.[172] British suspicions regarding Collins's involvement were suggested as documentation mentioning Collins had allegedly been found on the arrested men.[173] Further, Joe Sweeney, the pro-Treaty military leader in County Donegal, recalled that Collins informed him of his decision to order the shooting of Wilson. In addition, Sweeney stated that upon hearing the news that the order had been carried out, Collins seemed very pleased.[174] Collins sent Joe Dolan, a trusted member of the Squad, to London after the assassination to see if Dunne and O'Sullivan could be rescued from British custody – Dolan said he had 'a firm belief that Collins ordered the assassination'.[175] Dorothy Macardle wrote: 'popular belief attributed the assassination to the I.R.B. It was thought Michael Collins ordered it.'[176] Margery Forester agreed:

> There can be little doubt that such an order [for Wilson's assassination] had been given, most probably by Collins, in pre-Treaty days … But Collins was not a man who absent-mindedly left execution orders unrevoked. It is infinitely more probable that, far from doing so, he renewed the order to Dunne shortly before it was carried out, when the Belfast pogroms were at their height.[177]

Conversely, Emmet Dalton, one of Collins's closest confidants at the time, indicated that 'Collins was angry that the London IRA had taken an irresponsible attitude "at this time"'.[178] Further, Peter Hart has argued that there was no benefit to Collins to make such an order at this time, and that assassination was carried out by Dunne and O'Sullivan off their own bat.[179]

There is no clear and convincing evidence that Dunne and O'Sullivan were the tools of a conspiracy or of Collins giving the order in particular. The attack itself did not bear the hallmarks of a well-planned and organised assault, as had those by Collins's Squad throughout the war. Collins and Rory O'Connor separately briefly met Dunne in Dublin only two weeks before the assassination, but the results of those meetings are not known. One of the most infamous terrorist actions of the war and no one knows who gave the order.[180]

It must be said many of the British and Irish terror methods had immediate effect.[181] The Black and Tans and Auxiliaries so cowed the Irish that many simply ran away and deserted their homes and businesses at the thought the 'Tans' or 'Auxies' were coming to an area. On the other hand, local populations often asked the IRA/Volunteers to move along – IRA leaders were told that if they ambushed a lorry in the morning, the British would return at night to take their revenge on the local town and population, so the IRA would shift their operations elsewhere. As a result, the British were often able to effect their will on a population just by intimidation, while further Irish intimidation on the population often allowed them to remain in an area where they were not welcome.

Ronan Fanning, Professor at University College Dublin, in his 1975 lecture 'Transition from revolution to politics' said that 'violence will always hold the key to success'.[182] Fanning stressed that 'all revolutionaries demonstrate ambivalence toward democracy'.[183] In 2013 Fanning and Martin Mansergh[184] reviewed and discussed David Fitzpatrick's book *Terror in Ireland*[185] on an RTE radio show.[186] (Both questioned if 'political violence' should be substituted for 'terror' in the book's essays.) Fanning and Mansergh agreed that the War of Independence did 'not degenerate to a war of ambushes and assassinations', because the war did not 'degenerate' – that was the chosen strategy of the Irish leaders. Those leaders saw the defeat of the Easter Rising and a new and different strategy was necessary. The Irish 'believed that a strategy of assassinations and ambushes would work – and it did'. Fanning further noted the question in the introduction of the book 'Could a mutually acceptable settlement in Ireland be achieved without terror?', and Fanning answered, 'my answer, regretfully, is "No"'. Mansergh interjected, 'or not unless different people acted in very different ways'. Mansergh reiterated, 'Don't imagine for a second that violence doesn't produce results. It may not produce the results one wants – but it works.' Fanning concluded, 'war is hell, and hellish actions result'. Mansergh noted, 'and it doesn't have to be guerrilla war – it is in all wars'. War is dehumanising and brutal, and guerrilla war is particularly so. We don't like the thought of terror being effective – but it works. On both sides, military action could only go so far, but military action – and terror – was necessary in conjunction with political and propaganda pressures.

> There is not a shred of evidence that Lloyd George's Tory-dominated government would have moved from the 1914-style niggardliness of the Government of Ireland Act of 1920 to the larger, if imperfect generosity of the Treaty if they had not been compelled to do so by Michael Collins and his assassins. Indeed, the evidence points the other way.[187]

Insurgency breeds its own escalatory dynamics: excesses on one side produce excesses on the other side. The British forces used terrorism to continue the subjugation of Ireland, and the Irish used terror to achieve independence.[188] Each side blamed the other for what has been called the turn to terrorism. Indeed, it is in such contexts that the distinction between 'terrorist' and 'freedom fighter' becomes increasingly blurred.[189] Although initially such actions shocked the civilian population, the harsh responses from the British government resulted in a heightened civilian sympathy towards the Irish, though some of the Irish actions caused as much terror. Ernie O'Malley, one of the fiercest fighters of the Irish who spent much of the war going between Dublin and the country, wrote of the Irish:

> They faced their task squarely. They were fighting ruthlessness and they did not want to give mercy … That aspect of the fight in terms of cause and effect summed up for them the situation. The unnecessary cruelty of it made them bitter about other extravagant viciousness that shook them more than the ordinary aspects of the scrap … It would be hard to say which side was under the greatest tension.[190]

Terror seeks to control the future. Its eventual location and ultimate extent are undefined – its nature is open-ended. Terrorism's trauma is not merely absent in the non-occurrence of terror – rather it is just around the corner. 'It is not that it is not; it is not in a way that is never over'.[191] Trauma haunts the now, even as it fails to arrive: terror's trauma is directed toward the future as well as the past. This is what makes terrorism powerful and also what renders it traumatically affecting in a double sense: not only in the past, but in its potential to return as trauma and as another terrorist act. Encountered in literature, this futurity takes the form of a pervasive uncertainty, a sense that life is increasingly and irretrievably slipping out of control.

The war intensified as 1920 progressed – it became more brutal – and an increasingly ruthless IRA saw it as necessary to provoke publicity and international sympathy for their cause. But some on both sides recognised the 'descent into terror', and wished to distance themselves from their actions in Ireland. Lieutenant Frederick A.S. Clarke of the Essex Regiment (infamous in County Cork for its excesses and terror) said, 'I didn't like myself in Ireland. I don't think anybody else did either.'[192]

Notes

[1] S. Stewart, 'The difference between terrorism and insurgency', *Strategy* (26 June 2014); A. Merari, 'Terrorism as a strategy of insurgency', *Terrorism and Political Violence* 5 (4) (1993).

[2] See B. Hughes, 'Defying the IRA? Intimidation, coercion, and communities during the Irish Revolution', in E. Delaney and M. Luddy (eds), *Reappraisals in Irish History* (Liverpool, 2016).

[3] 'Propaganda by the deed' was the euphemism for terror coined by the Frenchman Paul Brousse in 1877: 'We must spread our principles, not with words but with deeds, for this is the most popular, the most potent, and the most irresistible form of propaganda'. M. Bakunin, *Bakunin on Anarchism* (Montreal, 1980), pp 195–6.

[4] C. Townshend, *Political Violence in Ireland. Government and Resistance since 1848* (Oxford, 1983).

[5] A. Schwenkenbecher, *Terrorism: A Philosophical Inquiry*, (New York, 2012).

[6] N. Machiavelli (trans. W.K. Marriott), *The Prince* (1532), p. 72.

[7] C.R. King, 'Revolutionary war, guerrilla warfare, and international law', *Case Western Reserve Journal of International Law* 4 (2) (1972); G.I.A.D. Draper, 'The status of combatants and the question of guerrilla warfare', *British Year Book of International Law* 45 (1971); R.R. Baxter, 'So-called "Unprivileged Belligerancy": spies, guerrillas and saboteurs', *British Yearbook of International Law* 28 (1951).

[8] M.C. Havens, C. Leiden and K.M. Schmit, *The Politics of Assassination* (Englewood Cliffs, NJ, 1970), p. 17.

[9] I.W.F. Beckett, *Modern Insurgencies and Counter-insurgencies: Guerrillas and their Opponents since 1750* (London, 2001), p. 75.

[10] B.M. Leiser, 'Terrorism, guerrilla warfare, and international morality', *Stanford Journal of International Studies* 12 (1977); C.E. Prisk, 'The umbrella of legitimacy', in M.G. Manwaring (ed.), *Uncomfortable Wars: Toward a New Paradigm of Low Intensity Conflict*

(Boulder, CO, 1991).

[11] D. Fitzpatrick (ed.), *Terror in Ireland, 1916–1923* (Dublin, 2012), p. 5.

[12] U.S. Government Counterinsurgency Guide (January 2009).

[13] B. Hanley, 'Terror in twentieth-century Ireland', in D. Fitzpatrick (ed.), *Terror in Ireland* (Dublin, 2012), p. 11.

[14] Schwenkenbecher, *Terrorism: A Philosophical Inquiry.*

[15] M. Danzer, 'The political consequences of terrorism: a comparative study of France and the United Kingdom', unpublished Masters dissertation, University of Bucharest (2019).

[16] M. Crenshaw (ed.), *Terrorism in Context* (Pennsylvania, 2005), p. 5.

[17] R. English, *Terrorism: How To Respond* (Oxford, 2009), pp 116–18.

[18] W.E. Trautman, 'Direct action and sabotage (1912)', in S. Salerno (ed.), *Direct Action and Sabotage: Three Classic IWW Pamphlets from the 1910s* (Chicago, 1997); K.R.M. Short, *The Dynamite War: Irish-American Bombers in Victorian Britain* (Dublin, 1979).

[19] Schwenkenbecher, *Terrorism: A Philosophical Inquiry.*

[20] *An t'Óglach,* 28 September 1918. *An t'Óglach* was the Irish Volunteers/IRA's own internal publication for members, although it was also distributed more widely to the public.

[21] C.S. Andrews, *Dublin Made Me* (Cork, 1979), p. 119.

[22] *Ibid.*

[23] 'The work before us', *An t'Óglach,* 1 February 1919.

[24] I. Cuenca-Sanchez, 'The dynamics of nationalist terrorism: ETA and the IRA', *Terrorism and Political Violence* 19 (2007).

[25] Though the Volunteers were the army of the Irish Republic, the term IRA was never officially adopted. The Volunteers continued to use that term, although the British ordinarily used 'IRA' or 'Sinn Féiners'. P. Béaslaí, 'The Anglo-Irish War', in G. Doherty (ed.), *With the IRA in the Fight for Freedom* (1970 edn), p. 15.

[26] *An t'Oglach,* 31 January 1919.

[27] F. Packenham, *Peace by Ordeal* (London, 1935), p. 49.

[28] *The Weekly Summary,* 8 October 1920.

[29] D. Leeson, *The Black and Tans: British Police and Auxiliaries in the Irish War of Independence, 1920–1921* (Oxford, 2012), p. 68.

[30] General H.H. Tudor, O/C of the Auxiliaries, was assigned to Palestine in 1922. Following the disbanding of the Auxiliaries in 1922, Churchill chose Tudor to be the overall civil and military commander in Palestine, though Colonel P.B. Bramley was the O/C of the British Gendarmerie in Palestine. The re-employment of disbanded RIC personnel as policemen was a deeply controversial issue in 1922, when reports of terror in Ireland were still fresh in the public mind. The Black and Tans and Auxiliaries had been widely associated in the international press with reprisal killings, destruction of property and general indiscipline. Most anxious was Palestine's high commissioner, Sir Herbert Samuel, who told Churchill that, while he had no objection to the recruitment of ex-RIC into the force, provided that the men selected were of good character, it would be: 'Most desirable, if it could be avoided, that no public announcement should be made connecting the Black and Tans with our Gendarmerie. Their reputation, as a Corps, has not been savoury and if any idea was created in the public mind in England or here that the Black and Tans, or any part of them, were being transferred as a body to Palestine, the new Gendarmerie might be

discredited from the outset' (Churchill Papers, CHAR, Samuel to Churchill, 11 December 1921); C. Townshend, 'In aid of civil power: Britain, Ireland, and Palestine 1916–1948', in D. Marston and C. Malkasian (eds), *Counterinsurgency in Modern Warfare* (Oxford, 2008); S. Gannon, 'The Black and Tans in Palestine – Irish connections to the Palestine Police 1922–1948', *The Irish Story* (20 February 2020), https://www.theirishstory.com/2020/02/20/the-black-and-tans-in-palestine-irish-connections-to-the-palestine-police-1922-1948/#.Xps24shKjGg.

[31] M. Hopkinson, *The Irish War of Independence* (Dublin, 2002), p. 79, quoted in the *Daily News,* April 1921.

[32] E. Holt, *Protest in Arms* (New York, 1960), pp 210–20.

[33] James Slattery: Witness Statement 445.

[34] S. Donovan, 'The multiple functions of terrorism: how the IRA used terrorism to resist British control while the British utilized terror to conquer the Irish people', https://www.trentu.ca.undergratuate/documents//S.Donovan.doc.

[35] B. Hughes, 'Make the terror behind greater than the terror in front? Internal discipline, forced participation, and the I.R.A, 1919–21', *Irish Historical Studies* **42** (161) (2018).

[36] McKenna Napoli, *Capuchin Annual* (1970); Kathleen McKenna: Witness Statement 643.

[37] K. Kearns, *Dublin Voices. An Oral Folk History* (Dublin, 1998), pp 99–100.

[38] *Ibid.*, p. 256.

[39] W. Sheehan (ed.), *British Voices From the Irish War of Independence 1918–1921: The Words of British Servicemen Who Were There* (Doughcloyne, 2007), pp 13–17.

[40] D. Duff, *Sword for Hire* (London, 1934), p. 64.

[41] C. Woodcock, *Experiences of an Officer's Wife in Ireland* (London, 1921; 1994), pp 48–50.

[42] M. Sturgis (ed. M. Hopkinson), *The Last Days of Dublin Castle: The Mark Sturgis Diaries* (Dublin, 1999), p. 123.

[43] E.S. Dowdell, 'Ireland under the new terror: what it means to live under martial law', *The London Magazine* (1921).

[44] Fitzpatrick, *Terror in Ireland*, p. 8.

[45] See K. Hughes, *English Atrocities in Ireland, a Compilation of Facts from Court and Press Records* (New York, 1920); T.R. Mockaitis, *British Counterinsurgency, 1919–60* (London, 1991), p. 37; T.R. Mockaitis, 'The origins of British counterinsurgency', *Small Wars and Insurgencies* **1** (3) (1990).

[46] T. Bowden, 'The Irish underground and the War of Independence 1919–1921', *Journal of Contemporary History* **8** (2) (1973); T. Bowden, 'Ireland: the impact of terror', in M. Elliott-Batemen, J. Ellis and T. Bowden (eds), *Revolt to Revolution: Studies in the 19th and 20th Century Experience* (Manchester, 1974).

[47] C. Townshend, *The British Campaign in Ireland 1919–1921: The Development of Political and Military Policies* (Oxford, 1975), pp 40–57.

[48] Mao Zedong, in E. Jocelyn and A. McEwen, *The Long March: The True Story Behind the Legendary Journey that Made Mao's China* (London, 2006), p. 46.

[49] Hopkinson, *The Irish War of Independence*, p. 79.

[50] Such use of provocation in guerrilla or terrorist warfare was not new. Walter Laqueur notes that Armenian revolutionaries of the 1880s and 1890s adopted a strategy based on provocation. They assumed their attacks on the Turks would instigate brutal retaliation, which would result in radicalisation of the Armenian population (W. Laqueur, *Age of Terrorism* (Boston, 1987), p. 43).

[51] J. Augusteijn, *From Public Defiance to Guerrilla Warfare: the Experience of Ordinary Volunteers in the Irish War of Independence* (Dublin, 1996), p. 251 *et seq.*, 294 *et seq.*, 310 *et seq.*; Hughes, 'Make the terror behind greater than the terror in front?'.

[52] T.E. Fitzgerald, 'The execution of spies and informers in West Cork, 1921', in D. Fitzpatrick (ed.), *Terror in Ireland* (Dublin, 2012), p. 181 *et seq.*; M. Murphy, 'Revolution and terror in Kildare, 1919–1923', in D. Fitzpatrick (ed.), *Terror in Ireland* (Dublin, 2012). While Murphy's essay deals mostly with the period after the Truce in July 1921, his statement that 'Revolutionary violence in Kildare was initially sporadic' could be applied throughout Ireland (p. 197).

[53] O'Malley Papers, P 17 b 88; Andrews, *Dublin Made Me*, p. 90.

[54] See P. Hart, *The IRA and its Enemies: Violence and Community in Cork: 1916–1923* (Cork, 1998); C. Townshend, 'The IRA and development of guerrilla war', *English Historical Review* 93 (371) (1979); D. Fitzpatrick, *Politics and Irish Life, 1913–1921: Provincial Experience of War and Revolution* (Dublin, 1977); C. O'Malley, *The Men Will Talk To Me* (Cork, 2010); Sheehan, *British Voices From the Irish War of Independence*; M. Ryan, *Tom Barry: Irish Freedom Fighter* (Cork, 2003); B. Keane, 'The IRA response to loyalist co-operation during the Irish War of Independence, 1919–1921'. Hart's book, *The IRA and its Enemies: Violence and Community in Cork, 1916–1923*, and the follow-up articles and reviews have been the subject of a voluminous and rancorous debate in Ireland since its publication in 1998. In academic journals, in the press and in the electronic media, Hart has been repeatedly accused of deliberately distorting evidence. The controversy turns on Hart's depiction of Irish revolutionary violence, and in particular upon a chapter entitled 'Taking it out on the Protestants', in which the IRA was portrayed as fundamentally sectarian. The articles and books are far too extensive for complete inclusion here, but one should be aware that there are many sides to the debate, and seek further information for a balanced view of the claims and counter-claims regarding 'informers' in the War of Independence (particularly in County Cork) and whether the IRA engaged in killings outside the bounds of war, which could be termed 'ethnic cleansing'. J. Regan, *The Irish Counter-revolution, 1921–1936* (Dublin, 1999); A. Bielenberg, 'Protestant emigration from the south of Ireland, 1911–1926', lecture given at 'Understanding our History: Protestants, the War of Independence, and the Civil War in Cork', Conference at University College Cork (13 December 2008); J. Regan, 'Irish public histories as an historiographical problem', *Irish Historical Studies* 37 (146) (2010).

[55] 'Record of the rebellion in Ireland in 1920–1921 and the part played by the army in dealing with it', Vol. 2, Imperial War Museum, Box 78/82/2, p. 12.

[56] 2nd Southern Division Orders, UCD Archive, O'Beirne Ranelagh Papers, p. 9.

[57] Cork No. 3 Brigade, War Diary, 14 May 1921, General Richard Mulcahy Papers, University College Dublin, MSS P7 A/II/2.

[58] M.G. Valiulis, *Portrait of a Revolutionary: General Richard Mulcahy and the Founding of the Irish State* (Blackrock, 1992), p. 53.

[59] T. Barry, *Guerilla Days in Ireland* (Dublin, 1949), p. 106.

[60] Tom Barry quoted in K. Griffith and T. O'Grady, *Ireland's Unfinished Revolution, An Oral History* (London, 1982), p. 143.

[61] *Ibid.*

[62] Hopkinson, *The Irish War of Independence*, pp 110–11.

[63] 'Record of the rebellion in Ireland', Vol. 2, 1922; Jeudwine Papers 72/82/1, Imperial War Museum. See footnotes 52, 54, 67 and 129 for more discussion on the contro-

versial debate regarding the activities of informers.

64 Hart, *The IRA and its Enemies*, pp 298–300.

65 *Ibid.*, p. 311.

66 P. Hart, 'Class, community and the Irish Republican Army in Cork, 1917–1923', in P. O'Flanagan, C.G. Buttimer and G. O'Brien, *Cork: History & Society* (Dublin, 1993), pp 963–81, see especially p. 979.

67 In many views and instances of the War of Independence, it is this either/or – a 'binary construct' – that is the difficulty for some commentators. History is seldom 'black or white' and one must understand that in many cases the evidence is not there for a definitive, one-sided view, and in other instances a more nuanced, objective and multi-faceted view is called for. There were some who were killed to settle scores, some who were killed as a result of internal feuds and some who were killed because they were passing information to the British. It would be reasonable for former soldiers, loyalists or Protestants to be more likely to give information to the British. The reasons for the killings, however, are not mutually exclusive – there were both informers killed, as well as those who were in the 'suspect classifications' as defined by Hart and others and who were killed but were not informers. It is important to note that of the 196 civilians killed by the IRA as 'spies or informers' nationwide, seventy-five per cent were Catholic and twenty-five per cent were Protestant (Anglican, Presbyterian or Methodist), approximately the ratio of Catholics to Protestants as found in the general population of the time. In County Cork, the number of Protestants killed (for whatever reason) was thirty per cent, and this larger proportion can be attributed to the larger loyalist and Protestant communities in Cork who were staunchly pro-British and, consequently, were more likely to assist the British forces.

68 County Inspector, West Cork Riding, January 1921, CO 904/114.

69 Major A.E. Percival, quoted in Sheehan, *British Voices From the Irish War of Independence*, p. 134.

70 'Record of the rebellion in Ireland in 1920–1', Vol. 1, March 1922; see also Letter to Strickland about this document, March 1 1922 Strickland Papers, EPS 2/3, Imperial War Museum. A second volume was submitted in April and printed in May 1922: 'Record of the rebellion in Ireland in 1920-1', Vol. 2, 1922, Jeudwine Papers 72/82/1, Imperial War Museum.

71 Report by the General Office Commanding-In-Chief on the Situation in Ireland for Week Ending 19th February, 1921, National Archives, CAB/24/120/25, p. 152.

72 Denis Lordan: Witness Statement 470; William Desmond: Witness Statement 832; Willie Foley: Witness Statement 1560; Anna Hurley-O'Mahoney: Witness Statement 540.

73 Barry, *Guerilla Days in Ireland*, p. 127.

74 P. Walsh (ed.), *Ireland (1921) with an introduction to the Anglo-Irish Treaty and the 'Lost World' of Imperial Ireland by Lionel Curtis and Henry Harrison on South Africa and Ireland* (Belfast, 2002), p. 60; L. Curtis, *Round Table* 11 (43), pp 496–7.

75 'Record of the rebellion in Ireland, the situation in Ireland at the end of 1919 to April 1920'.

76 S. Kalyvas, *The Logic of Violence in Civil War* (Cambridge, 2006), p. 27.

77 G. Clark, *Everyday Violence in the Irish Civil War* (Cambridge, 2014), p. 171.

78 See MCRs, IG, May–July 1921 (TNA: CO 904/115–16) where bodies are regularly referred to as having been found with the 'usual notice'.

79 A. Dolan, 'The shadow of a great fear: terror and revolutionary Ireland', in D. Fitz-

patrick (ed.), *Terror in Ireland* (Dublin, 2012).

[80] P. Óg Ó Ruairc, 'Spies & informers beware', *An Cosantóir* (March 2019).

[81] John Walsh: Witness Statement 966. One of the most striking features of the Bureau of Military History Witness Statements and Military Service Pensions Collection is the willingness of former IRA members to identify by name the people they killed and the circumstances of killing.

[82] C. Townshend, *The Republic: The Fight for Irish Independence, 1918–1923* (London, 2013), p. 265.

[83] P. Magee, quoted in R. English, *Does Terrorism Work?* (Oxford, 2016), p. 2.

[84] Lt Sheerin, 'Record of Derry City Battalion, Derry Brigade', Collins MSS A/0464/I, POS 915.

[85] Hart, *The IRA and its Enemies*, p. 243.

[86] *Ibid.*

[87] *Irish Post and Weekly Telegraph for Cavan*, 14 August 1920.

[88] Barron's Report of 15 October 1921, contained in a 'Note on the state of north-west Munster'; Memorandum by the Chief Secretary of Ireland, National Records of Scotland, Edinburgh, CAB 43/2.

[89] T.E. Lawrence, *The Science of Guerrilla Warfare* (1948); T.E. Lawrence, 'The evolution of a revolt', *Army Quarterly and Defence Journal* (October 1920).

[90] Kalyvas, *The Logic of Violence in Civil War*, p. 137.

[91] *Ibid.*, pp 54, 79, 189–91, 343–4, 357.

[92] Ernie O'Malley Notebooks, ECD, P17b/112, pp 74–83. It is not clear if the remark was made by Busteed or O'Malley, or to which shooting it refers.

[93] L. Deasy, *Towards Ireland Free* (Cork, 1973), p. 140.

[94] John O'Riordan: Witness Statement 1117.

[95] T. O'Reilly, *Rebel Heart: George Lennon Flying Column Commander* (Cork, 2009), p. 79.

[96] P.B. Leonard, 'The necessity of de-Anglicising the Irish Nation: boycotting and the Irish War of Independence', unpublished Ph.D thesis, University of Melbourne (2000).

[97] CI, MCR, Dublin, January 1919, CO 904/108.

[98] J.M. Regan (ed. J. Augusteijn), *The Memoirs of John M. Regan, A Catholic Officer in the RIC and RUC: 1909–1948* (Dublin, 2007); S. Waters (ed. S. Ball), *A Policeman's Ireland: Recollections of Samuel Waters, RIC* (Cork, 1999).

[99] P.J. Twohig, *Green Tears for Hecuba: Ireland's Fight for Freedom* (Ballincolig, 1994), p. 71 *et seq.*

[100] Éamon de Valera, Minutes of Dáil Éireann, Vol. 1 (10 April 1919).

[101] 'Committee of Enquiry into the Detective Organisation of the Irish Police Forces, December 1919–March 1920', CO 904/24/5.

[102] RIC IG Report for July 1920 for Counties Cork and Mayo and for August 1920, PRO CO 904/112; see also John Anderson Papers, PRO CO 094/188/1.

[103] Leonard, 'The necessity of de-Anglicising the Irish nation'.

[104] CI, MCR, Clare, October 1920, CO 904/103.

[105] Eamon Broy: Witness Statement 1280.

[106] Sir John Anderson Papers, 1 PRO, CO 904/188/97.

[107] The total numbers killed are contested but are relatively small in comparison to other guerrilla wars. Hopkinson lists 624 British killed and 724 Irish killed (civilians and IRA) (Hopkinson, *The Irish War of Independence*). The National Graves Association, *The Last Post* (New York, 1986), lists 585 republicans killed. There were 513 RIC con-

stables killed.

108 R. Asprey, *War in the Shadows* (London, 1994), p. 195.

109 L. Connolly, 'Hair taking: a weapon of war in Ireland's War of Independence?', *RTE Brainstorm* (February 2020), https://www.rte.ie/brainstorm/2020/0212/1115001-how-forced-hair-cutting-was-used-as-a-weapon-of-war-in-ireland/.

110 M. Coleman, 'Violence against women in the Irish War of Independence, 1919–1921', in D. Ferriter and S. Riordan (eds), *Years of Turbulence: The Irish Revolution and its Aftermath* (Dublin, 2015), pp 151–2.

111 *The Irish Citizen*, September 1920. *The Irish Citizen* was the leading female suffrage newspaper in Ireland. It was nationalist in sentiment but did not advocate violence.

112 Elizabeth Bloxam: Witness Statement 632.

113 L. Connolly, 'Sexual violence a dark secret in the Irish War of Independence and Civil War', *Irish Times* (10 January 2019).

114 Michael Walsh: Witness Statement 786.

115 Hughes, *Defying the IRA*, p. 140.

116 *The Weekly Summary*, TNA: CO 904/148–149.

117 Epitome of documents taken from Eileen McGrane, arrested 1 Jan. 1921, LHCMA: 7/24.

118 British National Archives (TNA), Cabinet Papers, CAB 24/109/26. Tudor, a clergyman's son from Devon, had no policing experience. He was in fact a life-long soldier, who had made a successful army career. It is generally accepted that Tudor's chief qualification for the position of 'police advisor' in Ireland was his close friendship with the War Secretary, Winston Churchill.

119 E. McCall, *The Auxiliaries: Tudor's Toughs, A Study of the Auxiliary Division of the Royal Irish Constabulary 1920–1922* (London, 2010).

120 Seán Kennedy: Witness Statement 885.

121 There seem to have been more documented cases during the Truce and Civil War than the War of Independence. See N. Murray, 'The rarely spoken about violence suffered by women during the Irish revolution', *The Irish Examiner* (12 September 2017): 'Professor Linda Connolly referred to a Cork IRA officer recounting knowledge of two cases of sexual violence by Crown Forces in the northside of the city, matters often used in the international propaganda campaign by the republican movement. One such case was that of Norah Healy, who was pregnant with her fifth child when she was raped in front of her husband at their Blackpool home. But seeing one of her attackers face-to-face when she visited a local police barracks, she was urged to let the matter slide by an Royal Irish Constable (RIC) sergeant. "Never mind, don't say anything now," he told her. Almost certainly even more so than today's low reporting of sexual violence, most such incidents went unrecorded and will be impossible to ever be numbered. But the fact that the case of Mary M was unearthed by University College Dublin historian Lindsey Earner Byrne as part of a study on poverty in early independent Ireland speaks volumes, says Prof Connolly. She believes the many historians of the military conflict have, for far too long, overlooked the question of women's experiences. "Stories of very violent assault on women do exist. You only have to look at some of the newspaper reports at the time, and these require serious consideration by any scholar of the period".' See also L.E. Byrne, 'The rape of Mary M.: a microhistory of sexual violence and moral redemption in 1920s Ireland', *Journal of the History of Sexuality* 24 (1) (2015).

122 S. Benton, 'Women disarmed: the militarisation of politics in Ireland, 1913–1923',

Feminist Review 50 (1995).

[123] George Berkeley: Witness Statement 424.

[124] Coleman, 'Violence against women in the Irish War of Independence', pp 151–2. Rape is seldom mentioned in the witness statements, and in none of the cases is any evidence provided. See George Berkeley: Witness Statement 971; Séamus Fitzgerald: Witness Statement 1737; Frank Henderson: Witness Statement 821; James Moloney: Witness Statement 1525.

[125] Clark, *Everyday violence in the Irish Civil War*, pp 136, 176, 197–9, 203.

[126] DP2100 (5 October 1933).

[127] M.K. Connery, 'Report to the Irish White Cross' (4 June 1922); C. Caruth, *Unclaimed Experience: Trauma, Narrative and History* (Baltimore, 2010), p. 72.

[128] Connery, 'Report to the Irish White Cross'.

[129] G. Foster, 'Ordinary brutalities', *Dublin Review of Books* (October 2017), p. 119. The Irish Grants Committee (IGC) was set up after the war to compensate the victims on both sides, and the files have an unmatched range and variety of first-hand civilian testimony, but the accounts must be treated with at least the same caution as the BMH Witness statements. Both are subject to faulty memory as well as some personal friction. Moreover, applicants for compensation would invariably portray themselves as victims and emphasise or exaggerate their losses at the hands of republicans. In addition, the terms of reference – notably, a requirement to prove loss on the basis of 'allegiance to the government of the United Kingdom' – framed and influenced testimony. The majority of claims were made for military service and awarded under the two Military Service Pension (MSP) acts. A Cumann na nGaedhael government brought in the first Act in 1924, in an effort to dispel unrest among pro-Treaty forces in the wake of demobilisation and the army mutiny. It was first limited to pro-Treaty Civil War veterans with pre-Truce (1916–21) service in one of the main separatist military organisations: the Irish Volunteers/IRA, Irish Citizen Army, Fianna Éireann or Hibernian Rifles. In late 1934 Fianna Fáil passed a second Pensions Act allowing applications from anti-Treaty Civil War veterans with pre-Truce service, neutral Easter Rising and War of Independence veterans whose service ended at the Truce, and for the first time from Cumann na mBan. A digitised collection of pension applications to the Irish Free State seeking compensation for 'wounded members, and the widows, children and dependents of deceased members, of Óglaigh na hÉireann including the National Army, the Irish Volunteers, and the Irish Citizen Army through the payment of allowances and gratuities' is being released in tranches. Over time, provision was enhanced and broadened to include members of the Hibernian Rifles, Cumann na mBan, Fianna Éireann and certain members of the Connaught Rangers. See 'Origin and Scope', Military Archives and the National Archives (2017), http://www.militaryarchives.ie/collections/online-collections/military-service-pensions-collection/about-the-collection/origin-and-scope. E. Morrison, 'The Bureau of Military History as a source for the Irish Revolution' (2012), http://www.bureauof-militaryhistory.ie/files/Bureau_of_Military_witness_statements%20as%20sources%20for_the_Irish%20Revolution.pdf .

[130] Clark, *Everyday Violence in the Irish Civil War*, p. 104.

[131] Pension applications were accepted from any male combatants for the period from 1916 to 1921 and from those who joined the National Army in the Civil War. Obviously, many anti-Treaty Volunteers chose not to apply before the 1934 Act.

[132] M. Coleman, 'Compensating Irish female revolutionaries, 1916–1923', *Women's His-*

tory Review **26** (6) (2017).

[133] Just as the availability of witness statements and pension applications in the early 2000s has allowed researchers to propose more complete and nuanced points of view of the entire War of Independence, such research has given an all-new understanding and appreciation of the need for more research on the violence against women during the war.

Marie Coleman writes, 'despite many bitter attacks and reprisals, serious and violent physical or sexual assaults against women were rare … Such violence was physical, psychological, and specific to gender (but falling short of sexual assault), rather than sexual or fatal … There is ample evidence attesting to physical assaults on women by the Black and Tans and Auxiliaries. Frequently this took the form of cutting off their hair … In September 1920 five members of Cumann na mBan in Galway were subjected to this unofficial punishment in reprisal for a similar attack carried out by the IRA on a woman who had given evidence to a military court. This incident indicates that the IRA was equally liable to commit such attacks and there are many instances of women who were friendly with the police or who worked for them being treated similarly. The majority of violence against women perpetrated by the IRA was the "victimisation of policemen's wives and barrack servants" … The first Dáil's efforts, albeit unsuccessful, to achieve foreign recognition for the republic would have been hampered by reports of callous treatment of women. In a similar vein, the British authorities in Ireland would have been well aware of the potential damage to Britain's reputation internationally if stories of rape and sexual assault of Irish women began to emerge. From the British viewpoint the avoidance of sexual violence allowed them to draw a clear contrast with their recent enemy, the autocratic Germany of the Kaiser, whose army had resorted to widespread rape and sexual assault in Belgium at the start of the First World War … Violence towards women was certainly a feature of the War of Independence, yet the evidence available indicates that it was limited in nature and scope. The targeted killing of females was very rare'(M. Coleman, 'Women escaped the worst of the brutalities in the War of Independence', *Irish Examiner* (27 November 2015); M. Coleman, 'Violence against women in the Irish War of Independence').

Professor Linda Connolly argues that 'women were in fact the subject of sexual assaults and violent attacks during the period which may have not been reported and therefore the evidence needs to be re-examined' (Connolly, 'Sexual violence a dark secret in the Irish War of Independence and Civil War'). A. Quinlan, 'Wartime sexual violence against women "ignored"', *Irish Times* (9 July 2018); L. Connolly, 'Towards a further understanding of the violence experienced by women in the Irish Revolution', Maynooth University Social Sciences Institute (January 2019); L. Connolly, 'Did women escape the worst of the brutalities between 1919–1921?' (September 2017), https://www.maynoothuniversity.ie/research/research-news-events/latest-news/did-women-escape-worst-brutalities-between-1919-1921; Murray, 'The rarely spoken about violence against women during the Irish revolution'.

See E.J. Wood, 'Variation in sexual violence during war', *Politics and Society* **34** (3) (2006); L. Ryan, '"Drunken Tans": representation of sex and violence in the Anglo-Irish War (1919–1921)', *Feminist Review* **66** (2000); A. Matthews, *Renegades: Irish Republican Women 1900–1922* (Cork, 2010); M. Loken, 'Rethinking rape: the role of women in wartime violence', *Security Studies* **26** (1) (2016); G. Machnik-Kékesi, 'Gendering bodies: violence as performance in Ireland's War of Independence (1919–1921)', unpublished Master of Arts thesis, Concordia University Montreal, Quebec,

134 J. Connors, *Seán Hogan. His Life: A Troubled Journey* (Tipperary, 2019), p. 87.

135 NLI MSS 900/9 (4).

136 Machnik-Kékesi, 'Gendering bodies: violence as performance in Ireland's War of Independence'.

137 See the execution of Mary Lindsay in Hart, *The I.R.A. and its Enemies*, pp 308–10; T. Sheehan, *Lady Hostage (Mrs Lindsay)* (Dripsey, 1990); and S. O'Callaghan, *Execution* (London, 1974), pp 26–7. See that of Kate Carroll in F. McGarry, *Eoin O'Duffy. A Self-made Hero* (Oxford, 2005), pp 65–6; and N. Meehan, 'She is a Protestant as well. Distilling British propaganda in accounts of the death of Kate Carroll, in April 1921', *The Aubane Historical Society* (8 August 2020). See that of Bridget Noble in E. O'Halpin, 'Problematic killing during the War of Independence and its aftermath: civilian spies and informers', in J. Kelly and M.A. Lyons (eds), *Death and Dying in Ireland, Britain and Europe: Historical Perspectives* (Dublin, 2013), pp 336–7. O'Halpin suggests there may be more, unconfirmed cases. See also, E. Morrison, 'Hauntings of the Irish Revolution: veterans and memory of the independence struggle and Civil War', in M. Corporal, C. Cusack and R. van den Beuken (eds), *Irish Studies and the Dynamics of Memory: Transitions and Transformations* (2016). The 'Record of the Rebellion in Ireland' addressed the killing of Mrs Lindsay with a view to informers coming forward: 'There was practically no chance of information being given to the troops; the case of Mrs Lindsay and *hundreds of others* was a perfectly sufficient deterrent' [emphasis added] ('Record of the rebellion in Ireland in 1920–1921 and the part played by the army in dealing with it', Imperial War Museum, Box 78/82/2. Lindsay was a Protestant. Carroll and Noble were Catholics.

138 General Orders (New Series), 1920, No. 13 'Women Spies', 9 Nov. 1920, UCDA: P7/A/45.

139 For example, 24-year-old Eileen Quinn, who was seven months pregnant and standing beside her three young children when she was killed by Black and Tans on 1 November 1920. Eileen was killed by the Black and Tans as they made their way from Gort back to their barracks in Galway City. Her husband Malachy was away at the fair in Gort and Eileen was standing with her children, Eva (4), Alfie (2) and Tessie (1), perhaps awaiting his return, when the British forces in trucks approached her house. A verdict of 'death by misadventure' was recorded. Local women tried valiantly to save both Eileen and her unborn child and it took her eight hours to die a painful death. It was believed locally that Eileen was murdered in retaliation for the killing of a Royal Irish Constabulary (RIC) man, Constable Horan, in the area just two days earlier. Constable Horan, a father of three young children, was killed in an IRA ambush in the same area. The report by Dublin Castle indicated it was '1 shot fired as a precautionary measure' and characterised by a military court as 'a manslaughter and accidental shooting by some occupant unknown of said police car'.

140 Communication from West Connemara Brigade IRA to General Headquarters, 14 February 1921, General Richard Mulcahy Papers, UCD archives, 7/A16-20.

141 Hughes, 'Defying the IRA?', p. 137. See M. Brennan, *The War in Clare 1911–1921: Personal Memoirs of the Irish War of Independence* (Dublin, 1980).

142 NLI MS 556(8), 'Women and children under the terror', 17 April 1920.

143 Machnik-Kékesi, 'Gendering bodies: violence as performance in Ireland's War of Independence'.

144 S. Aiken, 'The women who had been straining every nerve: gender-specific medical

management of trauma in the Irish Revolution (1916–1923)', in M. Terrazas Gallego, (ed.), *Trauma and Identity in Contemporary Irish Culture* (Bern, 2019).

[145] G. White and B. O'Shea, *The Burning of Cork* (Cork, 2006).

[146] *Cork Examiner*, 13 December 1920.

[147] *Freeman's Journal*, 20 January 1921.

[148] 'Charlie' letter to his mother, 16 December 1920, O'Donoghue Papers, NLI MS 31226.

[149] See J. McDermott, *Northern Divisions: The Old IRA and the Belfast Pogroms, 1920–1922* (Belfast, 2001).

[150] Major C.J.C. Street, *Ireland in 1921* (New York, 1921; London, 1922), p. 56.

[151] G.B. Kenna, *Facts and Figures of the Belfast Pogrom, 1920–1922* (Dublin, 1922).

[152] Hopkinson, *The Irish War of Independence,* pp 156–7.

[153] P. Hart, 'Operations abroad: the I.R.A. in Britain, 1919–1923', *English Historical Review* **115** (460) (2000).

[154] D. Gannon, 'The Irish Revolution in Great Britain', in J. Crowley, D. Ó Drisceoil and M. Murphy (eds), *Atlas of the Irish Revolution* (Cork, 2017), p. 520 *et seq.*

[155] J.A. Pinkman (ed. F.E. Maguire), *In the Legion of the Vanguard* (Dublin, 1998), pp 32–3.

[156] E. O'Malley, *On Another Man's Wound* (Dublin, 1936; 1979), p. 188.

[157] George Fitzgerald: Witness Statement 684.

[158] Paddy O'Donoghue: Witness Statement 847.

[159] E. Brady, *Ireland's Secret Service in England* (Dublin, 1924), pp 24–5, 27.

[160] *The Times,* 10 March 1921. Hart, 'Operations abroad: the I.R.A. in Britain, 1919–1923'; M. Rast, 'Tactics, politics and propaganda in the Irish War of Independence, 1917–1921', unpublished Masters thesis, Georgia State University (2011); G. Noonan, 'Republican terrorism in Britain, 1920–1921', in D. Fitzpatrick (ed.), *Terror in Ireland* (Dublin, 2012).

[161] *The Times,* 12 March 1921.

[162] D. Kirby, 'The IRA and Manchester: how terror unit waged war on the city', *The Manchester Evening News* (20 January 2013).

[163] G. Noonan, *The IRA in Britain 1919–1923, 'In the Heart of Enemy Lines'* (Liverpool, 2017), p. 86.

[164] *The Times,* 4 April 1921.

[165] *The Times,* 11 May 1921.

[166] *New York Times*, 4 July 1921.

[167] R. Taylor, *Assassination: The Death of Sir Henry Wilson and the Tragedy of Ireland* (London, 1961); P. Hart, 'Michael Collins and the assassination of Sir Henry Wilson', *Irish Historical Studies* **28** (110) (1992).

[168] http://www.nickelinthemachine.com/2008/10/knightsbridge-michael-collins-and-the-murder-of-field-marshall-sir-henry-wilson/.

[169] Dunne's report was smuggled out of prison and published in the *Sunday Press*, 14 August 1955. P. Hart, *The I.R.A. at War, 1916–1923* (Oxford, 2003), p. 194.

[170] Statements of A.A. Wilson and Ernest John Jordan, Lloyd George Papers, F/97/1/30.

[171] Dunne's prison letters, NLI, MS 2653. Statement of Robert Dunne (Reggie's father), Lloyd George Papers, F/97/1/30. Collins was greatly affected by attacks on Catholics in the North, and was engaged in many schemes that he thought would give them relief (G.B. Kenna, *Facts & Figures of the Belfast Pogroms 1920–1922* (1997 edn, ed. Thomas Donaldson), p. 130. Others, however, have written that Collins's efforts were

counterproductive. See R. Lynch, 'The Clones affray, 1922: massacre or invasion', *History Ireland* **12** (3) (2004). Lynch posits: 'The Clones affray also illustrates the shadowy and confused role of Michael Collins, who, stuck in his cocoon of conspiracy, continued in his deluded belief that an aggressive IRA policy could achieve similar results to those of the War of Independence. His failure to understand the Northern situation meant that his policy was at best a failure and at worst counterproductive, doing little else but confirming unionist prejudices and highlighting the Northern Catholic minority's vulnerability'.

[172] McDermott, *Northern Divisions: The Old IRA and the Belfast Pogroms, 1920–1922*, p. 191.

[173] The papers found on Dunne were determined to be irrelevant to the assassination. The Special Branch's investigation determined that the two men acted on their own. Conclusions of a Conference, CAB 23/30, c. 36 [22], and Appendix 3.

[174] M. Hopkinson, *Green Against Green: The Irish Civil War* (Dublin, 1988), p. 112 *et seq.*; Griffith and O'Grady, *Ireland's Unfinished Revolution*, p. 281. See notes of conversations with Sweeney held in 1962 and 1964, Mulcahy Papers, P7D/43.

[175] Joe Dolan: Witness Statement 900.

[176] D. Macardle, *The Irish Republic* (New York, 1937; 1965), p. 737.

[177] M. Forester, *Michael Collins, The Lost Leader* (Dublin, 1989), p. 316.

[178] M. Ryan, *The Day Michael Collins was Shot* (Dublin, 1989), p. 20.

[179] Hart, 'Michael Collins and the assassination of Sir Henry Wilson'.

[180] P. O'Sullivan and F. Lee, 'The execution of Field Marshal Sir Henry Wilson: the facts', *Sunday Press* (10 August 1958).

[181] See R. English, *Does Terrorism Work?* (Oxford, 2016).

[182] R. Fanning, 'Leadership and transition from the politics of revolution to the politics of party: the example of Ireland,1914–1939', paper delivered to the International Congress of Historical Societies, San Francisco (27 August 1975).

[183] Regan, 'Irish public histories as an historiographical problem'.

[184] Mansergh was a TD from the Tipperary South constituency, as well as a Senator and a Minister for State, and was instrumental in formulating Fianna Fáil policy during the negotiations for the Good Friday Agreement signed in 1998. In full disclosure, Mansergh launched the author's book, *Dublin Rising*, in 2015.

[185] Fitzpatrick, *Terror in Ireland*.

[186] RTE Radio 1, *Off the Shelf*, 16 February 2013.

[187] R. Fanning, 'Michael Collins – an overview', in G. Doherty and D. Keogh (eds), *Michael Collins and the Making of the Irish Free State* (Cork, 1998).

[188] R. W. White, 'From gunmen to politicians: the impact of terrorism and political violence on twentieth-century Ireland', *Journal of Conflict Studies* **27** (2) (2007).

[189] R. Clutterbuck, *Guerrillas and Terrorists* (Athens, OH, 1980), p. 24; R. Clutterbuck, *Terrorism and Guerrilla Warfare* (London, 1990).

[190] O'Malley, *On Another Man's Wound*, pp 292, 316.

[191] M. Richardson, 'Terrorism: trauma in the excess of affect', in J.R. Kurtz (ed.), *Cambridge Critical Concepts: Trauma and Literature* (Cambridge, 2018), p. 329.

[192] Liddell Hart Centre, King's College, 1/6, 1968. Clarke was ultimately promoted to Brigadier.

5. Trauma remains long after the event

We had to learn to kill in cold blood and we got used to it.

Joe Dolan, member of the Squad

Any discussion of terror in Ireland must consider the long-term human effects that the actions had on those who committed them, as well as on those upon whom they were committed and their families, and whether the Bloody Sunday killings and other actions by both the British and Irish should be classified as 'terror'. Just the use of the word 'terror' tends to imply a political or moral judgement, and is one of the reasons it is so controversial. It is a word that is imbued with fear, panic, outrage and a political fervour that is not seen in other historiography. Often, the term 'terrorism' is used as a polemical tool rather than as an analytical term.

Terrorism is not simply a particular form of political violence, but also has a marshalling of affect. That is, terrorism targets relations between individuals: the very capacity to affect and be affected. If terror's purpose is to disrupt the patterns and forms of everyday life, then its means are indirect – its force is both symbolic and affective. Terror in Ireland was exacerbated because the actions were at such close quarters. Most lives were taken at close range, many by a shot from a handgun, such as killing a man in bed with his wife.[1] That proximity to the violence caused a 'wounding of the mind' that affects one more, and longer, than violence that occurs from falling bombs or artillery. Many of those who partook in the violence and terror throughout Ireland remained haunted by the blood and fear that they saw on the faces of those killed or wounded right in front of them. Proximity heightens emotions.

To understand the use of terror in the Irish war, we must try to understand its context and meaning. Tactically, its initial and primary purpose was to intimidate the military/police opposition by, for example, throwing a grenade into a DMP/RIC barracks so all the policemen would

163

fear that every time a door or window was opened a grenade could come through it. At a slightly higher level it was used to eliminate political and military leaders and officials in order to destabilise the government.[2] Che Guevara addressed killing by insurgents:

> Terrorism should be considered a valuable tactic when it is used to put to death some noted leader of the oppressing forces well known for his cruelty, his efficiency in repression, or other quality that makes his elimination useful. But the killing of persons of small importance is never advisable, since it brings on an increase of reprisals, including deaths.[3]

So-called 'leadership targeting' is a most effective guerrilla tool, and was utilised in Dublin as well as throughout the country. Todd Andrews wrote in *Dublin Made Me*:

> Assassination, correctly applied by Michael Collins, was the real basis of our relative success.[4]

The selection of such targets reflected the IRA's concern with legitimacy and with preventing wanton violence. Its aim was not to kill massive numbers of people, but to confine its killing, where possible, to targets that could be justified as legitimate objects of military resistance. Where killing occurred, it was strategically intended. In addition to intimidating police and informers, IRA attacks were designed to provoke brutality from the British forces. Such an approach was simple in that it recognised the British weakness of over-reliance on individual agents for information and removed the threat these individuals' intelligence-gathering activities posed by eliminating the individuals themselves.[5] This 'selective assassination', refined by Collins, has been deemed the 'pivot of the war effort'.[6] Lord Londonderry, a Northern Ireland Minister in 1922, reached much the same conclusion:

> Mr Collins ... achieved his position ... by being one of the leaders of a campaign which Sinn Féin called war, and which I call assassination. He has maintained his position by challenging the

British government and by succeeding in compelling the British government to make terms and terms of a character far exceeding the wildest hopes of Mr Collins or any of his supporters.[7]

Terror lives long after the initial application of it and one must consider the nature of the terror used and what it does to the lives of those who commit it, as well as upon those upon whom it is committed. The effect of the trauma on each is different. For weeks after Bloody Sunday, Mrs Hettie Newberry, the wife of one of the British officers killed, claimed she was haunted by the sounds of gunfire and the laughing of the gunmen, and by the image of one of the killers washing her husband's blood from his hands in her sink. While that did not happen, it is the perception of what was happening among those on the ground that is most important. Three weeks after the events, she died while giving birth to a stillborn child.[8]

On the Irish side, Jane Boyle of 12 Lennox Street, Dublin, worked at Spiedel's Pork Shop at 92 Talbot Street, next door to Republican Outfitter's. It was directly in front of her shop that Seán Treacy was shot and died on 15 October 1920. Jane knew many of Collins's men, and when she knew there were British soldiers on the street she would hide guns for the IRA/Volunteers. Jane was taken to the match at Croke Park by her fiancé, Daniel Byron. She was knocked down in the stampede out of Croke Park that Sunday, and was shot to death. Her brother James stood over her broken body in the Mater Hospital. He saw she had a small bruise over her left eye, and her broken jaw had distorted the left side of her face. A bullet had pierced her back.[9] Jane was to be married to Daniel five days later – and she was buried in her wedding dress on that day. How safe could anyone feel attending any public meeting or sporting event? Grief and trauma can become a collective experience rather than just contained within an individual.

The morality of war is a slippery subject, especially to those who do the killing; in recent years, psychologists have coined the term 'moral injury' for a special kind of trauma they are seeing in veterans.[10] Unlike PTSD, moral injury doesn't arise from fearful experiences, but from the act of killing itself, especially from doing something that crossed a line with respect to their moral belief. Guilt, shame, disgust and anger are some of the hallmark reactions to moral injury, and these persist long after the injury, expressing themselves as depression or functional impairment.

Almost all rebellions are born in spilled blood, and the Irish fight was no different. While the figure of the shell-shocked man became a metaphor for the collective trauma of the First World War in post-war Britain, to the contrary, the newly conceived Irish Free State largely identified with the image of the heroic male guerrilla fighter, whose suffering and discomfort was rendered invisible. It was not until the 1970s that it was recognised that 'the most common post-traumatic disorders are not those of men in war, but of women in civilian life'.[11] There are relatively few contemporary studies on killing and its effects on young men acting as guerrillas in the Irish war, though recent wars in Afghanistan and Iraq have led to many medical and military studies of the effects on guerrilla warriors, and it is only recently that the particular travails of women have been studied.[12] What is interesting is how, as history unfolds, the previously hard-held facts and truths are being questioned and re-examined. It seems we are at that stage with the Irish War of Independence.

George Lennon, leader of a West Waterford flying column, wrote a memoir he so aptly entitled 'Trauma in Time', but he didn't publish it. Terence O'Reilly's *Rebel Heart: George Lennon Flying Column Commander* is the only study devoted to examining George Lennon's place in Irish affairs.[13] O'Reilly extensively quotes Lennon's mainly unpublished writings, including his memoir, which is best compared to Ernie O'Malley's *On Another Man's Wound*. The defining features of each work are honesty and empathy. Both writers are at their best when they recount how they were at one with their enemies. In Lennon's case one poignant instance involved a young RIC Sergeant, Michael Hickey, who had known George since he was a child. Hickey had been warned away from leading Black and Tan patrols, but he persisted. When Lennon and his men ambushed a group of Tans, Hickey was captured and his fate was sealed. Before shots rang out killing him, Hickey pleaded with Lennon:

> Sergeant Hickey: 'George, I knew you as a child … you are the only one who can save me.'
> George: 'I would give anything, anything in the world, Sergeant, but you know I cannot'.[14]

In later life, Lennon, the IRA flying column leader, renounced violence. Perhaps as a gesture of repentance, Lennon made a public commitment to promoting peace: he joined the Quakers, co-founded a Zen Center in Rochester, New York, and became an activist against the Vietnam War.[15] His memoirs acknowledge the damage done both to his enemies and to himself by killing for the cause, but he never spoke about his war experiences to his family. Only recently has evidence come to light that the Irish War Pensions Board diagnosed George Lennon with 'traumatic neurosis' in 1943. Now called post-ttraumatic stress disorder (PTSD), this condition is yet another mainly unrecognised legacy of the Irish war. It should be acknowledged that this psychic damage was suffered by combatants on both sides in the Irish war, including the Black and Tans. Many of these men were recruited after fighting in a war in which a defining phrase became 'shell shock'.[16]

There are abundant questions regarding contemporary understandings of what is now known as PTSD during and in the aftermath of the Irish revolutionary period. Even then, many considered the Black and Tans to be affected by what was called shell shock at the time, and what we now classify as PTSD.

> I was only a child about 6 years old at the time. The tenders would
> come around and they'd hop out and surround the whole place.
> Looking back on it now I see that a number of them must have
> been 'head cases' that were hospitalised out of the army and this
> kind of business – and it was all right to put them *here*. 'Cause like
> the things they did were *barbarous*. Like, on Seville Place there was
> the Gaelic Football Club and they raided that place on one
> occasion and took one of the men out and dragged him behind a
> tender. They made him run and then you're going to run out of
> breath, of course, and then they dragged him. His two hips were
> broken and he hobbled for the rest of his life … They took people
> out and they'd look for information. If they got the idea that the
> people *had* information and didn't *give* it – which very often *was*
> the case – the people were just taken out and found the next
> morning in a ditch on the roadside or up an alley. Oh, that
> happened on a wide scale.[17] [Emphasis in original.]

They didn't use the term PTSD in those times, but many on both sides had it. What the men and women saw and did remained with them for the rest of their lives. All trauma is deeply distressing. Those who suffered it felt as if it were happening all over again. Nothing prepared them for it, and it changed them forever – the psychological injury was unabated.

Of the Irish men on the morning's attacks, Charles Dalton was only seventeen when he was on the Bloody Sunday raid at 38 Pembroke Street. In his book, his feelings were expressed simply. He remembers sitting up the night before and that '[he] was wrought up, thinking of what we had to do the next morning, and I knew the other men were the same'. As the men waited before the raid, he wrote:

Outwardly we were calm and collected, even jesting with each other. But inwardly, I felt the others were as I was – palpitating with anxiety.

He described waiting to enter the house as:

The longest five minutes of my life. Or were they the shortest? I cannot tell but they were tense and dreadful.

He then went on to describe the shooting in the house:

In the hall, three or four men were lined up against the wall, some of our officers facing them. Knowing their fate, I felt great pity for them. It was plain they knew it too. As I crossed the threshold, the volley was fired ... the sights and sounds of that morning were to be with me for many days and night [sic] ... I remembered I had not been to Mass. I slipped out, and in the silence before the altar, I thought over our morning's work and offered up a prayer for the fallen.[18]

But Dalton's thoughts did not just run to time at the altar, or for 'many days and night'. On Sunday night, Dalton was distraught and couldn't sleep because he 'kept hearing the gurgling of the blood of the man he shot'. His friends tried to comfort him by saying it was just a faucet running in the upstairs flat.[19] Dalton wrote in his memoir that when it was over, 'I started to run. I could no longer control my overpowering need to run, to fly, to leave far behind me those threatening streets'. Later, he 'thought over our morning's work, and offered up a prayer for the fallen'.[20] Matty MacDonald told Ernie O'Malley that 'Charlie Dalton was very nervous. We went to the Capitol [Theatre] to ease his mind'.[21] 'I got the wind up rightly' was all Dalton admitted when Ernie O'Malley asked.[22] Yet for one who was blooded in the ways of the Squad, for one who was so afraid himself, Dalton made no allowance for those who had never been asked to kill or had seen killing like this before. He complained that 'in some instances the excuses put forward for the non-carrying out of instructions were not considered very satisfactory; in particular, those received from the Commandant of the 1st Battalion regarding two addresses they should have visited on the North Circular Road'. For Dalton, to make excuses not to kill was worse than the killing itself. Later, Dalton was involved in the killings of innocents in the Civil War. What effect did his actions on Bloody Sunday, and throughout the War of Independence, have on him as an intelligence officer in the Civil War? In the 1940s Dalton was judged to be 'permanently and completely insane' – he had taken to hiding under his bed, convinced that his enemies were coming to take their revenge.[23] Dalton died in hospital as a paranoid schizophrenic.

But Dalton was not the only one who had reservations about those who didn't 'show up'. C.S. (Todd) Andrews made a rare reference to the power of peer pressure in his memoir. Andrews was concussed while playing football the day before he was due to take part. His only concern was that he would not be able to fulfil his assignment the next morning:

> I felt that, short of actual death, I would be unable to persuade my
> comrades in the Company or in the Battalion that I had not faked
> an accident to avoid the mission. This, of course, was nonsense but
> I felt that I could not live with myself if I failed to turn up.[24]

'Maudie', the maid who let Dalton and the others into the house on Pembroke Street, came crying to him afterwards: 'I thought you only meant to kidnap them'. She admitted she felt so 'guilty that I was upset; I did not leave the house for days. You see, I felt I had a hand in it, and I couldn't bear my thoughts.'[25] It wasn't just those who had a gun in hand who were traumatised. Alternatively, how many others gloried in their small part in the fight for independence – those who carried a weapon to or from an ambush, for example?

Some others in Collins's Squad seemed to revel in killing. Vinnie Byrne, who gave newspaper and TV interviews until he was an old man, said:

It was the joy of my life when I was handed a .45 revolver and six rounds …

He said he:

Liked pluggin' British soldiers.[26]

Of Bloody Sunday, Byrne wrote in his statement:

As I opened the folding-doors, the officer, who was in bed, was in the act of going for his gun under his pillow. Doyle and myself dashed into the room, at the same time ordering him to put up his hands, which he did. Doyle dashed around by the side of the bed, and pulled a Colt .45 from beneath the pillow. Right behind us came Frank Saurin and he started collecting from papers etc., which was his job … I ordered the British officer to get out of bed. He asked me what was going to happen and I replied: 'Ah, nothing.' I then ordered him to march in front of me … I marched my officer down to the back room where the other officer was. He was standing up in the bed, facing the wall. I ordered mine to do likewise. When the two of them were together I thought to myself 'The Lord have mercy on your souls!' I then opened fire with my Peter [Mauser pistol]. They both fell dead.[27]

While some of the Irish who were on the attacks were reticent about their involvement, others provided copious details in their witness statements. Jim Slattery was one of those who wrote a very detailed report of his assignment on the day:

On the evening of 20th November, 1920, the Squad, the Active
Service Unit, and a lot of other Volunteers from individual units
were ordered to parade at a house in Gardiner Street, I believe. We
were addressed there by Dick McKee, who told us that an
operation had been planned for the following morning, Sunday at
nine a.m. to eliminate a number of British Intelligence Agents and
spies who were residing in houses throughout the city. He had the
names and addresses of the men who were to be executed. There
were members of the Intelligence Section present.

I was assigned to 22 Lower Mount Street, where 2 enemy
agents were located. One was Lieutenant McMahon, but I cannot
remember the other man's name. ['McMahon' was the alias of
Lieutenant H.R. Angliss.]

Tom Keogh and myself from the Squad, with six others from
"E" Company of the 2nd Battalion, proceeded to Lower Mount
Street, at the appointed hour on the following morning, 21st
November. We knocked at the door and a maid admitted us …
The housekeeper or some other lady in the house had seen a
patrol of [Black and] Tans passing by outside, and had started to
scream. The Tans immediately surrounded the house and tried to
gain admission. One of our young men, Billy McClean, fired at
them through the door and eased the situation for us for a little
while, although he got wounded in the hand himself. I think the
Tans fired first. [They were Auxiliaries, not Black and Tans.]

We succeeded in shooting Lieutenant McMahon, but could
not gain admission into the room where the other agent was
sleeping. There was a second man in McMahon's bed, but we did
not shoot him as we had no instructions to do so. We discovered
afterwards that he was an undesirable character as far as we were
concerned, and that we should have shot him.

We went downstairs and tried to get out but found the
British Forces at the front of the house. We went to the back of the
house, and a member of "E" Co, Jim Dempsey, and myself got
through by getting over a wall. We understood that the rest of our
party were following us, but after going a little distance we found
we were alone. What actually happened was that [Frank] Teeling

was the third man to scale the wall, and as he got up he was fired on from the house. We were all fired on, but Teeling was the only man who was hit. Teeling took cover in the garden. The other members of our party retired and got safely through the front door in the confusion. It was only hours afterwards that we discovered Teeling was wounded … Some time before the football match most of us met again, and it transpired that Teeling was on the missing list.[28]

William Stapleton was equally expansive. When he made his statement in 1953, he remembered the most specific details of the day:

On the Friday prior to Bloody Sunday my Company Captain, Tommy Kilcoyne, instructed me to report armed at Baggot St. Bridge on the following Sunday morning at, I believe, half past eight, and there I would meet Joe Leonard in charge of a party consisting of five members of my Company … I understood from Tommy Kilcoyne that on this particular Sunday a general effort was to be made in various parts of the city to liquidate members of the B. I. [British Intelligence] Service who resided in private houses and hotels throughout the city. I reported as instructed, and our party moved down to 92 Lower Baggot St., where the British agent we were interested in was residing. We knocked at the hall door, which was opened by somebody from upstairs, and entered … We knocked at the door of the front parlour, and, receiving no reply, knocked at the back parlour door. After some hammering on the door it was opened a little. It was evident that the occupant of the room was very cautious and suspicious because he tried to close the door again, but we jammed our feet in it. We fired some shots through the door and burst our way in. The two rooms were connected by folding-doors and the British agent ran into the front room and endeavoured to barricade the door, but some of our party had broken in the door of the front room and we all went into it. He was in his pyjamas, and as he was attempting to escape by the window he was shot a number of times. One of our party on guard outside fired at him from outside. The man's wife was standing in the corner of the room and was in a terrified and hysterical condition. The operation lasted about fifteen minutes.[29]

Prior to Bloody Sunday, the men of the Squad had learned to be callous types. Their training was brutal and short, as Byrne explained:

First of all, the men selected for squad work were brought on a few jobs and shown how they were carried out; secondly, each man had to prove his mettle, and was detailed to do an actual job himself.[30]

Each member of the Squad then killed, in what Joe Leonard called strict rotation.[31] Obsessive to the point of being fetishistic about revolvers, they had their favourite weapons and squabbled between killings about who was the best shot, about which was better – the Webley, the Mauser or the Colt. There were staunch supporters of the Peter the Painter, a lighter Mauser that was easier to conceal under their clothes. They all carried .45 caliber pistols, not .38s. It had taken Detective Inspector Patrick 'Dog' Smith, the first DMP detective to be assassinated in July 1919, two weeks to die from his wounds from a .38, so a .45 would be the weapon of choice after that.[32] They always brought a revolver as well as an automatic – the revolver in case the automatic ever stuck like they had learned that it did many times on the Germans during the war. For Joe Dolan, it was simple: 'We had to learn to kill in cold blood and we got used to it'.[33]

Not all who were 'invited' to join the Squad did so. Frank Henderson, who had fought in the Rising, been imprisoned and rejoined the fight after returning from Frongoch Prison, felt that shooting police would lie on his conscience and testified that 'some sincere men' refused to take part in street ambushes. From then on, he was sidelined to administrative tasks.[34] C.S. Andrews wrote that when Volunteers realised that shooting was involved, 'quite a few of them decided, on grounds of conscience, that they would not continue'.[35] The days of easy camaraderie and good times were being replaced by a kind of terror.[36]

Nevertheless, and in some cases paradoxically, the use of a gun and killing had a strange effect on some of them. Andrews, one of those on the Bloody Sunday raids, wrote he was 'left in a state bordering on ecstasy after firing his first shot'.[37] Another man who was not on the Bloody Sunday raids, Ernie O'Malley, was equally effusive about his weapons: 'his Webley had become as indispensable as his fountain pen, and with his Parabellum he felt a great warmth in my body and a rich joy as I filled my magazine'.[38] Even George Lennon, the West Wicklow column leader who later renounced violence, wrote suggestively of his weapon:

> What a strangely satisfying, almost wild, sensation it was to push forward the bolt, feeling the round slide smoothly out of the magazine and into the breach. You snuggled the butt voluptuously into your shoulder, took careful aim and pulled the trigger. The crash of the rifle was orgiastic.[39]

Did carrying a gun change the way some men viewed themselves? Was having a gun in hand nearly an erotic sensation?

It must be asked if actions 'learned' or 'suffered' in the intelligence and terror war of 1919–21 led to many of the excesses and atrocities of the Civil War of 1922–3. Modern discussion of terrorism delves deeply into what has been termed 'radicalisation'. Radicalisation involves the inculcation of a person (usually a young person) into this complex set of ritual practices, symbols and discourses. This inculcation is both *affective*, in engaging with the substrate of feeling and embodied states of a person linked to devotion to a cause or a god, and *cognitive* in drawing a person into the arguments that are often about the value of adherence and the ensuing rewards. Why were so many Irishmen prepared to kill for a cause? Were those Irish who went out on Bloody Sunday or on other assignments throughout the war 'radicalised' in their beliefs? Did they understand the ramifications of that cause and how had they been mobilised, inspired, groomed and trained?

Tom Barry, arguably the most successful flying column O/C, wrote that his reasons for joining the British Army in World War I were simple:

> I cannot plead I went on the advice of John Redmond or any other politician, that if we fought for the British we would secure Home Rule for Ireland, nor can I say I understood what Home Rule meant. I was not influenced by the lurid appeal to fight to save Belgium or small nations. I knew nothing about nations, large

or small. I went to the war for no other reason than that I wanted to see what war was like, to get a gun, to see new countries and to feel a grown man.[40]

Were Barry's reasons – to get a gun and to feel like a grown man – felt by many of those who joined the IRA? Were they driven to 'feel like a grown man', and gave little thought to killing and taking life?

What were those who went out to kill on raids and assassinations thinking? Or did they think anything at all? What did the men sent to do the killing believe – and need to believe – about the men they shot? Séumas Robinson wrote:

it was my conviction that, in revolutionary times, if the thing be morally right in itself and at the same time urgent and necessary, it would be legitimised subsequently.[41]

The fact of killing in wartime leads one to questions regarding the military necessity or morality of certain killings. Many people know, or come to realise, that there will always be 'collateral damage' and can live with that. Just as they know luck or chance play their part too. Car bombs and booby traps are a case in point. Military operations and bombardments are rarely 'surgical'. Did the Volunteers act with moral certainty? Their certainty – however clearly reasoned and understood or not – went a long way to mitigating their concern about killing. Morality and military goals became greyer. Ideals had long been downgraded to notions – notions were optional. The dead had to be spies because if they were not, then their killers were the murderers and assassins that British propaganda always said they were. They had to be spies; there were no mistakes, because otherwise how could these men justify what they had done? It had to be a coup for IRA intelligence with never any admission of mistakes. How many agonised – or even gave any thought – 'how do we know what we know'? How many of the men rationalised their actions that day – or on the days of violence thereafter?

The Squad members had been accustomed to attack their wanted men on the Dublin streets, but the other Dublin men were nervous on Bloody Sunday. For this type of work, some of them regarded it as a dirty job that had to be done to safeguard important officers and ministers. What did they think when they were briefed in various locations the night before they went out to kill – some for the very first time? Harry Colley wrote in his witness statement:

> It is well to place on record that Sean Russell, the O/C, explained to them that the men to be shot were members of a new secret service which the enemy had brought into this country; that many of them had great reputations as secret service men working for England during the recent war; that it was vitally necessary for the success of our fight they be removed; that no country had scruples about shooting enemy spies in war time; that if any man had moral scruples about going on this operation he was at full liberty to withdraw and no one would think any the worse of him; that he wanted every man to be satisfied in his conscience that he could properly take part in this operation.[42]

Dick McKee also felt it necessary to stiffen the Volunteers' resolve when he briefed them, warning:

> all those present of the gravity of the action to be taken on the next morning, Sunday. He explained that it was of vital importance to exterminate enemy intelligence officers who were residing in hotels and boarding houses in the centre of the city and who had become a terrible menace to our organisation and said further that he was conscious of the enormous dangers the men would encounter in dealing such a crushing blow to the enemy, and that the moral[e] effect produced would be worth any sacrifice sustained by us.[43]

Others were so dedicated to the cause and to their superiors that they unquestionably believed if the intelligence department chose to kill, then the target must have been properly identified and must have been guilty. Frank Thornton wrote the men knew they had been asked to 'do something which was outside the scope of the soldier', but he was explicit in carrying out his instructions:

The fact that we, who became aware of their activities earlier on, and smashed them by one military operation on Bloody Sunday, is sufficient answer I think to those who would try to confuse the issue by suggesting that they were shot purely because they had acted in the capacity of court-martial officers on some of our comrades.[44]

The enemy seemed clear – they thought they knew whom to kill and why. Their war could not have elusive or uncertain goals.

Many of the men viewed violence in the name of Ireland as righteous and holy, epitomising Patrick Pearse's blessing:

We must accustom ourselves to the sight of arms, to the use of arms. We may make mistakes in the beginning and shoot the wrong people, but bloodshed is a cleansing and sanctifying thing, and the nation which regards it as the final horror has lost its manhood. There are many things more horrible than bloodshed and slavery is one of them.[45]

One of those killed on Bloody Sunday was Thomas Herbert Smith, the house owner at 117 Morehampton Road in Dublin. Just at 9.00 10-year-old Percival William Smith opened the door at his home. Thomas's wife, Anna Marie Smith, stated at the military inquiry:

I saw some men coming up the stairs, who appeared to number about 20, with revolvers in their hands. They then told me to put my hands up and my husband came out on the landing and asked for a little time to put on some clothes, which they granted. I then asked [if] I could go into my baby in the next room and they pushed me roughly into it. I then heard about 8 shots. A minute or two later I heard John Caldow (who was staying with us) call out Kate (meaning his sister) run for the doctor. I then came out and saw John Caldow in [the] entrance to the room, lying on his back wounded. I passed him and saw my husband lying very badly wounded and Mr MacClean dead. My husband had no regular occupation and owned property. His age was 47. He did not take part in politics, but was very friendly with Captain MacClean who had just resigned from the army.

Ten minutes after he opened the door, Percy's father and an innocent man – one of these 'mistakes' killed on Bloody Sunday– lay dead. The reader must wonder about young Percy – and we should grieve for everyone lost to violence.

When members of their family chastened some of those Irish on the Bloody Sunday raids immediately afterward, they didn't understand their concern. Pat McCrea, one of Collins's favourite drivers, recounted:

> I was told that the British had raided the Tipperary Football team where they were staying in Gardiner's Row. We, therefore, decided that there would be no football match for us that day; that we would not attend it, as we thought there would possibly be trouble there. I returned home about 2 o'clock and lunched.
>
> After lunch I had been in the habit of going to football matches on a Sunday, and my family asked me was I not going to the match. I said no, that I was feeling tired and would lie down and have a rest. I lay on the couch in the room and fell asleep. I was awakened that evening about 4 o'clock. My wife came into the room crying, with a 'Stop Press' in her hand. I woke up and asked her what was the matter. Before speaking she handed me the 'Stop Press' and wanted to know was this the fishing expedition I had been on. [He told her he was fishing that morning.] Seeing that there was no use in concealing things any longer from her, I said: 'Yes, and don't you see we had a good catch', or words to that effect. She then said: 'I don't care what you think about it, I think it is murder'. I said: 'No, that is nonsense; I'd feel like going to the altar after that job this morning', and thus I tried to calm her. I don't think she put out any lights in the house during the following winter. I did not stay at home then for about a week. That Sunday night I slept in a grove in the demesne known as St. Anne's, which was nearby.[46]

Still, on the Irish side, some were uneasy with what they were going to do and they wrote of it later. Todd Andrews wrote he was:

> very excited by the assignment but the prospect of killing a man in
> cold blood was alien to our ideas of how a war should be
> conducted. We were very apprehensive, too, because it could be a
> dangerous operation. We were already being affected
> psychologically by the terror of the [Black and] Tans. I had
> increasing fears that we may be surprised by the Tans. If that
> happened and we were captured, we would have been shot or
> hanged. It is not an agreeable prospect for a nineteen year old
> unattuned to assassination … On the other hand, it was an article
> of national faith that separation had always been wrecked on a reef
> erected by informers and spies. I believed that it was justifiable to
> kill informers, spies, touts, and collaborators with the occupational
> forces.[47]

Andrews wrote of the contrast of emotions he felt that morning.
Deployed to kill, when Andrews broke into Lieutenant William Noble's
room he was ready to shoot on sight, but he:

> found the room empty except for a half-naked woman who sat up
> in bed looking terror stricken. She did not scream or say a word. I
> was very excited but, even so, I felt a sense of shame and
> embarrassment for the woman's sake. I was glad to get out quickly
> and moved to the next room where there was a man shaving.[48]

His ambivalence was further expressed when he wrote of his afterthoughts
on the day.

> As I went back to Terenure through quiet suburban roads and lanes
> well known to me I wondered whether I was glad or sorry that
> Nobel [sic] had not been at home. I would certainly have felt no
> remorse at having shot him, but I found it hard to get the memory
> of the terrified woman or indeed the equally terrified lodger from
> my mind.[49]

Andrews wasn't the only one on a raid where the men's sensibilities were challenged, and they didn't find the work easy. Mick O'Hanlon, who was on the raid at 28–29 Upper Pembroke Street, recalled:

> When we got in we found our man had a girl and that he was covering the door and the landing. None of us fired as she was in bed with him and covered him with her arms …

But this moment soon passed. O'Hanlon wrote callously:

> Mick Flanagan shot him.[50]

Some of those on the raids seemed to just walk away from the killings. But in their lives, there was often more trauma than before. While many seemed to be unphased by the killing, for others the killing took its toll. Liam Tobin had a nervous breakdown before Bloody Sunday could be carried out as he planned. He had become, according to David Neligan, 'gaunt, cynical, with tragic eyes, he looked like a man who had seen the inside of hell'.[51] Later, Colonel Charles Russell reported to the army inquiry in May 1924 that 'the very nature of their work' before the truce 'left [some men] anything but normal … if such a disease as shell-shock existed in the IRA … the first place to look for it would be amongst these men'.[52] From the end of 1923 the new Free State government was already worried enough to keep note of how many army men were involved in serious crimes.[53] The record of events in Oriel House, the actions of the Dublin Guard in Kerry during the Civil War, the fact that Collins himself thought of sending some of his Squad away, seems to suggest that many of these men no longer knew how to stop. Collins sent Mick McDonnell to California when his health collapsed.[54] Did they 'start' on missions like Bloody Sunday or another assassination? Did the Irish who went out on the Bloody Sunday morning raids realise that exposure to violence would engender more violence – in their lives and others?

Ernie O'Malley, one of the most noted gunmen of the War of Independence and the Civil War, was diagnosed with 'neurasthenia' (the medical term for PTSD used in the early twentieth century) when he applied for a pension in 1934:

As regards question of neurasthenia: his conduct would strike the average individual as strange. He wanders and has been wandering for some years past over the United States and Mexico, going from one job to another, seldom staying in one place long. He appears indifferent as regards making any provision for the future and although he works and studies he appears to have an antipathy to making any mater[ial] use of his knowledge.[55]

Dr Murray's letter seemed to provide the impetus for O'Malley's pension to be granted and Frank Aiken went further to advise O'Malley to apply for an additional pension for his military service. O'Malley continued to suffer from neurasthenia, as well as 'general nervousness', insomnia, impaired memory and 'the long-term effects of several gunshot wounds' for the rest of his life.[56] O'Malley's symptoms and lifestyle reflect exactly those who fought in later conflicts and who suffered from the trauma long after their wars were over.

Not just those with a gun in hand were traumatised. Understandably, Lily Mernin, who as Collins's 'Lt G' was one of the most active women in intelligence and was responsible for locating many of the British officers' addresses on Bloody Sunday, succumbed to the trauma of the times. Shortly afterwards, Collins exonerated her from her duties after her 'nervous breakdown' and arranged for her to take rest at a remove from the stress of the conflict:

The risks I was taking and the strain to which I was subjected had an injurious offset on my nerves and general health. At the end of 1921 I was dismissed from my post by the British – and shortly after had a nervous break down. Collins immediately gave me a sum of money to enable me to go away and take a holiday out of Ireland.[57]

The hunger strikes were probably the most harrowing episodes of any woman's imprisonment, and certainly the effects were long-lasting. Molly O'Reilly, who was 15 years old when she raised the Irish Republic flag over Liberty Hall on 16 April 1916, and served in the City Hall garrison during the Rising, was one of those who went on hunger strike during the

Civil War. She was arrested on 1 March 1923, and released, but when she was re-arrested on 8 August, she was sent to the North Dublin Union where she went on strike. When she was released on 22 November, she had been on strike for sixteen days – and was released in very poor health. The women received little medical attention in prison and none after release. Cumann na mBan put an advertisement in the newspapers for people to nurse the women back to health. Molly went to Mrs Melia in Summerhill, Co. Meath, and she spoon-fed her for months, nursing Molly back to health. A staunch republican to the end, Molly O'Reilly died on 4 October 1950, only 50 years old, and had suffered for her remaining years from the effects of her imprisonment and hunger strikes.[58]

How many Irish women availed themselves of the limited medical treatment for physical or mental afflictions caused by the trauma and terror of the times – or were able to do so if they wished? The medical management of patients in wartime is often difficult to determine, given the challenges in accessing records; hospital admissions records were not kept and patients were often registered under false names. As a result, one of the most revealing sources of data is the Military Service Pensions Collection, which holds approximately 300,000 files regarding individual pension, disability and special allowance applications; some of these include supporting medical documentation. While the Irish Grants Committee (IGC), which was founded in London in 1923 to compensate Irish loyalists, included shock in its definition of 'physical injuries', the Free State was far slower to recognise psychiatric casualties.[59] Moreover, it was even more difficult for a woman to prove a 'mental disability' than it was for a woman to prove 'active service'.

Many of the Irish refused to talk about the killings on Bloody Sunday, other assassination actions, or their involvement throughout the War of Independence. Both the pensions board and the Bureau of Military History requesting witness statements had difficulty in establishing who had taken part in Bloody Sunday because several of the men involved simply would not discuss it. Many never volunteered to talk even to their wives and families. Many outwardly seemed phlegmatic. Often their family members refused to ask. All family members desired to protect others from the trauma. Did they compartmentalise their actions in order to avoid the pain of understanding of what they did? Were the actions internalised because the killing had become automatic?

Professor Anne Dolan graphically wrote of the later experiences of one of the men on the Bloody Sunday attacks, Frank Teeling. Her lengthy account of the effects on Teeling points out the results that continued long after the day.

> Lieutenant Frank Teeling shot a man on 27 March 1923.
> Admittedly, in the closing weeks of the Irish civil war this was not an unusual thing for a Free State soldier to do. But the man Frank Teeling shot was not a republican. William Johnson was a member of the Citizens' Defence Force and he was shot because he brought a bag of tomatoes into the bar at the Theatre Royal.
> ... At his trial Teeling claimed he had acted in self-defence. The jury concurred with the judge that 'through drink he had allowed his mind to be dethroned', found him guilty of manslaughter instead of murder, and recommended mercy 'on account of the state of his mind'.
> It may be enough to put all this down to a heady combination of drink, revolvers and the stress of civil war. But there was a little more to Teeling's case than met the eyes of the judge and jury at his speedily expedited trial. Eight days before the shooting, the Department of Finance had made out a cheque for £250 to Lieutenant Frank Teeling. It had done so because the National Army wanted Teeling to disappear. He had, in the commander-in-chief's opinion, been 'publicly misconducting' himself, 'bringing serious discredit on us'. It was thought best to send him to Australia with £500 and to convince him that it would be a particularly bad idea ever to come back.
> ... Though one can wonder about Teeling's fate if he had cashed the cheque and gone about the life that William Johnson never got to lead because Teeling stayed, there is something more fascinating still about the offer itself. In March 1923 there seemed little shortage of soldiers 'publicly misconducting' themselves, yet few were presented with the prospect of a new life abroad with £250 in hand.
> Teeling was considered an exceptional case because every

member of the Executive Council was well aware of what was termed 'his past services to the State'. They all knew what Frank Teeling had done, what he had suffered for Ireland; they all knew that on 21 November 1920 he had stood with four other men at the bottom of a British soldier's bed and shot him until he was dead.

It could be argued that there is little or no connection between Teeling's whereabouts on Bloody Sunday morning 1920 and the shooting in the Theatre Royal almost two and a half years later ... Teeling had learned to kill without question for his cause: that was his 'past service to the State'. And while the offer of the money and the second chance may have acknowledged his efforts, the desire to get rid of him seemed to accept that this man no longer wanted, or knew how, to stop.[60]

Teeling's story is unique, but others have questioned the direction militarism took during and after 1919–21. Frank Gallagher, who was editor of the *Irish Bulletin*, author of *Four Glorious Years*, and who took the anti-Treaty side in the Civil War, wrote to Joseph McGarrity in 1938:

I know there are different views of how to best further the establishment of an Irish Republic. Some believe one of the ways is stealing up to an old man's door, calling him out, shooting him down and running away ... I have been through that kind of thing in the past, and know where it leads. Those who came to worship the gun before 1921 were the first to surrender to Britain at the treaty time. And they afterwards became those who committed the most terrible outrages on captured Republicans.[61]

One must repeatedly ask if killing hadn't become too easy to many – the simplest way out of difficulty. After killing so easily, how were they to readjust to civilian life? Was a gun in hand the answer – the only answer?

While few of the Irish talked of the events of Bloody Sunday or their participation in assassinations, it is generally accepted that these killings had a larger and more lasting effect on the men than did participation in ambushes, either in Dublin or in the countryside.[62] Some men in K

Company of Dublin's 3rd Battalion quickly began to regret that they had taken part.[63] Larry Nugent found it difficult to get any information about what had happened on Bloody Sunday from any of them: 'The men would not talk. Three men of K Company never returned to duty after the operation.' Twice in his Bureau of Military History witness statement Nugent stated that 'the men did not like this operation, but orders were orders and had to be obeyed'.[64] It was 'outside the ordinary scope of the soldier' and some reacted to the pressure better than others. Unsteady nerves and shaking beginner's hands explained why so many of the wounded survived. Even the dead were sometimes shot in unusual places, in parts of the body where a wound would never kill. The shootings were by nature often hurried and frenetic; the likelihood of failure was high. In Upper Mount Street one man had to have his gun taken away because his hand shook too much to fire. John Horgan suggested that Bloody Sunday was the one day that many old IRA men 'fell silently defensive about'.[65] Future Taoiseach Seán Lemass, who was a raider on Bloody Sunday, said: 'on both sides they did terrible things – and they knew it', and he cut short any inquiries about his actions with the answer 'firing squads don't have reunions'.

It wasn't only the men on urban ambushes or assassinations who were traumatised by their killing actions. One of the most famous ambushes of the war occurred on 28 November 1920 at Kilmichael, Co. Cork. Known as the first successful IRA ambush against the Auxiliaries, it has become the subject of numerous articles asking whether there was a 'false surrender' of the Auxiliaries after which some were killed. Nevertheless, it, too, caused such trauma amongst the IRA that it is another example of the results of the mental wounding of the time. Far from going on to relish battle, many of the victorious IRA men of the Kilmichael ambush were disinclined to go through similar experiences again. In the records of the Bureau of Military History, there is a revealing aside in the testimony of Peter Kearney, a former officer in the IRA's Cork Brigade, and an officer in the Third Flying Column in West Cork. He was not involved in the ambush but, writing in 1950, he referred to the effect of the events of that November evening on some of the Kilmichael veterans:

The 3rd Dunmanway Battalion had been falling away rather badly

since the Kilmichael ambush. A number of men out of that
battalion had fought at Kilmichael, but the strain had affected their
nerves, to such an extent that a number of the battalion officers
were practically useless from that time on, and no resistance was
being shown to the enemy, who were very overbearing.[66]

Terror lingered long into the lives of those who lived through those
times. Many questions must be asked of the terror and trauma itself. What
of those taken in the night, or who saw someone taken from their bed
throughout the War of Independence? What is remembered of the screams
of wives and children, or those waiting for loved ones to come home?
George Berkeley recalled:

> Crown agents in mufti went into the houses and shot men in front
> of their wives. Or, worse still, ordered the women into one room,
> and shot men in another room where on more than one occasion
> a husband bled to death while his wife heard him groaning on the
> other side of the partition.[67]

In another instance, a mother received a notice of death from the Black and
Tans intended for her son. A witness relayed that 'the suspense, fear and the
dread that the above notice will be executed are slowly but surely killing
her'.[68] Thus, even when not physically harming their female victims,
members of the Crown forces ensured that the trauma of these events, or
fear that they might take place in one's home, impressed themselves on the
minds of Irish women.

Women were particularly vulnerable to intimidation, terrorism and
trauma if they worked in British offices or were seen with British soldiers.
A sample of 120 non-lethal outrages directed specifically against women,
taken from précis compiled by the RIC of incidents against police, their
families and their tradesmen and suppliers, offers a snapshot of the nature
of punishment inflicted on women by the IRA. In each case the victims
had family in the RIC (twenty-two were policemen's wives), employment
in local barracks, trade links with Crown forces or courtships with a
policeman or soldier. In the eyes of the IRA, they were all assisting the
enemy and were potential sources of damaging information.[69] Reports to

the police noted that lethal violence had been directly threatened or implied: 'your days shall be numbered and ended'; 'your existence in this world will be short and sharp'; 'we warn you for the last time to cease or you will be sorry'. Other threatening behaviours suffered by the women in the sample comprised raids on their homes and damage to property.[70] Though violence against the 'female person' was comparatively rare in revolutionary Ireland, it also worth noting, as Gemma Clark does, the psychological effects of violence on the female relatives – wives, sisters, mothers – of the men who were its victims: 'Attacks on the home during the revolutionary period arguably affected women more seriously than they did the men at whom the violence purportedly was aimed'.[71] Even when not explicitly sexual, gender consistently underpinned violence against women.[72]

As the primary homemakers, women suffered trauma that invaded their 'domestic space', and more of these invasions occurred as a result of British actions than Irish actions. There are examples of domestic spaces being destroyed as a way to break the resolve, humiliate and punish Irish women perceived as IRA supporters. Geraldine Dillon wrote of 'parlours used as lavatories' by Crown forces. Moreover, 'reports on raids and burnings used sexualized language to emphasize female vulnerability and suggest the deliberate desecration of the private space'.[73] Thus, even when not physically harming their female victims, members of the Crown forces ensured that the trauma of these events, or fear that they might take place in one's home, impressed themselves on the minds of Irish women and their neighbours, exacerbating the effects of terror. Many of the Crown forces' victims were not deliberately selected – women in vulnerable situations were victims of spontaneous and opportunistic violence, which was intended to reverberate across the Irish population.

The British Labour Party sent a Commission to Ireland in 1921 (BLPCI) and its report was most damning regarding the conditions in Ireland. The BLPCI delegation reported that the terror experienced by the Irish population would have 'far-reaching effects on the health of the population' because a significant proportion of them were 'all nerves'. The specific issue of violence against women was examined by the BLPCI and it found the same reluctance of women to talk of their distress. The Commission reported that assaults on women were common and noted a particular incident of terror on a young girl by the Black and Tans. They raided her home and made her get out of her bed, and in the struggle her nightdress was ripped from top to bottom. The report went on:

> The cases of physical violence and brutal treatment, which we
> have cited, are, like the examples of other crimes which we have
> given, but examples. We could refer to more cases, but we believe
> that the reader of this report will agree with us that they suffice to
> show the infamous deeds which have been done in the name of
> law and order.[74]

Hanna Sheehy-Skeffington reported the same incident and went on to write 'she is young and pretty but was a complete nervous wreck for weeks after this experience'.[75]

The BLPCI report concluded:

> Unfortunately in their work of hunting down people, the agents
> of the British government often act in a way which is terrifying to
> women ... It is, however, extremely difficult to obtain direct
> evidence of incidents affecting females, for the women of Ireland
> are reticent on such subjects.[76]

The trauma of those 'terrifying acts' continued long after the raids.

Reports of sexual assaults on women were rare due to their reticence to talk of them, but there were some. One woman reported that she had been assaulted by Black and Tans while they were searching her home. She was taken from her bed and one of the men

> kept running his hands all over my body ... but I kept moving
> away from him until finally he raised my nightgown above my
> waist and kept it in that position for several minutes. All the time
> he was going through the actions of searching me, putting his
> hand under my blouse and all around my body and he kept
> repeating that I was not to be alarmed and that he would do no
> harm to me as he was a married man with five children. Finally he
> dropped the gown and resumed the search ... [77]

Even though reported rapes were rare, an unspoken but palpable terror spread throughout the female Irish population, and had the chilling effect of a profound feeling of dread and despair among large numbers of women in areas where rape and sexual assault occurred.[78]

A most heinous rape occurred in County Cork, where in July 1921 the *Irish Exile* reported a woman who was heavily pregnant was taken from her room by raiders wearing uniforms and in masks. Her husband was being held prisoner in another room when one of the raiders ordered her from her bedroom and forced her into the kitchen. Despite her apparent condition, and after she pleaded with him 'not to do anything as [she] was near her confinement', he 'then succeeded in criminally assaulting and raping [her]'. She was ordered back into her bedroom where she told her husband of her terror, and they subsequently reported the incident to the police at Shandon.[79]

In the propaganda battle, the Irish had a most useful tool in their republican newspaper, the *Irish Bulletin*. As the war intensified, allegations about British acts of violence against women became a growing concern for the *Irish Bulletin*. In April 1921 it devoted a special issue to 'Outrages on Irishwomen'. In response to British government claims that there 'had never been one bit of evidence' to support accusations of sexual violence, the paper published sworn affidavits by women who claimed they had been sexually abused by British soldiers. All the incidents involved night-time raiding parties. For example, in her testimony:

> Mrs Healy (full address given), a mother of four young children, described how a group of masked, uniformed men entered her home at 2.15 a.m. One of them forced Mrs Healy, who was in her night-clothes, into the kitchen where she succeeded in pulling the mask off his face. 'In spite of my every resistance he then succeeded in criminally assaulting and raping me'. The next day accompanied by her husband and solicitor, Mrs Healy went to the barracks to complain about the incident and to identify the man but the sergeant in charge refused to cooperate and sent her away. In another testimony 21 year old Miss Nellie O'Mahony (full address given) related how two uniformed men broke into her home at midnight on Christmas night 1920. 'The men seemed to

have some drink taken'. Miss O'Mahony described in considerable detail how one of the men lifted her night-dress and proceeded to 'put his hands all round my body'. Although she identified the men and made an initial complaint to the military barracks, she stated that: 'I did not pursue the matter further as, from the state of terror that exists consequent upon the deeds of the "Black and Tans", I was afraid and am afraid to pursue the matter further'.[80]

While many accounts hint at sexual assault, these two affidavits are quite explicit. The decision of these women to come forward and to allow their full names and addresses to be published must not only be weighed against the fear of reprisals but also the shame of breaking the taboo on such sexual experiences. It is probably no coincidence that both Mrs Healy and Miss O'Mahony had already told their families and had attempted to report the incidents to the authorities; clearly they were prepared to make the assaults public. The *Bulletin* claimed that they had evidence of many other sexual attacks where the women were not willing to publish their names and addresses.[81]

In July 1921 the *Irish Bulletin* carried the banner headline 'The War on Women and Children'. 'Women and children suffer greatly from these operations which are extensive and of frequent occurrence all over the south'. There followed lengthy accounts of such incidents. 'Cases of rape and attempted rape' were outlined by an unnamed investigator. 'In Cork, Limerick, Tralee and Dungarvan I came in contact with cases of this character'.

Some of the women 'were willing to give full particulars' and made sworn affidavits but they were reluctant to make the details public. The report concluded, however, that 'the threat of rape and attempted rapes had the effect of spreading a profound feeling of dread amongst large numbers of women in the districts where they occurred'. Under the subheading 'Mid-night raids, searching, etc.', the *Bulletin* went on to outline the impact of military raids on women and girls: 'These raids are a source of sleeplessness, nervous break-down, and in the case of expectant mothers, produce very grave results for mothers and children ... Women know that it is during curfew hours attempts of a sexual character have been made'.[82]

The most common assault on women and girls was hair cutting, and this was usually carried out using some form of physical violence, and both sides used this punishment, often for the pettiest of reasons. On the Irish side, members of the IRA and Cumann na mBan sheared women's hair as punishment for suspected informing, as well as being romantically involved with members of the Crown forces. IRA members in Tuam, Fingal, Galway and Dublin recounted 'shearing the hair off a young girl'.[83] A most unusual case was reported in the *Cork Examiner* in April 1921 under the heading 'Girl's Hair Cut Off – Allegations Against Police'.[84] A woman named as Delia Brown was awarded £400 compensation for having her hair cut off by a group of masked men. She alleged that the men were members of the police force. This case was unusual, first, because it went to court and, second, because the young woman won an extremely large amount of compensation for the time.

Raids on homes by the British, in conjunction with punishment doled out by the Irish, filled life with fear of physical and psychological abuse for many women. Some women recalled never laying 'down at night without the fear of having an invasion of these armed bands'.[85] For the IRA, in addition to serving the military function of neutralising espionage and threats to the republican movement, violence on women was effected on 'other' victims for breaching the IRA's view of appropriate femininity, and to serve as a warning to others who would dare to undermine the republicans' efforts or values.

All of these reports testify to the widespread fear and intimidation experienced by women in areas of southern Ireland. According to a wide range of sources, including independent witnesses such as the British Labour Party Commission and the American Commission, martial law, curfews and night-time raiding parties of armed men, frequently wearing masks, terrorised the local population, which was made up largely of women and children.[86]

The Irish also extended the war to the female members of RIC families. The BLPCI reported on violence to wives, children and girlfriends of RIC men, and their domestic servants bore the brunt of these actions. In many cases, the families had been made homeless and yet they were refused housing because the policy of ostracism left the Irish in fear for their own homes. In one case reported by the BLPCI, a policeman's widow was planning to take a sergeant's family into her home as a lodger, but was warned by an anonymous letter 'not to take this woman into her house' and that if she ignored the warning 'her house would be burned and she would be shot'. The women were reduced to living in an outhouse after their home had been destroyed, and the report said:

> Thirty masked men came to the huts and burned them. The sergeant's wife and her sister resided in one of the huts. The raiders gave them five minutes to clear out, and they were not allowed to take anything away ... The neighbors refused them admittance into their homes compelling them to remain in the little wash-house all night.[87]

A woman who had worked as a domestic servant in an RIC barracks was taken from her home on 7 August 1920 and taken to a field beside her home. She was held down, while one man held his hand over her mouth, and three other men put 'three pig rings into her buttocks with pincers'. She had been found guilty of 'supplying goods to the police'.[88]

Most women were reluctant to share stories of their traumatic experiences, and given the historian's dependence on archives, academic work that deals with this type of violence can often only cautiously conjecture.[89] While total numbers are probably quite low, individual cases are illuminating and stand out in the context of the overall low number of civilian and combatant casualties. Marie Coleman highlights one instance that is 'probably the clearest case of sexual assault, so serious that its consequence was fatal'. The victim's name was Kate Maher. On 21 December 1920 in Dundrum, Tipperary, Maher 'died as a result of a 'fracture of the base of the skull accelerated by haemorrhage from [a] wound in the vagina'.[90]

It was not just Irish men who were involved in offences against women. Ann Matthews recounts the story of a raiding party that included two women with three men. On 2 October 1920 the party raided the home of a couple named Bowes at Cadogan Road in Dublin and while one of the men held a pistol on the husband, one of the women cut off Mrs Bowes's hair. There was no reason given for this act of violence.[91]

Terrorism's particular force, its seeming suitability to a mediatised point in history, is bound up with its trauma and the capacity for that trauma to touch countless bodies far beyond the reach of any singular terrorist act. Yet to account for such trauma can be difficult. Health of all was often taxed beyond recovery, and time gleaned what the Black and Tans and Auxiliaries failed to reap – a harvest of early deaths, shattered nerves, rheumatoid and crippled bodies. Terror's traumas do not necessarily manifest in forms readily recognised by clinical models. They can be as fleeting as they are enduring, as subtly transformative as they are violently rupturing, as difficult to understand or diagnose as they are kept within the hearts of the individuals affected. One sees the toll of violence over time, and no one could be prepared for it.[92]

Destruction of property and boycotting were economic punishments and carried great societal and individual trauma. Aside from its social and psychological impact, ostracism from a community could be financially devastating for a small farmer, shopkeeper or publican. Other acts of punishment had a similar effect. Arson to property or crops could deprive the victim of a home and a livelihood, while cattle driving and animal maiming (acts of violence most often equated with agrarian agitation) 'struck at the heart of farm life by attacking the very thing … that generates wealth'.[93] In other cases, where the IRA assessed a levy on local farmers and businesses, the act of non-co-operation was intimidation and essentially financial: selling or purchasing prohibited goods or refusing to contribute money resulted in IRA action against those whom they deemed to be defaulters. For example, disobeying the Belfast boycott resulted in fines, more boycotting and 'blacklists' of offenders. Pre-emptive attacks on traders saw trains and railway stations raided and goods believed to be coming from boycotted Belfast firms either taken away by armed men or burned on site. The burning of goods, like other punishments with a potentially strong visual element, could be used as an act against the offender and a warning to others. The punishment, in the vast majority of cases, was either directly or indirectly financial – some, however, chose to move to Britain rather than pay the levies.

Application of terror did not always have to be violent. Potential levy defaulters usually faced a similarly fiscal dilemma. The first response to defaulting was the seizure of livestock, often of a much greater value than the amount levied. If cash was not forthcoming, the livestock was sold and the excess raised (it was said) returned to the defaulter. In the context of the arms levy, this mode of punishment made sense, offering immediate access to the money local Volunteers felt they had been denied and desperately needed to fund their war. Destruction of property or physical violence may have frightened recalcitrants or encouraged others to pay, but the money, which was, after all, the focus of the exercise, still needed to be secured.[94]

Along with 'actual physical harm' and 'actual threat', civilians were subject to intimidation by 'perceived environmental threat'. Many civilians feared that any unwarranted or suspicious behaviour would bring vengeance from an omnipotent IRA without them ever having been personally harmed or threatened.[95] J.H. Long wanted to bring food and water to wounded British soldiers but was told not to do so by his wife 'as there were spies of the I.R.A. all 'round'.[96]

The success of the IRA and the level of violence directed at the British depended on two factors: its ability to organise people behind them and the capacity to deal with the opposition it encountered in the community. Those factors, then, were connected with the IRA's integration within the community and the continued support for constitutional or military means of securing Irish independence.[97] But how many of those who killed did just what they were trained to do – without considering the humanity of those who were killed? How much of the community's acceptance was due to terror? One must accept that both sides used violence and terror. Sebastian Barry is hard to improve upon:

> We may or may not damn all sides of that era equally, but we must
> be prepared to acknowledge sins committed by those with whom
> we agree as well as those with whom we disagree.

Brian Hanley puts it thus:

> Any balanced discussion of terror in twentieth-century Ireland
> must identify all of its origins and agencies, not just those which
> confirm our own opinions and prejudices.[98]

Further, we should note the words of Knut Lier-Hansen, one of the heroes of Norwegian resistance in World War II, who wrote:

Warriors deserve our gratitude and support.

Wars can bring adventures that stir the heart –

But the truth is – war is composed of individual tragedies – of grief, waste and sacrifice.

We can't forget that *all* those killed and those injured physically or emotionally were human beings and recognise the trauma that so many suffered. We must acknowledge that *that* trauma haunted them for the rest of their lives. Terror's damage is contagious: it is not simply the victims of a bomb blast who suffer, but those touched by its rippling consequences and mediatised representations. While terrorism's trauma can be local and specific to the event, its distinctiveness as terror is contained in the excess of affect its violence produces. Terror terrorises when it overwhelms, when it becomes the dominant mode of relations to the wider world, the prism through which everything else refracts. Terror does not end at the event. Irish history can acknowledge the justness of the cause fought for but should fully admit to the cost. That burden includes the Irish warrior's own trauma as well as his enemy's suffering.

The traumatic effect of terror in Ireland was proven variously changeable, elusive, fleeting, enduring, intense and uncertain. We struggle to pin it down and force it to take specific form, but there is intensity in its evocation that is mutable and affecting. Understanding trauma through individual accounts proves too limiting for conceptualising all the complex ways in which terrorism and its traumas take up moments, lives, cities and cultures, and leaves them irrevocably marked.

Many times during the revolutionary period, Ireland and its people were 'changed utterly'.

Notes

[1] See J. Bourke, *An Intimate History of Killing: Face-to-Face Killing in Twentieth Century Warfare* (Granta, 1999).

[2] G. Costigan, 'The Anglo-Irish conflict, 1919–1921: A war of independence or systematized murder?', *University Review* 5 (1) (1968).

[3] C. Guevara, *Principles of Guerrilla Warfare*, http://www3.uakron.edu/worldciv/pascher/che.html.

[4] C.S. Andrews, *Dublin Made Me* (Cork, 1979), p. 60. See M.C. Havens, C. Leiden and K.M. Schmit, *The Politics of Assassination* (Englewood Cliffs, NJ, 1970).

[5] M.R. Cremin, 'Fighting on their own terms: the tactics of the Irish Republican Army 1919–1921', *Small Wars and Insurgencies* 26 (6) (2015).

[6] T. Bowden, *Beyond the Limits of the Law* (Harmondsworth, 1978), p. 159.

[7] T. Garvin, *1922: The Birth of Irish Democracy* (Dublin, 1996), p. 159.

[8] Recent research has questioned if the woman in the room with Newberry was his wife Hetty. In her book, Caroline Woodcock wrote 'One officer had been butchered in front of his wife. They took some time to kill him. Shortly afterwards she had a little baby. It was born dead, and a few days after she also died.' This must refer to the woman in the room when Newberry was shot. The initial police reports indicated the woman in the room was Newberry's wife. Her family, however, claims that Hettie Newberry was re-married in north London to Frank Warren in December 1922. According to the family, she died in 1928 from an alcohol-related illness, aged 52, and her family always said her illness was linked to the events she witnessed on Bloody Sunday. The Newberry family claimed the lady in the room was not his wife, but was carrying his child. The identity of Capt. Newberry's mystery companion at the time of his murder – and with her own reported death and stillborn child – is still to be resolved. The early Dublin Metropolitan Police report, compounded by the subsequent Hansard entry, has maintained the heroic but false image of a brave dutiful wife under extreme emotional/traumatic stress (http://www.bloodysunday.co.uk/murdered-men/newberry.html).

[9] M. Foley, *The Bloodied Field* (Dublin, 2014), p. 202.

[10] S.B. Norman and S. Maguen, 'Moral injury', PTSD: National Center for PTSD, https://www.ptsd.va.gov/professional/treat/cooccurring/moral_injury.asp.

[11] J.L. Herman, *Trauma and Recovery: The Aftermath of Violence – From Domestic Abuse to Political Terror* (New York, 1992), p. 28.

[12] M.O. Humphries and K. Kurchinski, 'Rest, relax and get well: a re-conceptualisation of Great War shell shock treatment', *War & Society* 27 (2) (2008); P. Leese, 'Why are they not cured? British shell-shock treatment during the Great War', in M. Micale and P. Lerner (eds), *Traumatic Pasts: History, Psychiatry, and Trauma in the Modern Age, 1870–1930* (Cambridge, 2001); S. Aiken, 'The women who had been straining every nerve: gender-specific medical management of trauma in the Irish Revolution (1916–1923)', in M. Terrazas Gallego (ed.), *Trauma and Identity in Contemporary Irish Culture* (Bern, 2019); J.J. Mathewson, 'How have the wars in Afghanistan and Iraq impacted the troops, their families, and the mental health community', https://www.counseling.org/docs/default-source/vistas/how-have-the-wars-in-iraq-and-afghanistan-impacted-the-troops.pdf?sfvrsn=28496b0b_14; E.W. Beal, MD, *War Stories from the Forgotten Soldiers* (Virginia Beach, 2019).

[13] T. O'Reilly, *Rebel Heart: George Lennon Flying Column Commander* (Cork, 2009).

[14] *Ibid.*, p. 126 *et seq.* Lennon wrote of the experience in a one act play he titled 'I and Thou'.

[15] D. Masterson, 'Opinion: remembrance and reconciliation: heroes in the Irish War of Independence', *The Irish Story* (13 March 2014), https://www.theirishstory.com/2014/03/13/opinion-remembrance-and-reconciliation-heroes-in-the-irish-war-of-independence/#.Xps92MhKjGg.

[16] On many pension applications, the term 'soldier's heart' was used, and would be called PTSD today.

[17] K. Kearns, *Dublin Voices. An Oral Folk History* (Dublin, 1998), Tom Byrne, pp 121–2.

[18] C. Dalton, *With the Dublin Brigade* (London, 1929), pp 106–8.

[19] *Ibid.*; Charles Dalton: Witness Statement 434. See Ernie O'Malley Papers, UCD archives, p/17/b/122/(22).

[20] Dalton, *With the Dublin Brigade*, pp 106–8.

[21] M. MacDonald, UCD archives, p/17/b/105/79.

[22] C. Dalton, UCD archives, p/17/b/122/(22).

[23] J. Dorney, 'How the Civil War "murder gang" tried to take over as judge, jury and executioners', *Irish Independent* (20 August 2017).

[24] Andrews, *Dublin Made Me*, p. 152.

[25] Dalton, *With the Dublin Brigade*, pp 116–17.

[26] Quoted in C. Younger, *Ireland's Civil War* (New York, 1979), pp 114–15; Vincent Byrne: Witness Statement 423.

[27] Vincent Byrne: Witness Statement 423.

[28] Jim Slattery: Witness Statement 445.

[29] William Stapleton: Witness Statement 822.

[30] Vincent Byrne: Witness Statement 423.

[31] Joe Leonard: Witness Statement 547.

[32] Jim Slattery: Witness Statement 445.

[33] Joe Dolan: Witness Statement 900; Younger, *Ireland's Civil War*, p. 114.

[34] Frank Henderson: Witness Statement 821.

[35] Andrews, Ernie O'Malley Papers, University College Dublin.

[36] M. Hopkinson, *The Irish War of Independence* (Dublin, 2002), p. 100.

[37] *Ibid.*, p. 164.

[38] E. O'Malley, *On Another Man's Wound* (Dublin, 1936; 1979), p. 245. O'Malley often wrote in the third person.

[39] O'Reilly, *Rebel Heart*, p. 49.

[40] T. Barry, *Guerilla Days in Ireland* (Dublin, 1949), p. 38.

[41] Séumas Robinson: Witness Statement 1721.

[42] Harry Colley: Witness Statement 1687.

[43] Joe Leonard: Witness Statement 547.

[44] Frank Thornton: Witness Statement 615.

[45] P. Pearse, 'The Coming Revolution', *Political Writings and Speeches* (Dublin, 1962).

[46] Pat McCrea: Witness Statement 413.

[47] Andrews, *Dublin Made Me*, pp 151, 153.

[48] *Ibid.*

[49] *Ibid.*, p. 153.

[50] *Ibid.*

[51] D. Neligan, *The Spy in the Castle* (London, 1999), p. 141.

[52] Evidence of Colonel Charles Russell before the army inquiry, 10 May 1924, General Richard Mulcahy Papers, University College Dublin, p7/c/29.

[53] Home Affairs returns of serious crime in Ireland with particular reference to responsibility of members of the army, July–Dec. 1923, Dublin NA D/T s3527.

[54] Oriel House was headquarters of the Free State's Criminal Investigation Department, and was staffed by many of the Squad members and intelligence officers from the 1919–21 period, who were fiercely loyal to Collins. Michael McDonnell: Witness Statement 225. See also Frank Thornton: Witness Statement 615 and Bernard Byrne: Witness Statement 631.

[55] Confidential medical examination of Ernest O'Malley by Dr Frank Murray, 19 September 1934, Military Archives of Ireland, Military Service Pensions Collection, MSPC /34A6/WDP/760. Medical reports on Ernest O'Malley, 14 September 1937 and 28 September 1939, 34A6/WDP/760, MSPC, MAI; R. English, *Ernie O'Malley*.

I.R.A. Intellectual (Oxford, 1998), p. 45.

[56] *Ibid.*, p. 35.

[57] MSP34REF4945, *c.* 1935.

[58] Arrest Order signed by Risteard Ua Maolcaha (General Richard Mulcahy), dated 8 August 1923. Letter from Clare Cowley, Molly's granddaughter.

[59] G. Clark, *Everyday Violence in the Irish Civil War* (Cambridge, 2014), p. 140. See the petitions to the Irish Grants Committee, which were compiled in the 1920s. N. Brennan, 'A political minefield: southern Irish loyalists, the Irish Grants Committee, and the British government, 1922–31', *Irish Historical Journal* 30 (119) (1997). See E. Morrison, 'The Bureau of Military History as a source for the Irish Revolution' (2012), https://www.militaryarchives.ie/collections/online-collections/bureau-of-military-history-1913-1921/wp-content/uploads/2019/06/Bureau_of_Military_wit ness_statements-as_sources-for_the_Irish-Revolution.pdf.

[60] A. Dolan, 'Killing and Bloody Sunday, November 1920', *Historical Journal* 49 (3) (2006).

[61] Frank Gallagher to Joseph McGarrity, 25 June 1938, NLI, MS 17,544.

[62] There are many lapses and difficulties in determining who took part on the Bloody Sunday raids in the Bureau of Military History Witness Statements, the Pension Applications, as well as private collections such as the Ernie O'Malley Notebooks, simply because the men refused to talk about it.

[63] Larry Nugent: Witness Statement 907.

[64] *Ibid.*

[65] J. Horgan, *Seán Lemass: The Enigmatic Patriot* (Dublin, 1997), p. 17.

[66] Peter Kearney: Witness Statement 444.

[67] George Berkeley: Witness Statement 994.

[68] NLI, MS 10,556 (4).

[69] B. Hughes, 'Make the terror behind greater than the terror in front? Internal discipline, forced participation, and the I.R.A, 1919–21', *Irish Historical Studies* 42 (161) (2018), p. 138.

[70] Mrs Roddy, Monaghan (ORO: CO 904/148); Alice Averill, Tyrone (/149); Mrs McNulty and Mrs Lynch, Roscommon (/150), Mrs Githin, Fermanagh; Alice Gourley, Tipperary, Mary Brien, Tipperary S.R. (/148); Jane Lynch, Mayo (/150); Winifred Molloy, Sligo (/148).

[71] Clark, *Everyday Violence*, p. 192.

[72] See A. Matthews, *Renegades: Irish Republican Women 1900–1922* (Cork, 2010), pp 159–67.

[73] Geraldine Dillon: Witness Statement 424.

[74] Labour Party of Great Britain, *The Report of the Labour Commission in Ireland* (London, 1921), p. 29.

[75] Hanna Sheehy-Skeffington, Statement on Atrocities against Women in Ireland, NLI ILB 300, p. 3.

[76] *Ibid*, p. 163; M. Ward, *Hanna Sheehy Skeffington: Suffragette and Sinn Féiner, Her Memoirs and Political Writings* (Dublin, 2015), pp 182–6.

[77] *The Report of the Labour Commission in Ireland*, p. 56.

[78] L.E. Byrne, 'The rape of Mary M.: a microhistory of sexual violence and moral redemption in 1920s Ireland', *Journal of the History of Sexuality* 24 (1) (2015).

[79] *Irish Exile*, July 1921.

[80] *Irish Bulletin*, 14 April 1921.

[81] L. Ryan, '"Drunken Tans": representation of sex and violence in the Anglo-Irish War

(1919–1921)', *Feminist Review* 66 (2000).

82 *Irish Bulletin*, 8 July 1921.

83 Michael Higgins: Witness Statement 1247; Thomas Markey: Witness Statement 1446; George Berkeley: Witness Statement 994.

84 *Cork Examiner*, 11 April 1921.

85 NLI, MS 556(8), 'War on women in Ireland'.

86 Ryan, '"Drunken Tans": Representations of Sex and Violence in the Anglo-Irish War'.

87 *The Report of the Labour Commission in Ireland*, p. 80.

88 *Ibid.*, p. 81.

89 G. Machnik-Kékesi, 'Gendering bodies: violence as performance in Ireland's War of Independence (1919–1921)', unpublished MA thesis, Concordia University, Montreal, Quebec, Canada (2017).

90 M. Coleman, 'Violence against women in the Irish War of Independence, 1919–1921', in D. Ferriter and S. Riordan (eds), *Years of Turbulence: The Irish Revolution and its Aftermath* (Dublin, 2015), p. 145.

91 Matthews, *Renegades*, p. 164.

92 M. Richardson, 'Terrorism: trauma in the excess of affect,' in J.R. Kurtz (ed.), *Cambridge Critical Concepts: Trauma and Literature* (Cambridge, 2018), p. 321.

93 Hughes, 'Make the terror behind greater than the terror in front?'; Clark, *Everyday Violence*, p. 140.

94 Hughes, 'Make the terror behind greater than the terror in front?'.

95 J. Darby, *Intimidation and the Control of Conflict* (Syracuse, NY, 1986), pp 52–7.

96 J.H. Long, Irish Grants Commission claim, PRO CO 762/27/14.

97 J. Augusteijn, *From Public Defiance to Guerrilla Warfare: the Experience of Ordinary Volunteers in the Irish War of Independence* (Dublin, 1996), p. 334.

98 B. Hanley, 'Terror in twentieth-century Ireland', in D. Fitzpatrick (ed.), *Terror in Ireland* (Dublin, 2012), p. 22.

6. Did the Irish 'win' the terror war?

The British reprisals, instead of turning the people against us as the cause of their miseries, had thrown them strongly behind us.

Michael Brennan

Studies of intelligence 'failures' in the twentieth century reveal that in most cases the problem is not an absence of intelligence, but the way in which intelligence is used: signals are missed, good intelligence is not distinguished from bad intelligence, and policymakers see what they want to see.[1]

One of the accepted judgements about the Irish War of Independence was that the intelligence resources of the British state did not have any tangible effect on the insurgency: 'Neither the Army nor the police were able to build the essential foundation for success in guerrilla warfare, a dependable intelligence service'.[2] Peter Hart has argued that the 'nearly unanimous' verdict on both the intelligence process and the end product has been as follows: '"British intelligence", out-witted and out-spied, emerges from most accounts of the revolution as a contradiction in terms: a disastrous compound of misdirection, malice and ignorance'.[3]

The Irish war is sometimes thought of as being disastrous for British intelligence, combined with a counterproductive policy of terror and reprisals, while Collins and his men and women consistently out-spied His Majesty's secret services, despite engaging in their own terror methods. Do the facts bear these conclusions out?

In the immediate post-war period the British made a detailed analysis of their intelligence performance in Ireland and, in a flurry of activity, papers were published, conferences held, reports commissioned and lectures given in which their failures were fully acknowledged. Initially, there were seven separate British intelligence organisations in Ireland reporting back to their headquarters with no fusion centre. In partial explanation of the British lack of intelligence, it must be noted that prior to and even at the height of the IRA's campaign, the Dublin Metropolitan Police 'G' Division in Dublin employed fewer than two dozen men exclusively dedicated to political work, while the RIC's Special Branch consisted not of a nationwide detective force along the lines of Scotland Yard but a confidential records office based in Dublin Castle, staffed by several clerks, a detective inspector and a chief inspector. It is known that as late as May 1920 the British chief of police in Dublin had an intelligence staff consisting solely of one officer. Its primary source of information, from the political detectives of G-Division of the DMP, all but dried up as Collins ordered the assassination of many of those detectives. The vast bulk of intelligence gathered by Special Branch was collected by ordinary RIC men throughout the country and forwarded to Crimes Special Branch's small office in Dublin Castle for analysis. Until the final year of Dublin Castle's rule, there was no 'secret service' in Ireland: Special Branch did not run undercover agents, rarely recruited informers and made little effort to penetrate the organisations of its enemies. The documents gathered there demonstrated the old-fashioned methods employed by the police: republican premises were kept under observation, train stations and other public places were watched, suspects were shadowed from town to town, and their speeches were recorded by policemen. In 1920 Field Marshal Sir John French, the Lord Lieutenant, complained: 'What masquerades for [an intelligence] service in Ireland is nothing but delusion and a snare'.[4]

By late 1920 intelligence officers were appointed to each divisional commissioner of the RIC to co-ordinate military and police intelligence. The military, present throughout Ireland in force, together with the Auxiliaries, had their own intelligence services staffed with young officers, many of them noted for their zeal in intelligence matters.[5] The British struggled with their ungainly intelligence system until they re-focused and restructured it – and by then it was too late. Only by late 1920, after Bloody Sunday, did dedicated efforts by the British improve and centralise their intelligence systems and start to turn the intelligence-gathering tide, until by the Truce of July 1921 they had overcome many of their disadvantages and were starting to gain the upper hand.

Although some individuals in British service were dismissed on dubious or malicious grounds of spying for the Irish, the files indicate that the quality of evidence demanded for prosecution, or even dismissal, was generally high:

little action was taken in many of these cases despite the RIC's efforts to gather incriminating evidence. Consequently, the British administration in Ireland remained penetrated by republican sympathisers despite its periodic attempts to purge potentially subversive employees.

On the Irish side, Collins's intelligence department brought success not only in the intelligence wars, but also in the eyes of the Irish people. One Volunteer said, 'For the first time in the history of separatism we Irish had a better intelligence service than the British ... This was Michael Collins's great achievement and it is one for which every Irishman should honour his memory'.[6]

There are, however, contrary views of the successes of Collins's intelligence operation. For example, Peter Hart, one of Collins's greatest critics of intelligence, asks:

> What did Collins's remarkable achievements actually enable him to do? His sources rarely gave him useful operational intelligence other than warning of some raids and spies. He did not acquire any particular insight into British planning or intentions. The result was a particularly negative and partial one, largely confined to Dublin's inner circles: security from G-Men and spies, not from British intelligence as a whole.[7]

IRA intelligence results mostly exceeded those of the British counter-intelligence effort, but the IRA's own counter-intelligence was less omnipotent than is popularly represented. The Bloody Sunday shootings did not just kill intelligence officers but also legal officers who were required when the British Army became immersed in law-enforcement. Moreover, Mulcahy reported to Collins on the state of Irish intelligence at the organisational level in early 1921:

> Intelligence: very faulty grasp generally. Neither officers, non-commissioned, nor men realise its imp. [sic]. Men who clamour for arms neglect this branch which they can perfect unarmed. Brigade Organisation: Vice-Commandant and Quartermaster do not ... fulfil proper functions: no definite agenda to work on; set orders not issued or issued imperfectly. Too much laissez faire attitude.[8]

Nevertheless, in terms of *covert* intelligence methods – the use of undercover officers and informants – the IRA was the clear winner. The British forces received little operationally useful information from their array of agents. Moreover, their intelligence agencies failed to recruit or place agents within the Irish leadership. In its internal history of the rebellion the army concluded:

> Secret Service was on the whole a failure in Ireland. For many reasons it was practically impossible to place a man in any inner circle. Consistent, regular and unsuspected informers, such as had been employed on other occasions, were almost unobtainable at any price.
>
> ... Irish persons who were prepared to act as secret service agents, i.e., as Sinn Féiners or as IRA were difficult to find.
>
> ... Owing to the terrorism of Sinn Féin and kindred organisations, even respectable and loyal people are afraid of speaking to a policeman.[9]

There were more *overt* intelligence gathering methods, however, and in this area the British were much more successful. The first of these was captured documents. Collins and the Irish had a tendency to commit things to paper, as they sought to prove their credentials as a *de facto* government and army.[10] Secondly, the British captured many IRA men, of all ranks, and these proved to be a valuable source of intelligence. The British concluded that:

> The best information, i.e., that on which the most successful operations, where the heaviest loss was inflicted on the IRA, were based, was that given by IRA deserters and prisoners under interrogation.[11]

In April 1921 General Macready estimated that eighty per cent of all British intelligence was a by-product of overt security measures such as raids, arrests and engagements with IRA units.[12] In his memoirs Ormonde Winter concurred, arguing that British intelligence gradually improved between Bloody Sunday and the Truce:

> It is fortunate that the Irish had an irresistible habit of keeping

documents. They would hide them in the most unexpected places, but they seldom avoided discovery by the trained sleuth.[13]

More importantly, Winter understood the importance of organised searches in terms of providing accurate and timely intelligence:

The word of an informer is, very frequently, unreliable, but the evidence deduced from a captured document is tangible, and can generally be regarded as conclusive. It was mainly documentary evidence that enabled the authorities to obtain and hold, in the face of appeals, the vast number of internees, and led to the successful prosecution of many agitators. Endeavours were made to inculcate into all concerned the value of forwarding to the Central Bureau all documents captured in raids.[14]

Clearly, one of the lessons drawn from the Irish War of Independence was the importance of captured enemy documents, which provided the British forces with a wealth of invaluable intelligence on the IRA – the British in fact made their best intelligence discoveries from those Irish documents. As the war continued and the pace of raids increased, intelligence gleaned from captured documents could lead to two or three further raids. The War Office report after the war stated:

In Dublin both the military and the police agreed that their most important sources of information were captured documents.
... After the first important capture which, to a great extent, was fortuitous, other searches were made from the addresses noted and names obtained, and the snowball process continued, new arrests and the obtaining of a more intimate knowledge of the plans, resources, and methods of the rebel organisation, besides material for valuable propaganda.
... These documents were not only the foundations on which the IRA List and Order of Battle were built, but seizure usually led to further raids and the capture of more documents until GHQ, IRA, were entirely demoralised. Up to 1920 Sinn Féin had taken few precautions to safeguard or destroy their papers and the

documents taken in Dublin in this period were of the highest importance in that they contained more details and completer [*sic*] and more accurate lists of names than was the case later. It is possible that, had the importance of documents been realised in country districts, and had those captured at this time been more carefully scrutinised and analysed, the source might have proved a fruitful one, but, unfortunately, many papers were destroyed, many were not examined, and this side of intelligence was not developed until the IRA had begun to take what steps they could to safeguard themselves.

… Fortunately, however, IRA officers often did keep documents that they could have destroyed with advantage and without loss of efficiency, and these provided excellent evidence against persons whom it was intended to try or intern.[15]

Some British troops in the country *were* able to recover documents, and they proved invaluable. In December 1920 Auxiliaries captured Ernie O'Malley in a raid in Kilkenny, where he was breaking his journey on his way back to Dublin. O'Malley customarily carried all his notes and papers with him. He was eating in a safe house when the Auxiliaries broke in, and his notebooks were on the windowsill. When the British examined O'Malley's notes, they found that the Kilkenny area had 'four brigades of eight battalions with 103 rifles, 4,900 rounds of rifle ammunition, 471 shot-guns and 3,490 rounds of shot-gun ammunition'. The notebook also listed all the names of the Kilkenny Brigade. As they left, the Auxiliary O/C announced 'We have the lot!' and they were delighted.

The Auxies were so pleased with what they found in the book that they ran to tell each other and decided to burn the premises. They set fire to hay, straw and outhouses and sent a Crossley tender to Woodstock for petrol to burn the dwelling house.

… The petrol having arrived, the occupants of the house were compelled to leave, and the Auxies spilled the petrol on the bedding, furniture, floors, etc. They broke windows to ensure a draught and, having set the house on fire, remained for some time watching the flames.[16]

In the days that followed, the Auxiliaries used the notebook to seek out and arrest most of the leaders of the Kilkenny Brigade. While in prison O'Malley met two other prisoners from the area, who told him that the Auxiliaries had arrested 'the whole countryside' and that, mad with rage, they were murdering half the people they took'. O'Malley had been a critic of slovenly organisation in the country and he never lived down his embarrassment.

In assessing the intelligence war, Charles Townshend wrote:

> Alongside organisation and armament, as the foundation of a guerrilla campaign, modern theory would place the creation of a comprehensive intelligence system. The IRA's achievement in this sphere is legendary – in both senses of the word, it now seems.
>
> ... In the first place, the organisation and functioning of the intelligence service within the IRA was far from faultless.
>
> ... Even the most celebrated achievements of IRA intelligence were not without flaw. The apogee of the organisation was Michael Collins's own network in Dublin, which was responsible for the assassination of twelve British officers on 'Bloody Sunday'. According to the IRA, these were members of a secret service group, which was about to put Collins's organisation 'on the spot'; while the [British] Government, displaying the characteristic mentality, denied that any were connected with secret service work, which was not going on anyway. More detached verdicts have usually fallen somewhere between the two ...[17]

A 'detached verdict' is necessary. Too often in reviewing Irish and British actions in the war, historians have viewed policies and results as black or white, right or wrong, heroes or villains, and friends or foes. In many views and instances of the War of Independence, it is this either/or – a 'binary construct' – that is the difficulty for some commentators. Such binary constructs are usually wrong. History is seldom 'black or white', and one must understand that in many cases the evidence is not there for a definitive, one-sided view, and in other instances a more nuanced, objective and multi-faceted view is called for. Moreover, results often do not reflect intentions.

Recent access to intelligence records has led some academics to conclude that British intelligence, while badly co-ordinated and inefficient, was more effective than has been credited. Against this is the image of Michael Collins and his agents and assassins running rings around British intelligence. How can the effectiveness of an intelligence organisation be measured – is it by the number of agents one side is able to infiltrate into the other side? The purpose of intelligence is to allow commanders to optimise their resources and capabilities – good intelligence is the key to good decision-making. Perhaps a better question to ask is 'which side optimised its resources to the fullest'? Which side was able to uncover the most accurate 'actionable intelligence', in today's terms? Did either side *win* the overall intelligence war? A more objective review of the Irish intelligence effort reveals successes, but also many failures. Likewise, there were many British intelligence failures, but also successes.

Politics were just as important within the British cabinet and parliament as within the Irish contingent. It was a common thread in the British government that the Irish situation in 1920 was 'one of disastrous failure on the part of a police force overmatched by a vicious and cunning foe and undermined by a weak government'. That view was a general one and shared by the head of the British Civil Service, Sir Warren Fisher, who prepared a report for Lloyd George on the state of British intelligence and the general administrative situation in Ireland. The British intelligence system suffered from many weaknesses from the outset: inexperienced officers, amateur techniques, poor security and lack of co-ordination. Fisher's report revealed a Dublin Castle political administration mired in stagnation, bureaucratic intrigue and sectarian bigotry, whose bunker mentality had completely 'demoralised the civil service'. 'With the notable exception of General Macready who had fortuitously now been imported, the Government of Ireland strikes one as almost woodenly stupid and quite devoid of imagination'.[18] Fisher saw that the British government thought it faced a straight choice between conciliation and massive force, though the military leaders could not guarantee success, especially as it would have to rely upon that 'demoralised civil service and police'. Fisher knew the British intelligence and governance problems went much deeper than the cabinet knew, and he felt that an alternative should be made available.

To achieve that end, in 1920 Fisher installed a new 'team' in Dublin Castle, led by Sir John Anderson, widely regarded as the most talented admin-istrator of the day.[19] Reporting to Anderson were Sir Alfred (Andy) Cope[20] and Mark Sturgis.[21] Fisher proposed many changes, and thought that over time his policy and personnel alternatives would eventually culminate in peace-feelers and negotiations with Sinn Féin and, if and when that hap-pened, he intended that the Dublin Castle administration should be ready. Cope was described as 'Lloyd George's special agent, charged with infor-mally exploring avenues of settlement with Sinn Féin'.[22] The three men often acted against the sanction of Hamar Greenwood, their ministerial su-perior. In fact, their brief was a secret and confidential attempt by the British government to find someone in Sinn Féin with whom they could negotiate. Since the trio favoured conciliation and negotiations leading to Dominion Home Rule, Fisher and Lloyd George had shrewdly left open the option of an eventual compromise peace.

Collins did not recruit a single policymaking member of the British mil-itary, police or government. Further, he knew little of the goings-on in the British cabinet, and never attempted to penetrate it. Collins's best insights into British government policy came from the British civil servant in Dublin Cas-tle, Andy Cope, who passed along information intentionally. Collins's contact with Cope can be underplayed, but what remains indisputable is that Cope's secret relationship with the leaders of the insurgency contributed directly to the decision by the British government to agree to a truce in July 1921.[23] Confirmation is provided by Mark Sturgis: 'Lady Greenwood asked me this morning in mockery –'Who *has* made the Truce – [South African Prime Minister Jan] Smuts or the Viceroy'? 'Neither' says I, 'but one Cope'.[24] Sturgis was adamant that 'the honour of peace' should go to 'Andy [Cope] first, last and all the time … he was the author of the whole thing'.[25] Cope's role was known at the time, and some of the British deemed him a traitor. When the Truce was announced, the conservative newspaper *The Morning Post* editori-alised: 'While they were still fighting in the illusion that the Government was behind them, Mr Cope was establishing friendly relations with their would-be murderers'.[26] In contrast, *The Times* later noted: 'the negotiations which he [Cope] undertook at considerable danger to himself were approved by his superiors and he was able to bring about a state of affairs whereby the treaty of 1921 could be signed'.[27] Cope's activities were anathema to the military and Charles Townshend opined:

Working to secret instructions from Lloyd George, who often, in Cabinet, disowned his moves, Cope tirelessly struggled to establish common ground for negotiations. But his dedication in this sphere limited his success in other directions, especially the vital one of liaison with the Army.[28]

The British post-mortem on the Irish War of Independence attributed their 'failures' to strategic intelligence limitations as well as military short-comings:

> The Army is only the spear point; it is the shaft of the spear and the force behind it that drives the blow home. During the last two years it would appear that the true state of affairs in Ireland was not realised in Great Britain, at all events, until it was too late. Consequently, the want of a suitable and clear policy was felt and sufficient importance was not, perhaps, attached to convincing the country of the need for putting one into force ...
>   ... The first lesson we learn is the necessity for a good intelligence system so that the Government advisors may be in a position to appreciate the situation justly and to put it squarely, fully and honestly before the Cabinet.[29]

Britain was always one step behind the evolving Irish political situation. Augustine Birrell was the Chief Secretary of Ireland in 1916, and was re-placed after the Easter Rising. At the hearing regarding that Rising, he said, 'I always thought that I was very ignorant of what was going on in the minds, and in the cellars if you like, of the Dublin population'. The same could be said of many in Dublin Castle who followed him. General Macready said of the Chief Secretary of the later war years, Sir Hamar Greenwood, that he was a rare presence in his own land.[30] Indeed, Matthew Nathan, Under-Secretary at Dublin Castle, testified to that same Royal Commission inquiring into the rebellion that 'Apart from its general ulti-mate futility, the conduct of the insurrection showed greater organisation, ability and military skill than had [previously] been attributed to the Vol-unteers'. The Volunteers of 1919–21 were even more organised. The British should have taken note of Sun Tsu's sixth-century BC warning: 'he who knows his adversary as well as himself will never suffer defeat'. With specific regard to intelligence, Dublin Castle legal advisor W.A. Wylie noted 'the inability of Lloyd George to fully understand the dimensions of the Irish situation was due to the fact that the intelligence system from which he derived his information was faulty'.[31]

As was shown in Ireland and the guerrilla wars that followed in the twentieth and twenty-first centuries, a 'government-in place' must recognise that intelligence and counter-intelligence can be a great contribution to the war-winner/war-loser. Perhaps the best lesson learned by both sides, however, was that, in the words of Colonel Ormonde Winter, intelligence 'alone cannot win a war. It is merely an aid to force, and it is only by action that the desired end can result.'[32] Winter was also right when he concluded, 'one of the outstanding difficulties in the suppression of political crime in Ireland was the fact that the British nation was not at war with Ireland, whilst Ireland was at war with the British nation'.[33] When Lord French asked Lloyd George if he would go so far as to declare war against the Irish, Lloyd George replied, 'You do not declare war against rebels'.[34] As a result, this meant the British government relied on the increasingly demoralised police forces to fight the guerrillas and the terror inherent in such warfare.

The British were involved in a 'war' from 1919 forward, and while they did not recognise that at the beginning, they were forced to do so at the end. With the British government reluctant to accept that a state of war existed and declare martial law across Ireland, it was left to the RIC, the Black and Tans and the Auxiliaries to respond to the furtive, unexpected attacks by the IRA with their own brand of terror. The possibility of martial law had been mooted since 1919, but the British military was hesitant because of inadequate troop numbers, political awareness of legal complications, and especially because to implement it would mean acknowledgement that something more than a 'police action' was happening. Understanding that they were on a 'legal tightrope', and that there was a need to exercise caution, the British commanders knew that using troops in support of civil power was risky, since not every action used to bring about order would be defensible afterwards. Aversion to martial law pushed the government into what was surely a worse alternative: the Black and Tans and the Auxiliaries.

While the British Army, like every other actor in the conflict, became brutalised by the cycle of attack and retaliation, it was the British paramilitary police forces who became the most feared and hated by the Irish public, and it was their paramilitary police, with their indiscipline and hostility to the general population, that did most to turn the civilian population against the Crown forces.[35] The Black and Tans and the Auxiliaries are often confused but they were distinct entities, and both introduced an atmosphere of stark terror throughout Ireland.[36] A further lesson the British learned was that a war cannot be 'won' using tit-for-tat violence and terror. The pattern of almost instantaneous response to ambushes or shootings set by the British proved counterproductive and a propaganda boon for the Irish.

Toward the end of 1920, the British were wearing down the Irish militarily – though the British did not know it. Bloody Sunday, the Kilmichael ambush and other Irish successes obscured the fact that the Irish were desperately short of ammunition, and the British had captured or killed many of their leaders. (Nevertheless, as examples of the terror caused by those events and the intimidating effects on the British soldiers as well as on civilians, it should be noted that on the afternoon of Bloody Sunday panicked British officers and their families packed their belongings and moved into Dublin Castle; the surviving intelligence agents were billeted in Dublin's Central Hotel; and, following the Kilmichael ambush, barricades were erected on both ends of London's Downing Street and the viewing gallery of Westminster was closed to the viewing public. Fear and intimidation due to terror could be seen in British 'officialdom', just as it could be seen in the civilian population.) As the war continued into 1921, those shortages of arms and men became acute across the country. Cooler and more realistic heads on both sides began to see the benefits of a political peace.

At the time the Truce was declared in July 1921, perhaps unsurprisingly, there was a widely shared belief among most British Army officers that the IRA was on the verge of total defeat. Many of the officers believed that the IRA would have been completely crushed within 'weeks' or 'at most six months'. Many British officers seem never to have accepted that their IRA counterparts were any good at military operations, a bias that continued throughout the war. For these men, the government's willingness to negotiate a settlement at this point was almost incomprehensible. This narrative came to dominate the post-conflict official reports assembled by the British military.

In the 'Record of the rebellion' compiled in 1922, the British Army argued that the IRA had been in a 'desperate position' at the time of the Truce:

> The rebel organisation throughout the country was in a precarious position … The flying columns and active service units … were being harried and chased from pillar to post, and were constantly being defeated and broken up by the Crown forces; individuals were being hunted down and arrested; the internment camps were filling up.[37]

Further, a September 1921 report complained:

> It is small wonder that the rebel leaders grasped at the straw that was offered, and agreed to negotiation.[38]

In some ways, those reports were attempts by the army to shift blame for what they considered a failure to the cabinet and government. The army had fought a war they did not understand, and for which they were unprepared. The army's military mission (and to a lesser extent that of the Black and Tans and Auxiliaries) was not to defeat the IRA, but rather to prevent the Irish from installing an alternative, revolutionary republican government in Ireland. The British political undertaking was not to defeat Sinn Féin, but to assist in the establishment of what modern counter-insurgent forces call 'stability' and to maintain it.[39] Further, British commanders had an ingrained sense of superiority, which kept them from seeing that their enemy was good at his job. The Irish in the cities, and the columns in the countryside, developed their own tactics, techniques and procedures (TTPs) far more quickly and ably than did the British.

British intelligence officers in Ireland had not been consulted prior to the Truce. Less than a week before the Truce was agreed, Ormonde Winter dismissed the peace hopes as 'snow on the dusty desert's face'. He wrote:

> There will be no peace settlement – of that you may be quite sure – at the present moment. But I do hope, sincerely, that the proceedings will be not too long dragged out. It will only afford them more breathing space, and more time to negotiate the

purchase of arms ... This is not merely an impatient diatribe, but
just to put in black and white my view that, at the present
juncture, there will be no peace. And that is all there is to it.[40]

The War of Independence ended abruptly, but not because of the military failure of the British forces, and that led many of them to feel their
government had betrayed them. Nevertheless, while the British military
and intelligence command thought that they had been 'sold out' by the
politicians (as military men often think is the case), in defence of the politicians, the statistics of the conflict were not supporting the military men's
view. (As time passed, this retrospective conviction on the part of the military that they had the IRA beaten, but had been betrayed by the politicians
of Westminster, would become a powerful myth within military and unionist circles. No army likes to feel humiliated, not so much through loss of
personnel, which is to be expected, but through feeling it was outmanoeu-
vred by an irregular force aspiring to military achievement.) In 1921 the
cabinet was receiving weekly casualty reports on Ireland, which showed
that fatalities at the hands of the IRA were steadily rising and not declining.
The economic cost of the conflict was also soaring and set to get much
higher. Perhaps more damaging, the promising statements and perceptions
about the progress of the conflict made towards the end of 1920 and early
part of 1921 had proved to be mirages, and only harbingers for far tougher
times. In February, Macready gave a pessimistic assessment: 'I cannot say that
I see any grounds for optimism for anything like a permanent settlement
of the country outside Ulster'. In further communication with the cabinet,
he was keen to dodge promising success, warning:

If the Government decide to place at my disposal all possible
troops and material, every effort will be made to stamp out the
extremists while the fine weather lasts, that is up to the end of
September, but I am not prepared to guarantee that this object will
be attained ...[41]

Earlier, Macready objected to the declaration of martial law throughout Ireland, deployment of more and more troops, increased executions and in-
terning suspected republicans:

213

There are of course one or two wild people about who still hold the absurd idea that if you go on killing long enough, peace will ensue. I do not believe it for one moment but I do believe that the more people are killed the more difficult a final solution becomes.[42]

Field Marshal Henry Wilson backed up Macready's hardly enthusiastic assessment, warning the cabinet: 'Neither General Macready nor I can promise any definite result'.[43]

By this time General Macready had learned what so many military men learn about fighting insurgents: 'to make war upon rebellion is messy and slow, like eating soup with a knife'.[44] Any guerrilla war is one of detachment, in which the counter-insurgents are often grasping at straws. The insurgents' assets are speed and time, not the hitting power of conventional forces, and these gave the Irish strategic rather than tactical strength. It took some time for the British politicians to decide they were not willing to give the RIC or the army a free hand in Ireland, but it took considerably longer for them to understand that they were going to have to negotiate with those whom they had publicly stated that they never would.[45] It is by no means certain that the police and army would have succeeded if they were given *carte blanche* in using even more terror, but clearly many in the army, at least, thought that they would have done so. The British Army 'Record of the rebellion', while largely condemning the government for its lack of direction, paradoxically stated:

> The infinite capacity of fit officers and men of the IRA for going
> on the run and staying there, was perhaps not fully seen at this
> time [September 1920]. It was not suggested now, or at any other
> time that any military action could finally pacify the country or
> solve the Irish problem. All that was claimed was, that given
> sufficient powers and numbers, the Crown forces could in course
> of time produce a situation in which a political solution might be
> offered with reasonable chance of success.[46]

Such an attitude belatedly demonstrated an advanced interpretation of the nature of counter-insurgency operations and goals. The British Army and the RIC (including the Black and Tans and Auxiliaries), however, never demonstrated such thoughts in practice. The 'Record' betrays the paradox of the British appreciation of how to conduct their operations: they seemed to understand that they could not solve a political problem with military force, but at the same time they attributed the political violence in Ireland to simple crime, which was to be resolved by the RIC. While there is no consensus today about the nature of political violence, there is clearly a difference between ordinary crime and political crime. That distinction seemed to elude the British. In fact, and at the time, many in the army and their actions never signified a belief that a political problem cannot be remedied with military force.

Even though the IRA never had the strength to face the British Army in open warfare, it never had to do so as the British were decisively engaged elsewhere – and some would argue over-extended – meeting their post-World War I military commitments. The British government needed to provide military forces to garrison and protect a worldwide empire while the Irish war was ongoing. British 'imperial over-stretch' prevented the British from massing sufficient forces to drown out the guerrilla forces. Britain was required to garrison a far-flung empire, provide forces for the newly nan-dated Mid-Eastern Territories, and an occupation force for the German Rhineland. In addition, the British government faced public pressure to reduce the unprecedented size of the British Army and control costs in the wake of a very expensive global war. In the end, the British government was restrained from taking the military and security steps they needed to take to control the Irish insurgency – not because they *could* not, but because they *would* not. Militarily far stronger than the IRA could ever hope to be, the British were shackled by political realities as much as – if not more than – their reduced military might and worldwide military commitments at the end of World War I.

Given such assessments, understandably the Secretary of State for War, Sir Laming Worthington-Evans, was less than enthused about the prospects of further war, and warned his cabinet colleagues:

The position of the military forces in Ireland is anything but satisfactory. There is a risk that a position of virtual stalemate may continue throughout the summer and autumn and that winter will be a time of decisive advantage to the rebels. Officers and men have had little or no rest—there is no back area into which they can be withdrawn ... I am anxious, therefore, to reinforce the troops in Ireland with everything not actually required elsewhere, so that an endeavour should be made to break the back of the rebellion during the three months, July, August and September ... I am strongly impressed by the advice of my military advisers that there is grave risk of failure ...[47]

Immediately after the Truce had been signed, General Macready summed up the general feelings within the military as to what had happened:

The feelings of Officers and men under my Command at the turn events have taken may I think be described as somewhat mixed. The prominent features are feelings of humiliation, disappointment, anxiety and, at any rate in the South West, of scepticism. Humiliation that even in so worthy a cause as the restoration of peace in this distracted country, it should be necessary to discuss terms with men they have been taught to consider the organisers of the murders of their comrades; disappointment that, just as it appeared possible that firm and decisive steps in dealing with the situation were about to be initiated, those responsible for the orgy of outrage of the past eighteen months should escape their just punishment; anxiety lest the snowball of concession should develop into an avalanche – and scepticism as regards the ability of the leaders of the I.R.A. to control their more militant followers.[48]

Scarcely two years after the Truce, Ireland's place in history and contributions to guerrilla-war techniques, tactics and procedures were firmly emplaced by two British officers who fought so hard against them. In October 1923 Major A.E. Percival, who served as Intelligence Officer of the 1st Battalion of the Essex Regiment in Cork, wrote to his friend, Major Bernard Montgomery, who served with the 17th Infantry Brigade in Cork. Percival was preparing two lectures on guerrilla tactics using Ireland as his model, and wrote to Montgomery asking his advice. Montgomery wrote back:

> My own view is that to win a war of this sort, you must be
> ruthless. Oliver Cromwell or the Germans would have settled it in
> a very short time. Nowadays public opinion precludes such
> methods, the nation would never allow it, and the politicians
> would lose their jobs if they sanctioned it. That being so, I consider
> that Lloyd George was right in what he did, if we had gone on we
> could probably have squashed the rebellion as a temporary
> measure, but it would have broken out again like an ulcer the
> moment we removed the troops. I think the rebels would probably
> [have] refused battles, and hidden their arms etc. until we had
> gone. [49]

In his memoir published in 1958, Montgomery looked back on his time in
Ireland with mixed feelings:

> In many ways this war was far worse than the Great War which
> had ended in 1918. It developed into a murder campaign in
> which, in the end, the soldiers became very skilful and more than
> held their own. But such a war is thoroughly bad for officers and
> men; it tends to lower their standards of decency and chivalry and
> I was glad when it was over. [50]

Despite the problems of the British in providing troops for all their other
worldwide commitments, in summer 1921 Collins and the other Irish re-
alists knew their strictly military position was perilous and they, too, were
seriously deterred from continuing the military campaign. Collins knew
the great advantages the British military had, and also knew that the British
had resources to call upon to increase their military presence in Ireland. He
knew the Irish could not compete in that battle.

> If this citing of our ability to outwit our enemies seems to place
> me in the category of those who imagine that in time we could
> have routed them out of the country, let me dissipate that idea
> quickly. I hold no such opinion. English power rests on military

might and economic control. Such military resistance as we were able to offer was unimportant, had England chosen to go at the task of conquering us in real earnestness. There were good reasons for her not doing so.[51]

The Irish War of Independence did not lend itself to an exclusive military solution, which is ephemeral, at best. The words 'winning' and 'victory' diminished in meaning as the British faced the awesome political/economic challenge that in 1919–21 they – particularly their military commanders in the field in Ireland – seemed unable to comprehend. In fact, while the IRA was not winning the war in May and June 1921, neither was it losing outright. The IRA was not defeated by mid-summer 1921; it is, however, hard to see how they could have fared against the planned British infusion of additional forces. The British would have been able to counter almost every action the Irish could have taken, but it is also unclear whether Macready's plans could ever receive the full governmental support that would have been necessary. Some drastic action had to be taken – either leave the field to the Irish or seek a showdown. Later, some of the British were still ambivalent about the course to take:

> The military was torn between those who thought it best to ride out the storm, letting politicians negotiate a settlement, and those who advanced sterner measures designed to stamp out the IRA completely.[52]

It is important to note that the British forces were expected to develop an answer to a *political* problem, and then they were expected to implement that answer. In today's terms, they needed to develop an 'exit strategy'. How was that to be defined? How were the British to measure their success? How were they to know when or how to withdraw their forces from Ireland? The British never were able to adequately answer those questions.

The British were also systemically disadvantaged by the fact that almost the whole of southern Ireland became sympathetic to the IRA. The IRA did use terror to intimidate and punish people, but by and large it had little need to do so. The public was not at all inclined to co-operate with the RIC, let alone its alien, non-Irish Black and Tan recruits. Without superior intelligence, which can come only from a public willing to take risks for the official side, counter-insurgency and counter-terrorism must fail.

In assessing the war, one must also gauge the effects of the terror used. Martha Crenshaw observed correctly that 'An initial problem in assessing the results of terrorism is that it is never the unique causal factor leading to identifiable outcomes. The intermingling of social and political effects with other events and trends makes terrorism difficult to isolate.'[53] Admittedly, it is impossible to isolate the net effect of terrorism and to assess accurately its relative contribution to the events leading to the Truce of July 1921. The evaluation of terrorism as a strategy depends on how that success is defined. Most terrorist groups strive to depose the current government and seize power. For the Irish, complete achievement of their goals was impossible (as it is usually for all such groups), but their strategy and tactics in using it succeeded in accomplishing partial objectives.[54] Three types of partial success can be credited to the Irish:

- achieving international attention to their grievances,
- acquiring international legitimacy, and
- gaining partial political concessions from the British.

It has to be underscored that the British cabinet only negotiated with Sinn Féin and concluded a settlement because of IRA violence. Governments can claim that they will not negotiate with rebels or 'terrorists', but the British government did exactly that in 1921. This situation had come about not only because of the failure of the British government to deliver in the political arena on Home Rule, or in the military arena against the IRA, but also because of its additional failure to develop any form of security policy as a basis for British forces to take the initiative and wage an effective campaign against the IRA. The British recognised that they were trying to gain the popular support of the people, but were never able to produce the security necessary for potential supporters to come forward in numbers. In the absence of a policy to provide order and security to the people of Ireland in 1919–21, a series of repressive security measures, including the Black and Tans and the Auxiliaries, were employed by the British authorities in a vain attempt to curb the nationalist campaign for independence and thereby maintain Ireland's place as an integral part of the United Kingdom. The Volunteers had made Ireland 'ungovernable' both civilly and militarily through their targeting of the RIC and other British forces. For all the rhetoric, it was violence that got Sinn Féin a seat at the negotiating table they refused at the Irish Convention in 1917, and were denied at the Paris Peace talks in 1919, as well as concessions not offered before.[55]

Further, some of the British who fought in the war never seemed to realise how much terror their actions brought upon the Irish population. Ironically, Field Marshal Bernard Montgomery, who fought in Ireland as a major and said 'I regarded all Irish as Shinners and it never bothered me a bit how many homes were burned', assessed the conduct of the Russian army in Germany after World War II. Seemingly blind to the actions of his command in Ireland, he wrote:

> From their behaviour it soon became clear that the Russians, though a fine fighting race, were in fact barbarous Asiatics who had never enjoyed a civilisation comparable to that of the rest of Europe. *Their approach to every problem was utterly different from ours and their behaviour, especially in the treatment of women, was abhorrent to us.*[56] [Emphasis added.]

Terror cannot be quantified nor qualified, and the war in Ireland certainly did not approach the terror of World War II, but Montgomery never seemed to understand that the trauma suffered by *every* man or woman is still horrific – and that *that* trauma contributed to the downfall of the British.

A contemporary guerrilla warrior, T.E. Lawrence, was more reasoned regarding his own actions in his personal evaluation of World War I:

> I hope that when the nightmare ends that I will wake up and be alive again. This killing and killing of Turks is horrible. When you charge them and find them all over the place in bits, and still alive many of them, and know that you have done hundreds in the same way before and must do hundreds more if you can.[57]

To win the support of the population, counter-insurgency forces must create incentives for co-operating with the government and disincentives for opposing it. The leaders of both the counter-insurgency and insurgent forces must stress the importance of focusing more on the social, economic and political development of the people than on simple material destruction. In a later Irish war, British General Frank Kitson noted that ideas are a motivating factor in insurgent violence: 'The main characteristic which distinguishes campaigns of insurgency from other forms of war is that they are primarily concerned with the struggle for men's minds'.[58] Insurgencies fight for political power as well as for an idea. According to US Marine General Charles C. Krulak, to fight back 'you need a better idea. Bullets help sanitize an operational area … They don't win a war.'[59]

Even though much of the 'Record' was an attempt to transfer 'blame' to the politicians, the army authors knew that they learned a great deal about counter-insurgency actions while fighting in Ireland, and this knowledge would be of great help in fighting in Palestine, World War II, Malaya, and other 'irregular wars' in which the army found itself fighting later in the twentieth century. While the strategy and tactics used in Ireland were not much of a factor in the British counter-insurgency in Malaya in the 1950s, winning the 'hearts and minds' of the people has become enshrined as a pivotal component of counter-insurgency warfare ever since General Sir Gerald Templer declared in 1952 that it would be the key to success in fighting the communists.[60] Templer famously remarked that 'The answer [to the uprising] lies not in pouring more troops into the jungle, but in the hearts and minds of the people'.[61] His plan of war was not to *terrorise* the population but to *control* them, offering the Malays independence. His view was that 'the shooting side of this business is only 25% of the trouble'.[62] He realised that it was not a popularity contest but that the counter-insurgents must provide, first, security for the population and then, second, the legitimacy of the government. Insurgency versus counter-insurgency is a struggle to see who can provide better governance for the population; Templer realised this and the population made its choice. The Malayan Emergency is still regarded as the shining paradigm of how to properly wage a counter-insurgency campaign, and Templer's emphasis on hearts and minds established a fixation on these operations in military circles.[63] Certainly, the IRA won, and the British lost, the hearts and minds of the Irish population in the War of Independence.

In her book *Tom Barry: Freedom Fighter* Meda Ryan recounts how both

Menachem Begin in Israel and Che Guevara in Cuba wrote to Barry for advice.[64] Diverse nationalist guerrilla movements in the decades that followed emulated Collins's pioneering urban terror tactics and the IRA's skilful use of propaganda. While governments regularly decry terrorism as ineffective, the terrorists themselves have an abiding faith in their violence, and for good reason. Terrorism's intractability is also due to the capacity of terrorist groups to learn from one another. Those terrorist groups that survive the onslaught directed against them by governments and their police, military and intelligence and security services do so because they absorb and apply lessons learned from their predecessors. Theirs is a trade and they learn it from one another. For instance, the Jewish terrorist group Irgun, led by Begin, consciously modelled itself on the IRA and studied the Irish War of Independence. Israel's Yitzhak Shamir so admired Collins that he took the code name 'Micail' during Israel's war for independence in the late 1940s.

By spring 1921 the IRA/Volunteers had become a force in Dublin and its flying columns had become feared throughout the counties of Cork, Kerry and Clare. The columns were mobile units of from ten to one hundred men, who could strike in devastating ambushes and then melt into a hinterland that they knew far better than the British military units who were deployed to fight them. Most IRA units were, however, chronically short of both weapons and ammunition.

> At this particular time things were so bad with all the units that it
> was a question of how long they could last, would we last a
> month, a fortnight? The only reason was we had little left to fight
> with. We had no ammunition; we had a few guns. So bad was it
> that they cut down Winchester ammunition to fit .45 and several
> members of the A.S.U. and other units met with serious accidents
> as a result.[65]

Earlier in the war, Collins had said 'without guns you might as well be dead'. Now the emphasis was on a lack of ammunition. Following the Custom House fire on 25 May 1921, the Irish military situation moved from acute to desperate, at least in Dublin. The British seized a small amount of arms and ammunition on that day, and the loss of men to death or capture was a loss the Dublin Brigade could not withstand. Overall, some commentators regarded the IRA 'effectively beaten in Dublin by June 1921'.[66] By that time, though a formidable opponent, the IRA had not been able to dislodge the British forces, and it became clear to Collins that the Irish could not defeat those forces in the field.

From the Irish viewpoint, the overall military position of the IRA by spring 1921 is not easy to assess. The regular exercise of British administrative authority had certainly been crippled, but for those of the IRA who thought in terms of driving the British into the sea, the IRA was still at square one. It could scarcely hope to take on its adversaries in anything more than platoon strength, and that only in a few areas. This requires being realistic about what can be done, and therefore what cannot. From the outset, some IRA members believed that since the British were still traumatised from fighting a war of attrition in Europe, then fighting a war of attrition against them in Ireland would lead to success, while other members felt that the British would simply get tired of pouring in the money and manpower necessary to put down the guerrillas and give in. Many of the foot soldiers, and some leaders, of the IRA continued to expect, or at least to wish for, the outbreak of a further insurrection and open warfare to drive British power out of Ireland. They resented the fact that the Dublin leadership had failed to consult with them and many claimed their military prospects were quite favourable. Mulcahy disagreed, saying that to drive the British from anything more substantial than a police barracks was beyond them.[67] The strategic function of the IRA's warfare was to defeat the British psychologically and politically – it was a war of attrition and exhaustion – but that exhaustion had to be capitalised upon politically. Every IRA 'outrage' was a blow against the British will to persist, however many had little meaning in and of themselves. Collins understood that the IRA could not liberate Ireland by military means – it followed that he was treading on thin ice among some of his most devoted followers. Collins was playing politics with violence. He calculated that the IRA's guerrilla warfare, which actually entailed very little warfare and large amounts of terror and reprisals, would provoke British counter-violence.[68] Terror begets terror.

As so often happened during the war, events moved somewhat in parallel, and by spring 1921 the British government was also considering some sort of political settlement. This represented a major change from Walter Long's statement of summer 1920 that 'the British would not bargain with murderers. The thing is unthinkable.'[69] Fisher's appointment of Sir John Anderson, Sir Alfred (Andy) Cope and Mark Sturgis to their positions in Dublin Castle from months before looked prescient and was beginning to bear fruit.

It became clear that the war had deteriorated into a mutually hurting stalemate that could go on forever, and by late May 1921 Cope's efforts were bringing the two sides closer, though the process proceeded in fits and starts, as one can imagine. At a London conference, the British cabinet met with General Macready, who outlined the draconian measures that he felt would be necessary if a military option were to go forward, and he indicated that he was prepared to implement such measures. These included provisions that any member of the Dáil, the IRA, the IRB or Sinn Féin was liable to be executed for treason, and anyone caught with arms would suffer the same fate.[70] Macready emphasised that such a plan could only be effective if implemented 'with utmost thoroughness' and that only by doing so could the morale of the soldiers and police be maintained.[71] Macready was blunt with the cabinet: either 'go all out or get out'.[72] It is unclear if Macready really thought such a plan utilising greater terror methods would work, or if he was pressuring the cabinet to make a decision. How the Irish would have reacted to the increased British troops or terror is, of course, unknown, but it is hard to visualise them being able to put up the necessary resistance to such British reinforcements.

By early spring 1921 the calls for negotiation were increasing to the degree that British intelligence did its best to keep de Valera from being harmed or arrested:

> the Intelligence Service has been ordered not employ their information to secure the arrest of certain individuals, amongst whom was Mr. de Valera. It was considered better that he should remain at large, in order that the authorities might have the head of Sinn Féin organisation with whom to treat should the occasion arise. This order was loyally obeyed despite the difficulty of trying not to see him.[73]

When de Valera was arrested in Blackrock on 22 June, he was quickly released on the intervention of Andy Cope.

> The arrest of the President was quite an accident though the
> military authorities were very keen on getting him. The moment
> was a very awkward one for the British Government as many
> factors were compelling them to put up at least an appearance of
> wanting to settle. Chief amongst these was the Imperial
> Conference, the leading spirit of which is very keen on an
> American alliance, which cannot be had without a settlement
> here. Consequently the President was released and the offer from
> Lloyd George forwarded to him.[74]

Likewise, when Arthur Griffith was arrested in June, he, too, was immediately released.

Cope and the 'peace faction' of Dublin Castle disagreed with prolonging the military action, and felt that a military solution would require strict martial law, more house searches, more customs inspectors to stop all IRA arms importation, identity passes to be carried by all persons at all times, and the reassignment of every available British soldier from around the world to Ireland. Colonel Sir Hugh Elles, Commandant of the Tank Corps Centre, was asked to visit Ireland, and to submit a report to the cabinet and he estimated that if such measures were put into effect, it might take two years to complete, but there could be no absolute assurance that the measures, as strict as they would have to be, would result in a favourable end to the war: 'If you pour in more troops on the present lines, you are simply throwing good money after bad'.[75] The initial reaction of British cabinet to the rising aspirations of the Irish population was to quell the movement through force, but repression is a crude tactic and its failure to impair the subsequent radicalisation of the Irish was catastrophic for the British. Despite considerable effort, by the middle of 1921 the British government had not managed to check the Irish national movement. The choice they faced was to compromise or to unleash hell. The British had to make that choice: would its military attempt to subjugate Ireland by threats, terror and more violence, or would the British attempt to make peace?

Sturgis's views of de Valera and Collins, and their status and roles in any negotiations, were reflected in an intelligence report from June 1921.[76]

> My private opinion is that things are in a very bad way and de

Valera knows it. The Volunteers are out of hand and robberies are being carried out without orders. De Valera is of the opinion that he will be able to arrange a scheme with the Northern Parliament and then present it to the British Government for their acceptance. I am sure he has no power over Collins, if he had, and if sincere would he not have ordered the murders to stop at once?[77]

Anderson and his acolytes knew that the time for a decision was imminent. He warned that 'military action to be effective must be vigorous and ruthless. Many innocent people will suffer and the element of human error cannot be eliminated.'[78] Sir Basil Thomson believed that the Irish were split and that Collins was leading a more militarist faction against the more moderate de Valera. On 13 May Thomson reported that the IRA was prepared to fight on and repudiate any settlement made by Sinn Féin. (In retrospect, his report may have been premature but also prescient, as the events after the Treaty show. His estimation, however, of Collins's militarism versus de Valera's moderation at this time was misinformed.[79] Further, Lloyd George relied on British intelligence that indicated Collins's intransigence would prevail over de Valera's supposedly more moderate views in Sinn Féin circles.[80])

On 22 May 1921 there were elections for both the Northern and Southern Parliaments under the Government of Ireland Act that had passed Westminster and received royal assent on 23 December 1920. The provisions of the Act provided a timetable for implementation and the Southern Parliament had to be established by 14 July. If it were not implemented then there was to be a declaration of a Crown Colony government, and with that the imposition of martial law in the twenty-six counties. By now, it became apparent that it was either that, or the declaration of a truce and negotiation. Constitutional and military realities had clarified the options for the British. The British decision to negotiate at this time represented an uncomfortable acknowledgement of *realpolitik,* as well as the dominance of the political over the military considerations.

Frank Thornton, one of Collins's most important lieutenants, wrote that the Truce came with dramatic suddenness:

Whether the truce was a good thing or not remains for historians to record, but, in my humble opinion, had it not taken place we would have found ourselves very hard set to continue the fight with any degree of intensity, owing to that very serious shortage of ammunition, because men, no matter how determined they may be or how courageous, cannot fight with their bare hands.[81]

Collins emphasised that suddenness of the Truce: 'When we were told of the offer of a truce, we were astounded. We thought you [the British] must have gone mad.' But there was trepidation, as well. Further, Collins said, 'once a Truce is agreed, and we come out into the open, it is extermination for us if the Truce should fail ... We shall be ... like rabbits coming out from their holes'.[82] Andy Cope, who was sent to establish a means for negotiations and was doing so, recognised the British view of that as well. He wrote to Cabinet Secretary Tom Jones arguing for a protracted Truce, indicating that that would sap the efficiency and fighting spirit of the IRA:

whose members would gradually return to their ordinary habits of civilian life ... The advantages of this from the Government's view are such that I think they should take no action themselves to terminate the Truce ...[83]

To succeed at its war the IRA did not need to be loved, but it needed to be respected, and preferably feared as well. In Ireland in 1919–21, as in all other irregular wars, most people would prefer the violence to cease and for the men of violence to go away. Popular support of active or semi-active kinds flows to the side that is feared the most – terrorism fosters that fear. If that side happens to embody an attractive ideology, that is a bonus. In Ireland, Britain was always fighting against history. The Irish had long memories of British atrocities and oppression. But, that said, unprodded, they were not exactly eager to rebel in 1919, though this is not to deny that they were far readier to assist the IRA in 1919 than they had been to rise to die in company with Patrick Pearse and his fellow martyrs in 1916. In 1919–21, Ireland, beyond the small ranks of IRA activists, was both happy enough to cheer on the 'lads' of the IRA, while avoiding any serious, and potentially dangerous, commitment themselves. As much to the point, though, British behaviour provided no convincing reasons to withhold support for the rebels. Official repression of the IRA was sporadic, half-hearted, and ineffective. British forces could not offer protection, and they did not appear to be winning.[84] The Irish strategy in the war demonstrated how an ill-equipped, and mostly ill-trained, but well-motivated movement can combine military and political approaches in a successful way, even against a much larger and technologically superior enemy.

The IRA's guerrilla war was a curious compound of the admirable and the unpleasant – the chivalrous soldier and the cruel killer, the selfless patriot and the swaggering jack-in-office, the devout Catholic and the self-conscious martyr.[85] In the end, its campaign overcame all practical failings. As Ernie O'Malley wrote, the folk imagination could give the smallest action a 'heroic and epical' quality, and the saga concealed many acts of cold-blooded violence, cowardice and betrayal.[86] The IRA was heir to a tradition of agrarian terrorism, a succession of secret societies to which it remained akin, and its elemental quality of political change was one of its main sources of strength.

In their respective analyses, military men on both sides felt that they had been betrayed. Some British military leaders felt that they had the IRA 'on the run' and would be victorious quickly. On the Irish side, many IRA leaders felt the same: that they had the upper hand and would soon drive the British out of Ireland. Both of these 'betrayal' positions can be attributed largely to the distorted perceptions of the proximity of success by the respective military forces – especially those officers on both sides who were not aware of the overall limitations of larger commands. Neither side was on the 'verge' of defeating the other militarily. It is dangerous to mix ideology and military operations. It clouds one's thinking and makes one see only what one wants to see. So often we observe that people make their decisions based on what the facts mean to them, not on the facts themselves. Ironically, it was another example of the sides mirroring one another.

Those 'betrayal' positions became the dogma for many in the British military and for the 'anti-Treaty' forces in Ireland's terrible Civil War of 1922–3. The fact that many IRA volunteers were unaware of the limitations of what could be achieved through physical force and political pressure would become an intractable problem after the Truce. Such 'stalemate-induced, compromise endings' to wars can often lead to attitudes towards former colleagues remaining unaltered by the settlement, with the violence living on after the agreed conclusion. As a result, the Irish on both the pro-Treaty and anti-Treaty sides often retained a fundamentally hostile reading of former friends and allies who landed in the opposing communities.

The Truce, and the follow-on Anglo-Irish Treaty of December 1921, had to be based on the extant facts and circumstances of the situation – *realpolitik*. Many Irish commanders felt that since the British 'agreed to' a Truce, that they had been fairly beaten. They thought the treaty negotiations to follow would be between that of a victorious Irish and a supplicant British delegation. However much the British commanders and politicians dismissed the Truce, or however some of the Irish viewed their position as victors, that cannot negate the essential truth of the situation. Regardless of what the positions on the battlefield were thought to be by either side, the fact was that the IRA fought the conflict until British politicians were ready to negotiate with them.

Collins and the Irish knew their first rule, especially in guerrilla war, was the avoidance of decisive strategic encounters. Von Clausewitz expressed it as: 'They must not attempt to crack the nut: they must only gnaw at the surface and borders'. Collins recognised that a guerrilla's task is to draw the opponent into a battle he cannot win. In Sun Tsu's words, 'Allowing the enemy to choose the field of battle will only serve *his* purpose, not yours'. The British could not win the political/propaganda war. The British reprisals and stories of atrocities and terror that were published in the world-wide press completely changed the British view of the war. The political will of the British was more soundly beaten than their military will. At times, Collins and the IRA outthought and outfought the British, but Collins knew that this was a war that could not be won militarily – it could, however, be lost in that way. Collins's strategy was to keep the IRA alive, avoid a catastrophic defeat, remain an expensive nuisance and embarrassment, or more, and prod the British into making strategic mistakes. This they did, obligingly. The IRA was helped not only by its own circumspection but also by British violence that undermined that government's legitimacy.[87] Ernie O'Malley wrote: 'Their campaign of terror was defeating itself'.[88] Michael Brennan elaborated: 'The British reprisals, instead of turning the people against us as the cause of their miseries, had thrown them strongly behind us'.[89]

Most guerrilla wars of the twentieth century failed, and those that did 'succeed' did so by an intentional combination of military, political and propaganda action. Military action is a means to the end – but it is not an end in itself. By its very nature, an insurgency is military only in a secondary sense, and political, ideological and administrative in a primary sense. As historian Bernard Fall put it, 'when a country is being subverted, it is not being outfought – it is being out-administered'.[90] In the most basic analysis, a guerrilla war is a competition for power – ultimately, not military power, but rather political power in the country. History has borne out the idea that confrontation between power, and those who are subject to power, is the only way anything changes. There are certain conditions in which a particular insurgency has a chance of succeeding even against the professional armed forces of a *status quo* government, because for one reason or another the government cannot utilise their full resources.[91] Given these considerations, and in retrospect, the Irish leaders were justified in planning a strategy of insurrection that would bring them up against the armed forces of Britain because those forces would be hamstrung to a considerable extent. The Irish War of Independence falls into that 'successful' category. This does not happen often, but any revolutionary triumph is generally rare.

In judging the Irish war, and what the positions of the belligerents were at the time of the Truce in July 1921, one must attempt to make an objective assessment of the Irish strategy. Were the Irish 'successful'? To obtain their political goals, the Irish needed to provide credible information to the audiences whose behaviour they hoped to influence. They played to two key audiences: the British government, whose policies they wished to impact, and the Irish population, whose support or obedience they sought to gain. Adrian Guelke has written 'success, or at any rate, the prospect of success is crucial to the legitimisation of violence'.[92] Looking back, can we 'legitimise' the Irish use of violence and terror? Richard English argues that what terror 'working' actually means is that the terrorists have achieved (*inter alia*):

- They determined the agenda, thereby preventing one's opponent from securing victory.
- They secured interim concessions.
- They acquired meaningful publicity.
- They gained or maintained control of the population.[93]

Others use more specific measures to determine success. Erica Chenoweth and Maria Stephan make clear that:

> For our study, to be considered a 'success', a campaign had to meet two conditions; the full achievement of its stated goals (regime change, end of occupation, or secession) within a year of the peak of activities and a discernible effect on the outcome, such that the outcome was a direct result of the campaign's activities.[94]

Charles Townshend wrote that tactical success could be assessed by the movement 'seizing attention'. He asked 'What message did the terrorism convey?'[95] Just as there are competing definitions of what constitutes terrorism, one can see that there are differing notions of what represents 'success'. Evidence is rarely so clear that this kind of question can be decided unambiguously.

Even after British successes against the IRA in early 1921, however, the violence and terror accelerated and by July 1921, both sides realised that a military victory was probably out of the question. It has been argued that the violence of 1919–21 produced a greater measure of freedom for what was to emerge as independent Ireland than would otherwise have been the case.[96] In mid-1921, and in light of internal and international public opinion that was uniformly opposed to the British continuing their fight, the only reasonable course for the British politicians was to make a deal. The IRA tactics had not beaten the British, nor won the war, but they had prevented defeat – this was their triumph.[97]

In warning against irregular wars, British Major C.E. Callwell wrote: 'Guerilla warfare is what the regular armies always have the most to dread, and when this is directed by a leader with a genius for war, an effective campaign becomes well-nigh impossible'.[98]

Faced with insurmountable military obstacles, Irish nationalism manifested itself in a new republican ideology and a more co-ordinated political–military relationship. The new military construct mobilised large numbers of potential fighters, but put very little of that strength in the field at any time – creating a protracted war rather than a more symmetrical challenge that could be resolved decisively through conventional military operations.[99] The Irish created an entirely new political–military system that posed great enough challenges to British rule to force negotiation and enable political concession. The creation of broad-based political movements to support revolution or resistance remains an effective strategy for non-state actors even today, and some would argue that it is almost an archetype for success.[100] The Irish careful political mobilisation, strategic co-ordination and calibrated use of violence and terror, along with a willingness to indicate the ability to fight a protracted war, was a powerful disincentive for the British. Many of the choices considered by both combatants in Ireland were replicated later in other irregular wars.

Richard English has argued that there is an historically grounded framework for successfully fighting terrorism. He lists seven key components, and one should ask if the British should have revised their handling of Ireland from the outset using those elements. He recommends:

- learn to live with it;
- where possible, address the underlying root problems and causes;
- avoid the over-militarisation of response;
- recognise that intelligence is the most vital element in successful counter-terrorism;
- respect orthodox legal frameworks and adhere to the democratically established rule of law;
- co-ordinate security-related, financial, and technologically preventative measures;
- maintain strong credibility in counter-terrorist public argument (i.e. propaganda).[101]

While English's study primarily deals with terrorism of the twenty-first century, one can see that the British were deficient in their responses in the Irish War of Independence. The British did not address the underlying root causes and problems; their responses were over-militarised; their intelligence was faulty, at best; the Black and Tans and Auxiliaries ignored the law for the most part; and they lost the propaganda war. The Irish were much better at propaganda and intelligence, allowing them to be more successful in countering the British terrorism and military efforts of a palpably more powerful army.

For those who seek to understand counter-insurgency, the Irish War of

Independence illustrates numerous lessons related to securing victory. Chief among these are:

- the importance of securing the support of the local population and understanding your opponent,
- the essential need to apply only the minimum necessary use of force,
- the value of intelligence operations,
- the necessity of providing a peaceful path to change, and
- the critical nature of having a clear operational goal.

From an insurgent standpoint, the war demonstrates the ways in which targeted use of terror, effective use of guerrilla tactics, the creation of well-defined political, military and intelligence organisations and the support of the people can make an insurgency much more dangerous and difficult to overcome.[102] The Irish use of terror in 1919–21 shows that the most successful terrorist campaigns are waged for causes, usually nationalist, that are accepted broadly by the public and supported by major political parties. Fringe groups seeking radical social change – whether the anarchists of the nineteenth century or Germany's Baader-Meinhof Gang of the 1970s – have little chance of success. The IRA had strong support among the people throughout the conflict, worked to avoid civilian casualties and treat the local population with respect and care, framed their struggle politically and religiously as part of a resurgent Irish nationalist movement in order to inspire and incentivise the population to support their efforts, ensured the underground government of Sinn Féin and Dáil Éireann represented the legitimate government of the people and utilised violence effectively on Crown forces to make the idea of British control over the Irish seem tenuous at best and illusory at worst.

In the narrative of the Irish War of Independence, credit/blame is usually applied depending on one's viewpoint. The first option is to hail Collins (particularly, but the other Irish as well) as fighting a one-sided intelligence/military war and winning all the intelligence battles in Dublin and throughout the country.[103] In the second version, the British (and particularly Lloyd George and the hard-liners in the cabinet and military) 'lost'

Ireland by their incompetence and betrayed those who wished to remain part of the 'Empire' for their own selfish means by resorting to terror and reprisals.[104] Like all absolutes, neither is strictly true. In fact, both the Irish and the British had successes and failures, both used terror strategically and tactically, and both the Irish and British evolved as the war went on.[105] While direct comparisons cannot simply be drawn between the Irish war and those that followed in the twentieth and twenty-first centuries, events in Ireland and in other 'asymmetric wars' certainly prove that weaker insurgent forces can use imagination, improvisation and local expertise to challenge a materially better-resourced and armed adversary.

Collins should be credited with having an evident appreciation of the necessity of acquiring information from disparate sources and their analysis as the primary elements of intelligence; penetrating the British intelligence service; understanding the need for ruthlessness when required; and in maintaining the security of his own service.[106] His intelligence service did not contribute a great deal directly to the operations of units outside of Dublin, but that was mostly owing to the circumstances extant in 1919–21. Most operations were on a local level, and each was planned and conducted in conjunction with local conditions and intelligence. Guerrilla war is a localised war.

Collins was bold, but not reckless. It should be understood that he was not a superman, that the IRA was vulnerable to British spying insertions, and that by the time of the Truce in 1921, Collins's Irish intelligence operation was almost equalled by the upgrade in British intelligence. Such an objective review also suggests that, had the Truce not gone into effect in July 1921, the British efforts to find and capture Collins within a short period could have been successful. Hart suggests that 'time simply ran out' on the British. Although slow at the start, British military intelligence towards the end of the campaign put severe pressure on the insurgents, although its counter-intelligence and security efforts left a lot to be desired. It is well worth mentioning that it is a general rule in strategic history that both sides learn by experience. Collins appreciated that the British were capable of strategic and then tactical improvement. The outcome could therefore be the result of a race between British political war weariness due to accusations of terror in the international press and the British learning curve in counter-insurgency. Collins was ahead in covert intelligence gathering, but it may have been a close-run thing. If the Irish intelligence war was judged as a horse race, the British were in the lead at the start of the race, the Irish caught up and actually pulled ahead in the middle, and at the end of the race the British recovered to almost a dead heat.

Insurgencies are psychological and political more than they are military struggles. The Irish needed to remain active in the War of Independence for longer than the nerves of liberal Britain could stand, and they succeeded. Irish governance, not military victory, was always the goal. If success can be defined as doing more with less, then Michael Collins must be counted as among the great guerrilla planners of the twentieth century. He understood the limits of what could be achieved by violence – and when to forgo violence for negotiation. While Collins always said he was 'a soldier not a politician' to the end of his life, he epitomised what we would now recognise as a modern-day multi-national CEO – one who was always willing to make a deal – and to 'deal' with the anti-Treaty IRA as willingly as with the British. The remarkable thing is not that he failed, but that he almost succeeded.

Hart conceded that 'Collins was brilliant, and we must be aware of the limits of his reach. His secret service may well have bested his vaunted rivals, but theirs was one battle not the whole war.'[107] Hart, however, wrote further:

> Irish republicans invented modern revolutionary warfare, with its mass parties, popular fronts, guerrilla warfare, underground governments, and continuous propaganda campaigns. What Michael Collins and company did in post-Great War Ireland, Mao, Tito, and Ho Chi Minh would do during and after the next world war.[108]

Credit belongs to many of the Irish, but 'it's doubtful the revolt would have succeeded without the genius of one man: the Irish Republican Army's *de facto* military commander, Michael Collins, described by one of his foes as a man "full of fascination and charm—but also of dangerous fire"'.[109]

Fifty years after the Irish War of Independence Henry Kissinger wrote cogently about the U.S. role in Vietnam, and this could be said of any guerrilla war – before or after:

- We fought a military war; our opponents fought a political one.

- We sought physical attrition; our opponents aimed for our psychological exhaustion.

- In the process, we lost sight of one of the cardinal maxims of guerrilla warfare:

- The guerrilla wins if he does not lose.

- The conventional army loses if it does not win.[110]

There is no better description of the Irish War of Independence.

Overall, the IRA was able to mobilise public support throughout the war, slowly at first, then the Irish public fell more in step with the Irish separatist aspirations. Initially, this was an expression of constitutional nationalism that was embodied in the protests against conscription in 1918.[111] The identification of Sinn Féin with popular issues in 1917–18 also led to support for more radical policies. Such support, however, was not universal – intimidation, violence and terror were necessary during arms raids beginning in 1917, and after 1918 to enforce the alternative Irish administration and boycott of British institutions. Direct defiance of British rule, such as non-payment of taxes, needed a large measure of enforcement. Nevertheless, the need for public support meant the Irish rarely inflicted serious injuries on innocents and the focus on 'hearts and minds' prevented most injuries from being reported to the British.[112] O'Donoghue wrote 'one thing they [the British] lacked which the IRA had in generous measure – the co-operation of the people and without it they were blind and impotent'.[113]

Indiscriminate violence and terror utilised by the British forces wounded the population to a much greater extent than similar IRA violence, and helped justify the Irish military campaign, at least in international opinion. The 'emotive' effect of the British violence was far stronger. Combined with the fear and intimidation their own violence created, the IRA could safely operate in many areas.[114] In Dublin, the divided loyalty of the population did inspire violence against some anti-republican civilians, but the relatively anonymous environment ensured a relative safe functioning of the IRA. The success of the IRA and the level of violence it directed at the reluctant Irish population and the British depended on two factors: its ability to organise people behind them and the capacity to deal with the opposition it encountered in the community. Those factors, then, were connected with the IRA's integration within the community and the continued support for constitutional or military means of securing Irish independence, but targeted terror was one of the tactics they used.[115]

Collins and the Irish were astute enough to avoid what they saw as excess terror, especially against the common people of Ireland. Collins's restraint, his recognition of the need to conduct the war as much in public opinion as in military action and, most of all, his realism were his strengths. Unlike most guerrilla leaders, he knew when to stop fighting even though he had not achieved all of his goals.

It is important that one does not overestimate nor underestimate the violence of the War of Independence. It was a savage and vicious war on both sides, and both eschewed the norms of war recognised at the time, leading to a breakdown in law. The IRA took great pains to identify itself as the legitimate military arm of a representative Irish government fighting against a foreign invader, but a further examination indicates not only that the Irish used terrorism themselves but also that it was their policy to provoke British terrorism for propaganda and political purposes. The response of the Irish, British and international press to terrorism cannot be overemphasised in explaining Lloyd George's agreement to negotiate with the Irish. In modern terms referencing guerrilla war and terrorism, the Irish succeeded in winning 'the battle of the narrative'.

All wars must teach lessons. If they do not, then they were fought in vain and those who fought them, and those who died, did so for nothing.

The first lesson of the Irish War of Independence concerns the gathering and utilisation of intelligence. Their skill, resourcefulness, cunning, and sometimes luck, provided the Irish with the means to take on a far larger and better-equipped British opponent.

The second lesson is that physical injury and mental anguish bring with them uniquely different problems. Individually, each can cripple. A physical injury suffered as a result of the war immobilised many, whereas psychological trauma incapacitated by inflicting fear or taking away the individual's desire to continue their life. Separately, they were destructive, but taken together they were devastating. After the war ended, the effects of the mass trauma it inflicted lingered across societies for years. For those who suffered through the trauma of the times, all trauma compounds on each other. The terror war ended, but the trauma did not.

Notes

1 R.K. Betts, 'Analysis, war and decision: why intelligence failures are inevitable', *World Politics* **31** (1) (1978).
2 C.Townshend, *The British Campaign in Ireland 1919–1921:The Development of Political and Military Policies* (Oxford, 1975), p. 205.
3 P. Hart (ed.), *British Intelligence in Ireland, 1920–21:The Final Reports* (Cork, 2002), p. 1.
4 R. Popplewell, 'Lacking intelligence: some reflections on recent approaches to British counter-insurgence 1900–1960', *Intelligence and National Security* **10** (2) (1995).
5 J. McGuigan, 'Michael Collins on file?', *History Ireland* **19** (4) (2011).
6 E. O'Halpin, 'Collins and intelligence, 1919–1923', in G. Doherty and D. Keogh (eds), *Michael Collins and the Making of the Irish State* (Cork, 1998), p. 71.
7 Hart, *British Intelligence in Ireland*, p. 11.
8 Memorandum of Richard Mulcahy, IRA Chief of Staff, 7 March 1921, Mulcahy Collection, UCD Archives, P7/A/32.
9 'Record of the rebellion in Ireland in 1920–1921 and the part played by the army in dealing with it', Imperial War Museum, Box 78/82/2.
10 P. McMahon, *British Spies and Irish Rebels—British Intelligence in Ireland: 1916–1945* (Suffolk, 2008), p. 46 *et seq.*
11 'Record of the rebellion in Ireland in 1920–1921'.
12 Macready letter to Greenwood, 27 April 1921, IWM, HHW 32/2D/36.
13 Sir O.Winter, *Winter's Tale* (London, 1955), p. 234.
14 *Ibid.*, p. 16.
15 'Record of the rebellion in Ireland in 1920–1921'.
16 Thomas Treacy: Witness Statement 1093; *Irish Press*, 15 December 1936.
17 C.Townshend, 'The IRA and development of guerrilla war', *English Historical Review* **93** (371) (1979).
18 Report of Warren Fisher to Lloyd George, Lloyd George Papers, F/31/1/32/32-2; M. Foy, *Michael Collins's Intelligence War* (Stroud, 2006; Dublin, 2007), p. 86. See E. O'Halpin, *Head of the Civil Service: A Study of Sir Warren Fisher* (London, 1989).
19 Sir John Anderson Papers, CO 904/188.
20 Sir Alfred Cope: Witness Statement 469.
21 Mark Sturgis Diaries, UK PRO 30.59, 1–5. Sturgis was a British civil servant from the Treasury who was appointed joint Assistant Secretary along with Cope in May 1920. Interestingly, he was not gazetted in that position until after the Truce in July 1921, partially in deference to Cope. His diaries that he kept of this period were published in 1998. He was careful, however, to limit any specific references to Cope's contacts with the leaders of Sinn Féin.
22 J.M. Curran, *The Birth of the Irish Free State, 1921–1923* (Alabama, 1980), p. 424.
23 G. Sloan, 'Hide, seek, and negotiate: Alfred Cope and counterintelligence in Ireland,

1919–1921', *Journal of Intelligence and National Security* **33** (2) (2018).

[24] Mark Sturgis Diaries, PRO 30.59, 1–5.

[25] M. Sturgis (ed. M. Hopkinson), *The Last Days of Dublin Castle: The Mark Sturgis Diaries* (Dublin, 1999), pp 170, 201. For a review of Cope's secretive peace parleys, see Macready letter to Wilson, 19 May 1921, IWM, HHW 2/2D/63. For a discussion of Cope's giving information to the Irish, and an opinion that it was 'treasonous', see Sloan, 'Hide, seek, and negotiate: Alfred Cope and counterintelligence in Ireland, 1919–1921'.

[26] *The Morning Post,* 15 July 1921.

[27] *The Times,* 14 May 1954.

[28] Townshend, *The British Campaign in Ireland*, p. 80.

[29] W. Sheehan, *Hearts and Mines: The British 5th Division, Ireland, 1920–1922* (Cork, 2009), pp 138–9.

[30] Gen. N. Macready, *Annals of an Active Life,* 2 vols (New York, 1925), pp 470–1.

[31] L. Ó Broin, *W.E. Wylie and the Irish Revolution, 1916–1921* (Dublin, 1989), pp 47–53.

[32] 'Report on the Intelligence Branch of the Chief of Police from May 1920 to July 1921', Col. Ormonde de l'Épée Winter, Public Records Office, WO 35/214, p. 13.

[33] *Ibid.*

[34] Notes of a conversation at Downing Street on 30 April 1920, Cabinet minutes, National Archives, CAB 23/21/62.

[35] P. O'Brien, 'Masters of chaos: British Special Forces during the Irish War of Independence', *An Cosantóir* (March 2019).

[36] D. Leeson, 'Imperial stormtroopers: British paramilitaries in the Irish War of Independence, 1920–1921', unpublished Ph.D thesis, McMaster University (2003).

[37] 'The Record of the rebellion in Ireland', WO 141/93.

[38] 'Record of the military situation in Ireland at the end of 1921'.

[39] W.H. Kautt, *Ground Truths. British Army Operations in the Irish War of Independence* (Sallins, 2014), pp 7–8.

[40] Sir Ormonde Winter letter to Cabinet, 1 July 1921, HO 371/60.

[41] 'Memorandum "A" by the Commander-In-Chief, the Forces in Ireland', PRO CAB 24/123.

[42] M. Hopkinson, *The Irish War of Independence* (Dublin, 2002), p. 183.

[43] 'Memorandum by the Chief of the Imperial General Staff', PRO CAB 24/123.

[44] T.E. Lawrence, 'The evolution of a revolt', *Army Quarterly and Defence Journal* (October 1920).

[45] Kautt, *Ground Truths,* p. 5.

[46] 'Record of the rebellion in Ireland in 1920–1921 and the part played by the army in dealing with it, a new campaign: September 1920', Imperial War Museum, Box 78/82/2.

[47] 'Ireland and the general military situation', memorandum by the Secretary of State for War, May 1921, PRO CAB 24/123; T. Jones (ed. K. Middlemas), *Whitehall Diary, Volume III, Ireland 1918–1925* (London, 1971), p. 71.

[48] 'Report by the General Officer Commanding-in-Chief on the situation in Ireland for the week ending 9th July, 1921'.

[49] B.L. Montgomery letter to A.E. Percival, 14 October 1923, Montgomery Papers, Imperial War Museum; Lt Gen. A.E. Percival, two lectures on 'Guerrilla Warfare – Ireland 1920–1921', Imperial War Museum, Folder 411, pp 19–23.

[50] Field Marshal B.L. Montgomery, *The Memoirs of Field Marshal the Viscount Montgomery*

(London, 1958), p. 345.

[51] H. Talbot, *Michael Collins' Own Story* (London, 1923), p. 90.

[52] Field Marshal B. Montgomery, in N. Hamilton, *Monty – The Making of a General* (London, 1982), p. 276.

[53] M. Crenshaw, 'Introduction: reflections on the effect of terrorism', in M. Crenshaw (ed.), *Terrorism, Legitimacy and Power: The Consequences of Political Violence* (Middletown, CT, 1983), p. 5.

[54] A. Merari, 'Terrorism as a strategy of insurgency', *Terrorism and Political Violence* 5 (4) (1993).

[55] W.H. Kautt, *Militarising Policemen. The Various Members of the RIC and their Response to IRA Violence in Ireland, 1919–1921* (2003).

[56] K. Telfer, *The Summer of '45: Stories and Voices from VE Day to VJ Day* (London, 2015), p. 243.

[57] T.E. Lawrence letter to T.E. Leeds, 24 September 1917.

[58] Gen. F. Kitson, *Bunch of Five* (London, 1977), p. 290.

[59] Gen. C. Krulak, quoted in E. Thomas, R. Nordland and C. Caryl, 'Operation Hearts and Minds', *Newsweek*, 29 December 1992/5 January 1993.

[60] B. Lapping, *End of Empire* (London, 1985), p. 224.

[61] N.R. Ampssler, 'Hearts and minds: Malayan campaign re-evaluated', https://www.defenceviewpoints.co.uk/articles-and-analysis/hearts-and-minds-malayan-campaign-re-evaluated.

[62] S.C. Smith, 'General Templer and counter-insurgence in Malaya: hearts and minds, intelligence and propaganda', *Intelligence and National Security* 16 (3) (2001).

[63] R. Stubbs, *Hearts and Minds in Guerrilla Warfare: The Malayan Emergency, 1948–1960 (Singapore, 1989)*, pp 155–64. It must be understood that the Malay insurgency, and Templer's method of combating it, was characterised by geographical and demographic factors that were peculiar to it and were not often possible to replicate in later insurgencies. Under the Briggs Plan employed by Templer, however, the British administration replaced soldiers with civilian police who gained the trust of the community by building long-term relationships. The British also developed an information campaign to portray the police as civil servants whose job it was to protect civilians. By 1953 these efforts had reduced violence and increased trust in the government and have been used in successful counter-insurgency actions ever since to win 'hearts and minds'.

[64] M. Ryan, *Tom Barry: Irish Freedom Fighter* (Cork, 2003), p. 25.

[65] Daniel McDonnell: Witness Statement 486.

[66] Foy, *Michael Collins's Intelligence War*, p. 220.

[67] Commanders in the field mostly disagreed. They thought the IRA was 'winning' and soon would have a military victory. See L. Deasy, *Brother Against Brother* (Cork, 1998), p. 11 *et seq*; E. O'Malley, *The Singing Flame* (Dublin, 1978), p. 13.

[68] C.S. Gray, 'The Anglo-Irish War, 1919–1921: lessons from an irregular conflict', *Comparative Strategy* 26 (5) (2007), available at: DOI: 10.1080/01495930701750208.

[69] Walter Long Papers, PRO 947/308.

[70] Tom Jones Diary, 15 June 1921.

[71] *Ibid*.

[72] Macready, *Annals of an Active Life*, pp 470–90.

[73] Tom Jones Diary, 25 June, 1921; T.P. Coogan, *De Valera, Long Fellow, Long Shadow* (London, 1995), p. 216. For arrest and release of de Valera, see CO 904/23/7.

[74] Documents on Irish Foreign Policy. Reprinted from *Official Correspondence Relating to*

240

the Peace Negotiations June–September 1921 (Dublin, 1921).

[75] Memorandum by Colonel Sir Hugh Elles to the Cabinet. Submitted to the Secretary of State for War, 24 June 1921, PRO CAB/24/185 C.P. 3075.

[76] Mark Sturgis Diaries, UK PRO 30.59, 1–5.

[77] Irish Intelligence Summary, Report No. 259, 1 July 1921, Lloyd George Papers, HGLO, F/46/9/25.

[78] Sir John Anderson letter to Hamar Greenwood, 15 June 1921, PRO CO 904/232.

[79] Sir Basil Thomson to the Cabinet, 23 June 1921, PRO CAB 24/125 CO 3074.

[80] Cabinet discussions, 27 April 1921, in Jones, *Whitehall Diary, Volume III*, p. 53-55.

[81] Frank Thornton: Witness Statement 615.

[82] R. Taylor, *Michael Collins* (London, 1958; 1970), p. 110.

[83] Letter from Andy Cope to Tom Jones, 24 August 1921, Tom Jones Papers, National University of Wales.

[84] Gray, 'The Anglo-Irish War, 1919–1921: lessons from an irregular conflict'.

[85] Townshend, 'The IRA and development of guerrilla war'.

[86] *An tÓglach*, 6 May 1921.

[87] M.R. Cremin, 'Fighting on their own terms: the tactics of the Irish Republican Army 1919–1921', *Small Wars and Insurgencies* 26 (6) (2015).

[88] E. O'Malley, *On Another Man's Wound* (Dublin, 1936; 1979), p. 326.

[89] M. Brennan, *The War in Clare 1911–1921: Personal Memoirs of the Irish War of Independence* (Dublin, 1980), pp 80–1.

[90] B. Fall, 'The theory and practice of counterinsurgency', *Naval War College Review* (April 1965).

[91] Gray, 'The Anglo-Irish War 1919–1921: Lessons from an Irregular Conflict'.

[92] G. Adrian, *The Age of Terrorism and the International Political System* (London, 1995), p. 172.

[93] R. English, *Does Terrorism Work?* (Oxford, 2016), p. 30.

[94] E. Chenowith and M. Stephan, *Why Civil Resistance Works* (New York, 2011), p. 14.

[95] C. Townshend, *Terrorism: A Very Short Introduction* (Oxford, 2002), p. 8; 'The process of terror in Irish politics', in N. O'Sullivan (ed.), *Terrorism, Ideology and Revolution* (Brighton, 1986), p. 339.

[96] R. Fanning, *Fatal Path* (London, 2013), pp 1–6, 356–8.

[97] J.B. Bell, *The Secret Army* (London, 1972), pp 62–71.

[98] C.E. Callwell, *Small Wars: Their Principles and Practice* (London, 1903), p. 126.

[99] F. O'Donoghue, 'Guerilla warfare in Ireland 1919–1921', *An Cosantoir* 23(1963).

[100] M. Boot, *Invisible Armies: An Epic History of Guerrilla Warfare from Ancient Times to Present* (New York, 2013), pp 246–59.

[101] See R. English, *Terrorism: How To Respond* (Oxford, 2009).

[102] C. Mattern, 'Strange creatures are we, even to ourselves: understanding insurgency and counterinsurgency efforts in the Irish War of Independence', *Small Wars Journal* (20 October 2019).

[103] T.P. Coogan, *Michael Collins, The Man Who Made Ireland* (London, 1992), pp xi–xii.

[104] P. Gudgin, *Military Intelligence: The British Story* (London, 1989), p. 52.

[105] Townshend, 'The IRA and development of guerrilla war'.

[106] O'Halpin, 'Collins and intelligence 1919–1923'.

[107] Hart, *British Intelligence in Ireland,* p. 13.

[108] P. Hart, *The I.R.A. at War, 1916–1923* (Oxford, 2003). pp 3–4.

[109] M. Boot, 'Kick the bully: Michael Collins launches the War of Independence'

http://www.historynet.com/kick-the-bully-michael-collins-launches-the-1921-irish-rebellion.htm.

[110] H. Kissinger, 'The Viet Nam negotiations', *Foreign Affairs* (January, 1969).

[111] K. Griffith and T. O'Grady, *Ireland's Unfinished Revolution, An Oral History* (London, 1982) [originally published as *Curious Journey, An Oral History of Ireland's Unfinished Revolution*], p. 33.

[112] J. Augusteijn, *From Public Defiance to Guerrilla Warfare: the Experience of Ordinary Volunteers in the Irish War of Independence* (Dublin, 1996), p. 277.

[113] F. O'Donoghue, 'Guerilla warfare in Ireland', *An Cosantoir* (1963).

[114] B. Ryan, *A Full Private Remembers the Troubled Times* (Hollyford, 1969), p. 40.

[115] Augusteijn, *From Public Defiance to Guerrilla Warfare*, p. 334.

Select bibliography

Newspaper and archive sources
An t'Óglach.
Birmingham Post.
Cork Examiner.
The Daily Mail.
Freeman's Journal.
History Ireland.
Imperial War Museum.
Irish Bulletin.
Irish Citizen.
Irish Exile.
Irish Independent.
Irish Press.
The Irish Times.
London Daily Herald.
Manchester Guardian.
Military Archives, Cathal Brugha Barracks, Military Service Pension
    Collection (MSPC).
Military Archives, Cathal Brugha Barracks, Records of the Irish Grants
    Commission.
Military Archives, Cathal Brugha Barracks, Witness Statements.
Montreal Gazette.
National Library of Ireland (NLI).
New Statesman.
The New York Times.
Public Record Office, Kew, London (now the National Archives).
The Times.
Weekly Standard.

Primary sources

The American Commission on Conditions in Ireland, Interim Report (1921).

'Arrangements governing the cessation of active operations in Ireland which came into force on 11 July 1921', 1921 CMD, 1534 XXIX 427.

Ernest Blythe Papers, University College Library.

British Cabinet, 'Irish situation committee reports and minutes, 1920–1921', Cabinet Series No. 23 and 27.

British Cabinet, 'Weekly survey of the state of Ireland memorandum', 29 July 1921, PRO CAB 24/126/72.

British Parliamentary Archive Papers, 'The Irish uprising, 1914–1921'.

Cathal Brugha Papers, University College Library.

Máire Ní Shuibhne Brugha Papers, University College Library.

Dáil Éireann, Minutes of Proceedings of the First Parliament of the Republic of Ireland, 1919–1921.

Dáil Éireann, Correspondence Relating to Peace Negotiations, June–September 1921.

Department of Foreign Affairs, *Documents on Irish Foreign Policy* (ed. C. Crowe, R. Fanning, M. Kennedy, D. Keogh, E. O'Halpin), National Archives.

Department of Foreign Affairs, *The Anglo-Irish Treaty December 1920–December 1921* (ed. C. Crowe, R. Fanning, M. Kennedy, D. Keogh, E. O'Halpin), National Archives.

Directorate of Intelligence, 'Report on revolutionary organisations in the United Kingdom', 20 May 1920, NAUK CAB 24/106/110.

Frank Gallagher Papers, National Library of Ireland.

General Staff, Irish Command, 'The Irish Republican Army (from captured documents only)', June 1921, PRO WO 141/40.

Hicks, W.W., 'Memorandum on British Secret Service Activities in this Country, November 2, 1920', Doc. 9771-745-45, Declassification no. 740058, 15 April 1987.

Intelligence Notes, 1913–1916: Preserved in the State Paper Office, edited by Breandán Mac Giolla Choille (Dublin: Oifig an tSoláthair, 1966).

'Ireland and the general military situation', Memorandum by the Secretary of State for War, May 1921, PRO CAB 24/123.

Irish Intelligence Summary, Special Supplementary Report 259, 1 July

1921.

'The Irish situation', Memorandum by the Secretary of State for War, 3 November 1920, PRO CAB 23/23/2.

Lt Gen. Sir Hugh Jeudwine Papers, Imperial War Museum, Box 72/82/2.

Captain Robert Jeune Papers, PRO 76/172/1.

Labour Party of Great Britain, *The Report of the Labour Commission in Ireland* (London, 1921).

Walter Long Papers, PRO 947/308.

Nevil Macready correspondence with Field Marshal Henry Wilson, Imperial War Museum.

Macready Committee Report, Cabinet Paper 1317, 19 May 1919, 'Formation of a special force for service in Ireland', PRO WO 32/9517.

'Memorandum on the procedure, examination of, certification and assessment of claims under the Military Service Pension Act, 1934', undated, *c.* 1942, S 9243, TSCH, NAI.

'The Military situation in Ireland', Memorandum by Colonel Sir Hugh Elles, 24 June 1921, PRO CAB 24/125/77.

General Richard Mulcahy Papers, University College Dublin. Following the publishing of Piaras Béaslaí's book *Michael Collins and the Making of a New Ireland* in 1927, many contested Béaslaí's views. In the 1950s Risteard Mulcahy, son of the general, asked General Mulcahy to read the book and to annotate it. General Mulcahy's descriptions of Collins show his development as a leader and how their relationship ripened. Mulcahy's notes covered two volumes compiled by his son. General Mulcahy's comments are cited in endnotes as 'Béaslaí critique, Vol. __, p. __'.

National Graves Association, *The Last Post* (New York, 1986).

Batt O'Connor Papers, University College Library.

Rory O'Connor Papers, University College Library.

Florence O'Donoghue Papers, National Library of Ireland.

Duirmuid O'Hegarty Papers, University College Library.

Seán T. O'Kelly Papers, National Library of Ireland.

Ernie O'Malley Papers, including the 'Ernie O'Malley Notebooks', University College Library.

'Outrages, Ireland', Cmd 63 and 709 (1920).

'Outrages, Ireland. Return showing the number of serious outrages',

Cmd 1165 (1921).

Lt Gen. A.E. Percival Papers, 'Guerrilla warfare in Ireland, 1919–1921', Imperial War Museum, Folder 411.

'The present military situation in Ireland and the proposed military policy during the coming winter', Memorandum by General Nevil Macready, 6 August 1920 PRO CAB 24/110/50.

'Record of the rebellion in Ireland in 1920–1921 and the part played by the army in dealing with it', Imperial War Museum, Box 78/82/2.

'Report by the General Officer Commanding-in-Chief, the situation in Ireland for the week ending 14th May 1921', PRO CAB 24/123.

'Report by the General Officer Commanding-in-Chief on the situation in Ireland for the week ending 9th July 1921', PRO CAB 24/131.

Report of the Proceedings of the Irish Convention (Dublin: His Majesty's Stationery Office, 1918).

'Report on Bloody Sunday', PRO WO 35/38.

'Report on the Intelligence Branch of the Chief of Police from May 1920 to July 1921', Colonel Ormonde de l'Epee Winter, PRO WO 35/214.

'Report on revolutionary organisations, 23 June, 7 July 1921', PRO CAM 24/125, 126.

Royal Commission on the Rebellion in Ireland, Report (1916), Cmd. 8279, Minutes of Evidence, Cmd 8311.

Royal Irish Constabulary, Auxiliary Division Register, PRO HO 184/50–1.

Royal Irish Constabulary List and Directory (Dublin: His Majesty's Stationery Office, 1920).

Royal Irish Constabulary Manual or Guide to the Discharge of Police Duties (Dublin: His Majesty's Stationery Office, 1909).

Hanna Sheehy-Skeffington, 'Statement on atrocities against women in Ireland', NLI ILB 300.

Sinn Féin Party Papers, University College Dublin Library.

Sinn Féin and Other Republican Suspects 1899–1921: Dublin Castle Special Branch Files CO 904 (193–216), the United Kingdom, Colonial Office Record Series Vol. 1 (Dublin, 2006).

General Sir E.P. Strickland Papers, 'The Irish rebellion in the 6th Divisional Area: from after the 1916 Rebellion to December 1921', Imperial War Museum.

Mark Sturgis Diaries, PRO 30.59, 1–5.

U.S. Army Field Manual FM 3–25, *Counterinsurgency* (2006).

U.S. Department of Defense, *Counterinsurgency*, Joint Publication 3–24 (22 November 2013).

Sir Henry Wilson Papers, Imperial War Museum, DS/MISC/80, HHW/2/2B.

Online sources

Ampssler, N.R., 'Hearts and minds: Malayan campaign re-evaluated', https://www.defenceviewpoints.co.uk/articles-and-analysis/hearts-and-minds-malayan-campaign-re-evaluated.

The Auxiliaries (Auxiliary Division of the Royal Irish Constabulary), www.theauxiliaries.com/index.html.

Benest, Col. D., OBE, 'British Atrocities in Counter Insurgency', https://www.militaryethics.org/British-Atrocities-in-Counter-Insurgency/10/.

Boot, M., 'Kick the bully: Michael Collins launches the War of Independence', http://www.historynet.com/kick-the-bully-michael-collins-launches-the-1921-irish-rebellion.htm.

'Ned Broy: the greatest spy of Ireland's freedom struggle', https://youtu.be/E1IEl7NArLw.

Bloody Sunday – Initial Press Reports, http://www.gaa.ie/centenary/bloody-sunday-archive/1920-initial-press-report-bloody-sunday/.

Bureau of Military History Pension Collection, http://www.bureauofmilitaryhistory.ie/bmhsearch/search.jsp; http://www.militaryarchives.ie/collections/online-collections/military-service-pensions-collection/search-the-collection.

Connolly, L., 'Did women escape the worst of the brutalities between 1919–1921?', Maynooth University Social Sciences Institute (September 2017), https://www.maynoothuniversity.ie/research/research-news-events/latest-news/did-women-escape-worst-brutalities-between-1919-1921.

Connolly, L., 'Towards a further understanding of the violence experienced by women in the Irish Revolution', Maynooth University Social Sciences Institute (January 2019), http://mural.maynoothuniversity.ie/10416/1/Linda%20Connolly_final.pdf.

Connolly, L., 'Hair taking: a weapon of war in Ireland's War of Independence?', *RTE Brainstorm* (February 2020), https://www.rte.ie/brainstorm/2020/0212/1115001-how-forced-hair-cutting-was-used-as-a-weapon-of-war-in-ireland/.

Donovan, S., 'The multiple functions of terrorism: how the IRA used terrorism to resist British control while the British utilized terror to conquer the Irish people', https://www.trentu.ca.undergratuate/documents//S.Donovan.doc.

Gannon, S., 'The Black and Tans in Palestine – Irish connections to the Palestine Police 1922–1948', *The Irish Story* (20 February 2020), https://www.theirishstory.com/2020/02/20/the-black-and-tans-in-palestine-irish-connections-to-the-palestine-police-1922-1948/#.Xps24shKjGg.

Guevara, C., *Principles of Guerrilla Warfare,* http://www3.uakron.edu/worldciv/pascher/che.html.

Keane, B., 'The IRA response to loyalist co-operation during the Irish War of Independence, 1919–1921', https://www.academia.edu/27954537/The_IRA_response_to_loyalist_co-operation_in_County_Cork_during_the_Irish_War_of_Independence.

Keown, B., '"I would rather have my own mind": the medicalization of women's behavior in Ireland, 1914–1920', *Nursing Clio* (25 October 2017), https://nursingclio.org/2017/10/25/i-would-rather-have-my-own-mind-themedicalization-of-womens-behavior-in-ireland-1914-1920/.

Macmillan, M., Reith Lectures, https://www.cbc.ca/radio/ideas/making-sense-of-the-warrior-the-reith-lectures-by-margaret-macmillan-1.4852055.

Masterson, D., 'Opinion: remembrance and reconciliation: heroes in the Irish War of Independence', *The Irish Story* (13 March 2014), https://www.theirishstory.com/2014/03/13/opinion-remembrance-and-reconciliation-heroes-in-the-irish-war-of-independence/#.Xps92MhKjGg.

Mathewson, J.J., 'How have the wars in Afghanistan and Iraq impacted the troops, their families, and the mental health community', https://www.counseling.org/docs/default-source/vistas/how-have-the-wars-in-iraq-and-afghanistan-impacted-the-troops.pdf?sfvrsn=28496b0b_14.

Mattern, C., '"Strange Creatures we are, even to ourselves": understanding insurgency and counterinsurgency efforts in the Irish War of Independence', *Small Wars Journal* (20 October 2019), https://smallwarsjournal.com/jrnl/art/strange-creatures-we-are-even-ourselves-understanding-insurgency-and-counterinsurgency.

Morrison, E., 'The Bureau of Military History as a source for the Irish Revolution' (2012), https://www.militaryarchives.ie/collections/online-collections/bureau-of-military-history-1913-1921/wp-content/uploads/2019/06/Bureau_of_Military_witness_statements-as_sources-for_the_Irish-Revolution.pdf.

Norman, S.B. and Maguen, S., 'Moral injury', PTSD: National Center for PTSD, https://www.ptsd.va.gov/professional/treat/cooccurring/moral_injury.asp.

Ward, M., 'Hair cutting and women in the Irish War of Independence', *The Irish Story*, 31 January 2020, https://www.theirishstory.com/2020/01/31/hair-cutting-and-women-in-the-war-of-independence/#.XpyPnchKjGg.

Secondary sources

Abbott, R., *Police Casualties in Ireland, 1919–1922* (Cork, 2000).

Adams, G., *The Politics of Irish Freedom* (Dingle, 1986).

Adrian, G., *The Age of Terrorism and the International Political System* (London, 1995).

Aiken, S., 'The women who had been straining every nerve: gender-specific medical management of trauma in the Irish Revolution (1916–1923)', in M. Terrazas Gallego (ed.), *Trauma and Identity in Contemporary Irish Culture* (Bern, 2019).

Ainsworth, J., 'British security policy in Ireland, 1920–1921: a desperate attempt by the Crown to maintain Anglo-Irish unity by force', Queensland University of Technology, School of Humanities and Social Science, 11th Irish–Australian Conference (25–30 April 2000).

Ainsworth, J., 'The Black & Tans and Auxiliaries in Ireland, 1920–1921: their origins, roles and legacy', paper presented to the Queensland History Teachers' Association, Brisbane, Queensland (12 May 2001).

Alexander, Y. and O'Day, A. (eds), *Ireland's Terrorist Dilemma* (Dartrecht, 1986).

Andrew, C., *Her Majesty's Secret Service: The Making of the British Intelligence*

249

Community (New York, 1986).

Andrew, C. and Dilks, D. (eds), *The Missing Dimension. Governments and Intelligence Communities in the Twentieth Century* (London, 1984).

Andrews, C.S., *Dublin Made Me* (Cork, 1979).

Arreguin-Toft, I., *How the Weak Win Wars: A Theory of Asymmetric Conflict* (Cambridge, 2005).

Asprey, R., *War in the Shadows* (London, 1994).

Augusteijn, J., *From Public Defiance to Guerrilla Warfare: The Experience of Ordinary Volunteers in the Irish War of Independence* (Dublin, 1996).

Augusteijn, J. (ed.), *The Irish Revolution* (Basingstoke, 2002).

Augusteijn, J., 'Political violence and democracy: an analysis of the tensions within Irish republican strategy, 1914–2002', *Irish Political Studies* **18** (1) (2003).

Bakunin, M., *Bakunin on Anarchism* (Montreal, 1980).

Ball, S. (ed.), *A Policeman's Ireland: Recollections of Samuel Waters, RIC* (Cork, 1999).

Barry, T., *Guerilla Days in Ireland* (Dublin, 1949).

Barry, T., *'The Reality of the Anglo-Irish War, 1920–21 in West Cork': Refutations, Corrections, and Comments on Liam Deasy's 'Towards Ireland Free'* (Tralee, 1974).

Bartlett, T. and Jeffrey, K. (eds), *A Military History of Ireland* (Cambridge, 1996).

Baxter, R.R., 'So-called "Unprivileged Belligerancy": spies, guerrillas and saboteurs', *British Yearbook of International Law* **28** (1951)

Beal, E.W., MD, *War Stories from the Forgotten Soldiers* (Virginia Beach, 2019).

Béaslaí, P., *How It Was Done—I.R.A. Intelligence: Dublin's Fighting Story* (London, 1926).

Béaslaí, P., *Michael Collins and the Making of a New Ireland* (London, 1926).

Béaslaí, P., 'The Anglo-Irish War', in G. Doherty (ed.), *With the IRA in the Fight for Freedom* (1970 edn).

Beckett, I.W.F., *Modern Insurgencies and Counter-insurgencies: Guerrillas and their Opponents since 1750* (London, 2001).

Bell, J.B., *The Secret Army* (London, 1972).

Bell, J.B., 'Revolts against the Crown: the British response to imperial insurgency', *Parameters (Journal of the Army War College)* **9** (1) (1974).

Bell, J.B., *The Gun in Politics: An Analysis of Irish Political Conflict, 1916–*

1986 (New Brunswick, 1991).

Bennett, R., *The Black and Tans: The British Special Police in Ireland* (New York, 1959).

Benton, S., 'Women disarmed: the militarisation of politics in Ireland, 1913–1923', *Feminist Review* 50 (1995).

Betts, R.K., 'Analysis, war and decision: why intelligence failures are inevitable', *World Politics* 31 (1) (1978).

Bielenberg, A., 'Protestant emigration from the south of Ireland, 1911–1926', lecture given at 'Understanding our History: Protestants, the War of Independence, and the Civil War in Cork', Conference at University College Cork (13 December 2008).

Boot, M., *Invisible Armies: An Epic History of Guerrilla Warfare from Ancient Times to Present* (New York, 2013).

Borgonovo, J., 'Revolutionary violence and Irish historiography', *Irish Historical Studies* 38 (150) (1996).

Borgonovo, J. (ed.), *Florence and Josephine O'Donoghue's War of Independence: A Destiny that Shapes our Ends* (Cork, 2006).

Borgonovo, J., *Spies, Informers and the Anti-Sinn Féin Society* (Dublin, 2008).

Borgonovo, J., 'Separating fact from folklore: in the name of the Republic', *Irish Examiner* (27 March 2013).

Bourke, J., *An Intimate History of Killing: Face-to-Face Killing in Twentieth Century Warfare* (Granta, 1999).

Bourke, J., *Rape: Sex, Violence, History* (New York, 2007).

Bowden, T., 'Bloody Sunday, a reappraisal', *European Studies Review* 2 (1) (1972).

Bowden, T., 'The Irish underground and the War of Independence 1919–1921', *Journal of Contemporary History* 8 (2) (1973).

Bowden, T., 'Ireland: the impact of terror', in M. Elliott-Batemen, J. Ellis and T. Bowden (eds), *Revolt to Revolution: Studies in the 19th and 20th Century Experience* (Manchester, 1974).

Bowden, T., 'The I.R.A. and the changing tactics of terrorism', *Political Quarterly* 47 (1976).

Bowden, T., *The Breakdown of Public Security: The Case of Ireland 1916–1921 and Palestine 1936–1939* (London, 1977).

Bowden, T., *Beyond the Limits of the Law* (Harmondsworth, 1978).

Boyce, D.G., *Englishmen and Irish Troubles: British Public Opinion and the*

Making of Irish Policy: 1918–1922 (Cambridge, MA, 1972).

Brady, E., *Ireland's Secret Service in England* (Dublin, 1924).

Breen, D., *My Fight for Irish Freedom* (Dublin, 1924).

Brennan, M., *The War in Clare 1911–1921: Personal Memoirs of the Irish War of Independence* (Dublin, 1980).

Brennan, N., 'A political minefield: southern Irish loyalists, the Irish Grants Committee, and the British government, 1922–31', *Irish Historical Journal* 30 (119) (1997).

Brewer, J.D., *The Royal Irish Constabulary: An Oral History* (Belfast, 1990).

Brinton, C., *The Anatomy of Revolution* (New York, 1948).

Browne, C., *The Story of the 7th. A Concise History of the 7th Battalion Cork No. 1 Brigade I.R.A. from 1915–1921* (Macroom, 1971).

Burleigh, M., *Blood and Rage: A Cultural History of Terrorism* (New York, 2009).

Butler, E., *Barry's Flying Column* (London, 1971).

Byrne, L.E., 'The rape of Mary M.: a microhistory of sexual violence and moral redemption in 1920s Ireland', *Journal of the History of Sexuality* 24 (1) (2015).

Callwell, C.E., *Small Wars: Their Principles and Practice* (London, 1903).

Callwell, Major Gen. Sir C.E., *Field Marshall Sir Henry Wilson: His Life and Diaries* (2 vols) (London, 1927).

Campbell, C., *Emergency Law in Ireland, 1918–1925* (Oxford, 1994).

Carey, T. and de Burca, M., 'Bloody Sunday 1920: new evidence', *History Ireland* 11 (2) (2003).

Carroll, F.M., *American Opinion and the Irish Question, 1910–1923* (Dublin, 1978).

Carroll, F.M. (ed.), *The American Commission on Irish Independence 1919. The Diary, Correspondence and Report* (Dublin, 1985).

Caruth, C., *Unclaimed Experience: Trauma, Narrative and History* (Baltimore, 2010).

Chenowith, E. and Stephan, M., *Why Civil Resistance Works* (New York, 2011).

Chesterton, G.K., *What are Reprisals?* (pamphlet, undated, no place of publication).

Clark, G., *Everyday Violence in the Irish Civil War* (Cambridge, 2014).

Clarke, K., *Revolutionary Woman* (Dublin, 1991).

Von Clausewitz, C. (ed. and trans. M. Howard and P. Paret), *On War*

(Princeton, 1984).

Clutterbuck, R., *Guerrillas and Terrorists* (Athens, OH, 1980).

Clutterbuck, R., *Terrorism and Guerrilla Warfare* (London, 1990).

Coleman, M., *The Irish Revolution, 1916–1923* (Dublin, 2013).

Coleman, M., 'Military service pensions for veterans of the Irish Revolution, 1916–1923', *War in History* 20 (2013).

Coleman, M., 'Violence against women in the Irish War of Independence, 1919–1921', in D. Ferriter and S. Riordan (eds), *Years of Turbulence: The Irish Revolution and its Aftermath* (Dublin, 2015).

Coleman, M., 'Women escaped the worst of the brutalities in the War of Independence', *Irish Examiner* (27 November 2015).

Coleman, M., 'Compensating Irish female revolutionaries, 1916–1923', *Women's History Review* 26 (6) (2017).

Collins, M., *The Path to Freedom* (Dublin, 1922).

Collins, M. (ed. F. Costello), *Michael Collins: In His Own Words* (Dublin, 1997).

Comerford, M., 'Women in struggle', *Éire Amach na Casca* (pamphlet, Republication Publications, 1986).

Conlon, L., *Cumann na mBan and the Women of Ireland, 1913–1972* (Kilkenny, 1969).

Connolly, L., *The Irish Women's Movement* (New York, 2002; Dublin 2003).

Connolly, L., 'Sexual violence a dark secret in the Irish War of Independence and Civil War', *Irish Times* (10 January 2019).

Connolly, L., 'Sexual violence in the Irish Civil War: a forgotten war crime?', *Women's History Review* (2020) (DOI 10.1080/09612025. 2020.1735613).

Connors, J., *Seán Hogan. His Life: A Troubled Journey* (Tipperary, 2019).

Coogan, T.P., *Michael Collins, The Man Who Made Ireland* (London, 1992).

Coogan, T.P., *De Valera, Long Fellow, Long Shadow* (London, 1995).

Costello, F., 'The republican courts and the decline of British rule in Ireland, 1920–1921', *Éire-Ireland* 25 (2) (1990).

Costigan, G., 'The Anglo-Irish conflict, 1919–1921: a war of independence or systematized murder?', *University Review* 5 (1) (1968).

Coyle, A. (ed.), *Evidence of Conditions in Ireland, Comprising the Complete Testimony, Affidavits, and Exhibits placed before the American Commission on Conditions in Ireland* (Washington, 1921).

Cremin, M.R., 'Fighting on their own terms: the tactics of the Irish Republican Army 1919–1921', *Small Wars and Insurgencies* **26** (6) (2015).

Crenshaw, M., 'The causes of terrorism', *Comparative Politics* **13** (4) (1981).

Crenshaw, M. (ed.), *Terrorism, Legitimacy and Power: The Consequences of Political Violence* (Middletown, CT, 1983).

Crenshaw, M. (ed.), *Terrorism in Context* (Pennsylvania, 2005).

Crenshaw, M., *Explaining Terrorism: Causes, Processes, and Consequences* (London, 2011).

Cronin, M., Duncan, M. and Rouse, P., *The GAA: A People's History* (Cork, 2009).

Cronin, S., *Three Murders in Dublin Castle* (Dublin, 2002).

Crowe, C. (ed.), *Guide to the Military Service (1916–1923) Pensions Collection* (Dublin, 2012).

Crozier, General F.P., *Impressions and Recollections* (London, 1930).

Crozier, General F.P., *Ireland Forever* (London, 1932).

Crozier, General F.P., *The Men I Killed* (London, 1937).

Cuenca-Sanchez, I., 'The dynamics of nationalist terrorism: ETA and the IRA', *Terrorism and Political Violence* **19** (2007).

Cullen, M. and Luddy, M., *Female Activists, Irish Women and the Change, 1900–1960* (Dublin, 2001).

Curran, J.M., *The Birth of the Irish Free State, 1921–1923* (Alabama, 1980).

Curtis, L., 'Ireland', *Round Table* **11** (43) (1920–1).

Dalton, C., *With the Dublin Brigade* (London, 1929).

Danzer, M., 'The political consequences of terrorism: a comparative study of France and the United Kingdom', unpublished Masters dissertation, University of Bucharest (2019).

Darby, J., *Intimidation and the Control of Conflict* (Syracuse, NY, 1986).

Dawson, R., *Red Terror and Green* (London, 1920, 1972).

Deasy, L., *Towards Ireland Free* (Cork, 1973).

Deasy, L., *Brother Against Brother* (Cork, 1998).

Delaney, E. and Luddy, M. (eds), *Reappraisals in Irish History* (Liverpool, 2016).

De Montmorency, H., *Sword and Stirrup* (London, 1936).

Denning, B., 'Modern problems of guerrilla warfare', *Army Quarterly* (January 1927).

Dennis, P. and Grey, J. (eds), *An Art in Itself: The Theory and Conduct of*

Small Wars and Insurgencies, Australian Army Military Conference (Sydney, 2006).

Dolan, A., 'Killing and Bloody Sunday, November 1920', *Historical Journal* 49 (3) (2006).

Dolan, A., 'The British culture of paramilitary violence', in R. Gerwarth and J. Horne (eds), *War in Peace: Paramilitary Violence in Europe after World War I* (Oxford, 2012).

Dolan, A., 'The shadow of a great fear: terror and revolutionary Ireland', in D. Fitzpatrick (ed.), *Terror in Ireland* (Dublin, 2012).

Dolan, A., 'Spies and informers beware …', in D. Ferriter and S. Riordan (eds), *Years of Turbulence: the Irish Revolution and its Aftermath* (Dublin, 2015).

Donnelly, J.S. Jnr, '"Unofficial" British reprisals and IRA provocation, 1919–1920: the cases of three Cork towns', *Éire-Ireland* 45 (1) (2010).

Dorney, J., 'How the Civil War "murder gang" tried to take over as judge, jury and executioners', *Irish Independent* (20 August 2017).

Dowdell, E.S., 'Ireland under the new terror: what it means to live under martial law', *The London Magazine* (1921).

Doyle, E.J., 'The employment of terror in the forgotten insurgency: Ireland 1919–1922', unpublished Masters dissertation, U.S. Defense Intelligence College, Bethesda, MD (1969).

Draper, G.I.A.D., 'The status of combatants and the question of guerrilla warfare', *British Year Book of International Law* 45 (1971).

Duff, D., *Sword for Hire* (London, 1934).

Dwyer, T.R., *Tans, Terror and Troubles: Kerry's Real Fighting Story, 1913–1923* (Cork, 2001).

Dwyer, T.R., *The Squad and the Intelligence Operations of Michael Collins* (Cork, 2005).

Dwyer, T.R., 'When the horror of war hits homes', *Irish Examiner* (25 March 2013).

Elliott-Bateman, M., 'Ireland: the impact of terror', in M. Elliott-Bateman, J. Ellis and J. Bowman (eds), *Revolt to Revolution – Studies in the 19th and 20th Century European Experience* (Manchester, 1974).

English, R., *Ernie O'Malley. I.R.A. Intellectual* (Oxford, 1998).

English, R., *Armed Struggle: A History of the I.R.A* (London, 2003).

English, R., *Terrorism: How To Respond* (Oxford, 2009).

English, R., *Does Terrorism Work?* (Oxford, 2016).

English, R. (ed.), *Illusions of Terrorism and Counter-Terrorism* (Oxford, 2016).

Fagan, T. (ed.), *Rebels and Heroes. Hidden Stories from Dublin's Northside* (Dublin, 2016).

Fall, B., 'The theory and practice of counterinsurgency', *Naval War College Review* (April 1965).

Fanning, R., 'Leadership and transition from the politics of revolution to the politics of party: the example of Ireland,1914–1939', paper delivered to the International Congress of Historical Societies, San Francisco (27 August 1975).

Fanning, R., 'Michael Collins – an overview', in G. Doherty and D. Keogh (eds), *Michael Collins and the Making of the Irish Free State* (Cork, 1998).

Fanning, R., *Fatal Path* (London, 2013).

Fennell, T., *The Royal Irish Constabulary: A History and Personal Memoir* (Dublin, 2003).

Fierro, M.R., 'British counterinsurgency operations in Ireland 1916–1921: a case study', unpublished Masters dissertation, US Naval War College, Newport, RI (1997).

Figgis, D., *Recollections of the Irish War* (London, 1927).

Finnane, M., *Insanity and the Insane in Post-Famine Ireland* (Croom Helm, 1981).

Fishel, J.T. and Manwaring, M.G., 'The SWORD model of counterinsurgency: a summary and update', *Small Wars Journal* (2008).

Fitzgerald, T.E., 'The execution of spies and informers in West Cork, 1921', in D. Fitzpatrick (ed.), *Terror in Ireland* (Dublin, 2012).

Fitzpatrick, D., *Politics and Irish Life, 1913–1921: Provincial Experience of War and Revolution* (Dublin, 1977).

Fitzpatrick, D., 'Ireland since 1870', in R.F. Foster (ed.), *The Oxford Illustrated History of Ireland* (Oxford, 1989).

Fitzpatrick, D., 'Militarism in Ireland, 1900–1922', in T. Bartlett and K. Jeffery (eds), *A Military History of Ireland* (Cambridge, 1997).

Fitzpatrick, D., 'The price of Balbriggan', in D. Fitzpatrick (ed.), *Terror in Ireland* (Dublin, 2012).

Fitzpatrick, D. (ed.), *Terror in Ireland, 1916–1923* (Dublin, 2012).

Foley, M., *The Bloodied Field* (Dublin, 2014).

Foot, M.R.D., 'Michael Collins and irregular warfare', lecture given to the Irish Military History Society (1969).

Foot, M.R.D., 'The IRA and the origins of the SOE', *War and Society: Historical Essays in Honour and Memory of J.R. Western 1928–1971* (New York, 1973).

Foot, M.R.D., 'The Irish experience', in M. Elliott-Batemen, J. Ellis and T. Bowden (eds), *Revolt to Revolution: Studies in the 19th and 20th Century European Experience* (Manchester, 1974).

Forester, M., *Michael Collins, The Lost Leader* (Dublin, 1989).

Foster, G., 'Ordinary brutalities', *Dublin Review of Books* (October 2017).

Foster, R.F., *Modern Ireland, 1600–1972* (London, 1988).

Fox, R.M., *Rebel Irishwomen* (Dublin, 1935).

Foy, M.T., *Michael Collins's Intelligence War* (Stroud, 2006; Dublin, 2007).

Fraser, T.G. and Jeffery, K. (eds), *Men, Women and War* (Dublin, 1993).

Fromkin, D., 'The strategy of terrorism', *Foreign Affairs* 53 (4) (1975).

Gallagher, F. (writing as David Hogan), *Four Glorious Years* (Dublin, 1953).

Gallagher, F., *The Anglo-Irish Treaty* (London, 1965).

Gannon, D., 'The Irish Revolution in Great Britain', in J. Crowley, D. Ó Drisceoil and M. Murphy (eds), *Atlas of the Irish Revolution* (Cork, 2017).

Gardiner, A.G., 'Stop the terror', *Daily News* (6 November 1920).

Garvin, T., *1922: The Birth of Irish Democracy* (Dublin, 1996).

Gaucher, R., *The Terrorists* (London, 1968).

Giáp, V.N., *People's War, People's Army, The Military Art of People's War* (New York, 1971).

Gleeson, J., *Bloody Sunday* (London, 1962).

Gough, General H., 'The situation in Ireland', *Review of Reviews* 63 (1921).

Gray, B. and Ryan, L., 'Dislocation "woman" and women in representations of Irish nationality', in A. Byrne and M. Leonard (eds), *Women and Irish Society: A Sociological Reader* (Belfast, 1997).

Gray, C.S., 'The Anglo-Irish War, 1919–1921: lessons from an irregular conflict', *Comparative Strategy* 26 (5) (2007) (DOI: 10.1080/01495930701750208).

Griffith, K. and O'Grady, T., *Ireland's Unfinished Revolution, An Oral History* (London, 1982) [originally published as *Curious Journey, An Oral History of Ireland's Unfinished Revolution*].

257

Griffith, P., 'Small wars and how they grow in the telling', *Small Wars and Insurgencies* **2** (2) (1991).

Grog-Fitzgibbon, B., *Turning Points of the Irish Revolution. The British Government, Intelligence and the Cost of Indifference, 1912–1921* (London, 2008).

Gudgin, P., *Military Intelligence: The British Story* (London, 1989).

Hamilton, N., *Monty – The Making of a General* (London, 1982).

Hammes, Col. T.X., 'The way to win a guerrilla war', *Washington Post* (26 November 2006).

Hammond, J.L., 'A tragedy of errors', *The Nation* (8 January 1921).

Hammond, J.L., 'The terror in action', *The Nation* (30 April 1921).

Hanley, B., 'The rhetoric of republican legitimacy' in F. McGarry (ed.), *Republicanism in Modern Ireland* (Dublin, 2003).

Hanley, B., 'Terror in twentieth-century Ireland', in D. Fitzpatrick (ed.), *Terror in Ireland* (Dublin, 2012).

Hare, S., 'Martial law from the soldier's point of view', *Army Quarterly* **7** (October 1923 and January 1924).

Hart, P., 'Michael Collins and the assassination of Sir Henry Wilson', *Irish Historical Studies* **28** (110) (1992).

Hart, P., 'Class, community and the Irish Republican Army in Cork, 1917–1923', in P. O'Flanagan, C.G. Buttimer and G. O'Brien, *Cork: History & Society* (Dublin, 1993).

Hart, P., *The IRA and its Enemies: Violence and Community in Cork: 1916–1923* (Cork, 1998).

Hart, P., 'Operations abroad: the I.R.A. in Britain, 1919–1923', *English Historical Review* **115** (460) (2000).

Hart, P. (ed.), *British Intelligence in Ireland, 1920–21: The Final Reports* (Cork, 2002).

Hart, P., *The I.R.A. at War, 1916–1923* (Oxford, 2003).

Hart, P., *Mick* (London, 2006).

Hartline, M.C. and Kaulbach, M.M., 'Michael Collins and Bloody Sunday: the intelligence war between the British and Irish intelligence services', *CIA Historical Review Program*, accessed 2 July 1996, approved for release 1994.

Harvey, A.D., 'Who were the Auxiliaries?', *The Historical Journal* **35** (3) (1992).

Havens, M.C., Leiden, C. and Schmit, K.M., *The Politics of Assassination*

(Englewood Cliffs, NJ, 1970).

Hawkins, R., 'Dublin Castle and the R.I.C. (1916–1922)', in T.D. Williams (ed.), *The Irish Struggle 1916–1926* (London, 1966).

Henderson, F., 'Irish leaders of our time, 5: Richard McKee', *An Cosantóir* **5** (1945).

Herlihy, J., *The Royal Irish Constabulary* (Dublin, 1997).

Herlihy, J., *The Royal Irish Constabulary: A Complete Alphabetical List of Officers and Men, 1816–1922* (Dublin, 1999).

Herlihy, J., *The Dublin Metropolitan Police: A Complete Alphabetical List of Officers and Men, 1836–1925* (Dublin, 2001).

Herman, J.L., *Trauma and Recovery: The Aftermath of Violence – From Domestic Abuse to Political Terror* (New York, 1992).

Hittle, J.B.E., *Michael Collins and the Anglo-Irish War: Britain's Counter-insurgency Failure* (Chicago, 2007).

Holt, E., *Protest in Arms* (New York, 1960).

Hopkinson, M., *Green Against Green: The Irish Civil War* (Dublin, 1988).

Hopkinson, M., *The Irish War of Independence* (Dublin, 2002).

Horgan, J., *Seán Lemass: The Enigmatic Patriot* (Dublin, 1997).

Hughes, B., 'Persecuting the Peelers', in D. Fitzpatrick (ed.), *Terror in Ireland* (Dublin, 2012).

Hughes, B., 'Defying the IRA? Intimidation, coercion, and communities during the Irish Revolution', in E. Delaney and M. Luddy (eds), *Reappraisals in Irish History* (Liverpool, 2016).

Hughes, B., 'Make the terror behind greater than the terror in front? Internal discipline, forced participation, and the I.R.A, 1919–21', *Irish Historical Studies* **42** (161) (2018).

Hughes, K., *English Atrocities in Ireland, a Compilation of Facts from Court and Press Records* (New York, 1920).

Humphries, M.O. and Kurchinski, K., 'Rest, relax and get well: a re-conceptualisation of Great War shell shock treatment', *War & Society* **27** (2) (2008).

Issacharoff, S. and Pildes, R.H., 'Targeted warfare: individuating enemy responsibility', *New York University Law Review* **88** (5) (2013).

Jeffery, K., 'British military intelligence following World War I', in K.G. Robertson (ed.), *British and American Approaches to Intelligence* (London, 1987).

Jeffery, K., 'Intelligence and counter-insurgency operations: some reflections on the British experience', *Intelligence and National Security* **2** (1) (1987).

Jeffery, K., 'Some problems and lessons of the Anglo–Irish War in the twentieth century', in P. Dennis and J. Grey (eds), *An Art in Itself: The Theory and Conduct of Small Wars and Insurgencies* (London, 2006).

Jocelyn, E. and McEwen, A., *The Long March: The True Story Behind the Legendary Journey that Made Mao's China* (London, 2006).

Jones, T. (ed. K. Middlemas), *Whitehall Diary, Volume I, 1916–1925* (London, 1969).

Jones, T. (ed. K. Middlemas), *Whitehall Diary, Volume III, Ireland 1918–1925* (London, 1971).

Kahn, D., 'An historical theory of intelligence', in P. Gill, S. Marrin and M. Phythian (eds), *Intelligence Theory, Key Questions and Debates* (Abingdon, 2009).

Kalyvas, S., *The Logic of Violence in Civil War* (Cambridge, 2006).

Kautt, W.H., *The Anglo–Irish War, 1919–1921: A People's War* (Westport, 1999).

Kautt, W.H., *Militarising Policemen. The Various Members of the RIC and their Response to IRA Violence in Ireland, 1919–1921* (Kansas, 2003).

Kautt, W.H., *Ground Truths. British Army Operations in the Irish War of Independence* (Sallins, 2014).

Kavanagh, S., 'The Irish Volunteers' intelligence organisation', *Capuchin Annual* (1969).

Kearns, K., *Dublin Voices. An Oral Folk History* (Dublin, 1998).

Kee, R., *The Green Flag* (combining three separate volumes entitled *The Most Distressful Country*, *The Bold Fenian Men* and *Ourselves Alone*) (London, 1972).

Kenna, G.B., *Facts and Figures of the Belfast Pogrom, 1920–1922* (Dublin, 1922).

Keyes McDonnell, K., *There is a Bridge at Bandon. A Personal Account of the Irish War of Independence* (Cork, 1972).

Kilcullen, D., 'Counterinsurgency *Redux*', opinion paper of Kilcullen, Chief Strategist in the Office of the Coordinator for Counterterrorism, U.S. State Department, Washington D.C. (undated).

King, C.R., 'Revolutionary war, guerrilla warfare, and international law', *Case Western Reserve Journal of International Law* **4** (2) (1972).

Kirby, D., 'The IRA and Manchester: how terror unit waged war on the city', *The Manchester Evening News* (20 January 2013).

Kissane, C., 'An eye for and eye: the IRA's campaign in 1920's Britain', *The Irish Times* (17 December 2017).

Kissinger, H., 'The Viet Nam negotiations', *Foreign Affairs* (January, 1969).

Kitson, Gen. F., *Bunch of Five* (London, 1977).

Kostal, D., 'British intelligence in Ireland 1919–1921: integration of law enforcement and military intelligence to support force protection', unpublished Masters dissertation, US Joint Military Intelligence College, Bethesda, MD (2004).

Kotsonouris, M., *Retreat from Revolution: The Dáil Courts, 1920–1924* (Dublin, 1994).

Kydd, A.H. and Walter, B.F., 'The strategies of terrorism', *International Security* **31** (1) (2006).

Laffan, M., *The Resurrection of Ireland: The Sinn Féin Party, 1916–1923* (Cambridge, 1999).

Lankford, S., *The Hope and the Sadness: Personal Recollections of Troubled Times in Ireland* (Tower Books, 1980).

Lapping, B., *End of Empire* (London, 1985).

Laqueur, W., *Age of Terrorism* (Boston, 1987).

Larrabee, A., 'Why historians should exercise caution when using the word "terrorism"', *The Journal of American History* **98** (1) (2011).

Lawlor, D., 'Why the Black and Tan stain has never washed out of the Irish psyche', *Irish Independent* (9 May 2002).

Lawlor, D., 'The Black and Tans – nine things to know', *An Phoblacht* (19 November 2016).

Lawrence, T.E., 'The evolution of a revolt', *Army Quarterly and Defence Journal* (October 1920).

Lawrence, T.E., *The Science of Guerrilla Warfare* (1948).

Lawson, Lt Gen. Sir H., *A Report on the Irish Situation* (pamphlet, London, 1921).

Lawson, Lt Gen. Sir H., *A Second Report on the Situation* (pamphlet, undated).

Leese, P., 'Why are they not cured? British shell-shock treatment during the Great War', in M. Micale and P. Lerner (eds), *Traumatic Pasts: History, Psychiatry, and Trauma in the Modern Age, 1870–1930* (Cambridge, 2001).

Leeson, D., 'Death in the afternoon: the Croke Park Massacre, 21

November 1920', *Canadian Journal of History* (April 2003).

Leeson, D., 'Imperial stormtroopers: British paramilitaries in the Irish War of Independence, 1920–1921', unpublished Ph.D thesis, McMaster University (2003).

Leeson, D., 'The "scum of London's underworld?", British recruits for the Royal Irish Constabulary, 1920–1921', *Contemporary British History* **17** (1) (2003).

Leeson, D., *The Black and Tans: British Police and Auxiliaries in the Irish War of Independence, 1920–1921* (Oxford, 2012).

Leiser, B.M., 'Terrorism, guerrilla warfare, and international morality', *Stanford Journal of International Studies* **12** (1977).

Leonard, J., '"English dogs" or "poor devils"? The dead of Bloody Sunday morning', in D. Fitzpatrick (ed.), *Terror in Ireland* (Dublin, 2012).

Leonard, P.B., 'The necessity of de-Anglicising the Irish Nation: boycotting and the Irish War of Independence', unpublished Ph.D thesis, University of Melbourne (2000).

Levie, H.S., 'An international law of guerrilla warfare: the global politics of law-making', *Maryland Journal of International Law and Trade* **9** (1985).

Loken, M., 'Rethinking rape: the role of women in wartime violence', *Security Studies* **26** (1) (2016).

Lowe, T.A., 'Some reflections of a junior commander upon the campaign in Ireland 1920 and 1921', *Army Quarterly* (1922).

Lowe, W.J., 'The war against the RIC, 1919–1921', *Éire-Ireland* **37** (3) (2002).

Lowe, W.J., 'Who were the Black and Tans', *History Ireland* **12** (3) (2004).

Luddy, M., and Murphy, C., *Women Surviving: Studies in Irish Women's History in the 19th and 20th Centuries* (Dublin, 1990).

Lynch, R., 'The Clones affray, 1922: massacre or invasion', *History Ireland* **12** (3) (2004).

MacAodh, S., 'I.R.A. wipe out "G" Division', *An Phoblacht* (6 September 2001).

MacAodh, S., 'Murder in the Castle', *An Phoblacht* (22 November 2001).

Macardle, D., *The Irish Republic* (New York, 1937; 1965).

McCall, E., *The Auxiliaries: Tudor's Toughs, A Study of the Auxiliary Division of the Royal Irish Constabulary 1920–1922* (London, 2010).

McCarthy, Á., 'Hearths, bodies and minds: gender ideology and women's committal to Enniscorthy Lunatic Asylum, 1916–1925', in A. Hayes and D. Urquhart (eds), *Irish Women's History* (Dublin, 2004).

McCoole, S., *Hazel, A Life of Lady Lavery* (Dublin, 1996).

McCoole, S., *Guns and Chiffon* (Dublin, 1997).

McCoole, S., *No Ordinary Women, Irish Female Activists in the Revolutionary Years* (Dublin, 2003).

McDermott, J., *Northern Divisions: The Old IRA and the Belfast Pogroms, 1920–1922* (Belfast, 2001).

McDonald, H., *Gunsmoke and Mirrors: How Sinn Féin Dressed Up Defeat as Victory* (Dublin, 2008).

MacEoin, U. (ed.), *Survivors: The Story of Ireland's Struggle as Told Through Some of Her Outstanding Living People. Notes 1913–1916.* (Dublin, 1966).

McGarry, F., *Eoin O'Duffy. A Self-made Hero* (Oxford, 2005).

McGarry, F., 'Keeping an eye on the usual suspects: Dublin Castle's "Personality Files", 1899–1921', *History Ireland* 14 (6) (2006).

McGuigan, J., 'Michael Collins on File?', *History Ireland* 19 (4) (2011).

Machiavelli, N. (trans. W.K. Marriott), *The Prince* (1532).

Machnik-Kékesi, G., 'Gendering bodies: violence as performance in Ireland's War of Independence (1919–1921)', unpublished MA thesis, Concordia University, Montreal, Quebec, Canada (2017).

McInnes, C. and Sheffield, G.D., *Warfare in the Twentieth Century: Theory and Practice* (London, 1988).

Mack, A., 'Why big nations lose small wars: the politics of asymmetric conflict', *World Politics* (January 1975).

McKenna, J., *Guerrilla Warfare in the Irish War of Independence, 1919–1921* (Jefferson, NC, 2011).

McKillen, B., 'Irish feminism and national separatism', *Éire-Ireland* 17 (1982).

McMahon, P., *British Spies and Irish Rebels—British Intelligence in Ireland: 1916–1945* (Suffolk, 2008).

Macready, N., *Annals of an Active Life,* 2 vols (New York, 1925).

Mahon, Sir B., 'The Irish welter as I found it: an indictment of British methods', in W.G. Fitzgerald (ed.), *The Voice of Ireland* (Dublin, 1924).

Malcom, E., *The Irish Policeman, 1822–1922: A Life* (Dublin, 2006).

Martin, H., *Ireland in Insurrection* (London, 1921).

Mattern, C., 'Strange creatures are we, even to ourselves: understanding insurgency and counterinsurgency efforts in the Irish War of Independence', *Small Wars Journal* (20 October 2019).

Matthews, A., *Renegades: Irish Republican Women 1900–1922* (Cork, 2010).

Meehan, N., 'She is a Protestant as well. Distilling British propaganda in accounts of the death of Kate Carroll, in April 1921', *The Aubane Historical Society* (8 August 2020).

Merari, A., 'Terrorism as a strategy of insurgency', *Terrorism and Political Violence* **5** (4) (1993).

Mitchell, A., *A Revolutionary Government in Ireland: Dáil Éireann 1919– 1922* (Dublin, 1995).

Mockaitis, T.R., 'The origins of British counterinsurgency', *Small Wars and Insurgencies* **1** (3) (1990).

Mockaitis, T.R., *British Counterinsurgency, 1919–60* (London, 1991).

Moloney, E., *A Secret History of the IRA* (London, 2002).

Montgomery, Field Marshal B.L., *The Memoirs of Field Marshal the Viscount Montgomery* (London, 1958).

Moran, M., *Executed for Ireland. The Patrick Moran Story* (Cork, 2010).

Morrison, E., 'Hauntings of the Irish Revolution: veterans and memory of the independence struggle and Civil War', in M. Corporal, C. Cusack and R. van den Beuken (eds), *Irish Studies and the Dynamics of Memory: Transitions and Transformations* (2016).

Morrison, E., 'Witnessing the Republic. The Ernie O'Malley Notebook Interviews and the Bureau of Military History compared', in C. O'Malley, *Modern Ireland and Revolution, Ernie O'Malley in Context* (Dublin, 2016).

Mulcahy, R., 'Mulcahy and Collins – a conjunction of opposites', *History Ireland* **13** (2) (2008).

Murray, N., 'The rarely spoken about violence suffered by women during the Irish revolution', *The Irish Examiner* (12 September 2017).

Murphy, B.P., *The Origin and Organisation of British Propaganda in Ireland, 1920* (Dublin, 2006).

Murphy, J.F. Jr., 'Michael Collins and the craft of intelligence', *International Journal of Intelligence and Counterintelligence* **17** (2) (2010).

Murphy, M., 'Revolution and terror in Kildare, 1919–1923', in D. Fitzpatrick (ed.), *Terror in Ireland* (Dublin, 2012).

Neligan, D., *The Spy in the Castle* (London, 1999).

Neumann, P.R. and Smith, M.L.R., *The Strategy of Terrorism: How It Works, and Why It Fails* (London, 2008).

Nic Dháibhéid, C., *Terrorist Histories: Individuals and Political Violence since the 19th Century* (New York, 2016).

Noonan, G., 'Republican terrorism in Britain, 1920–1921', in D. Fitzpatrick (ed.), *Terror in Ireland* (Dublin, 2012).

Noonan, G., *The IRA in Britain 1919–1923, 'In the Heart of Enemy Lines'* (Liverpool, 2017).

O'Brien, G., *Irish Governments and the Guardianship of Historical Records, 1922–72* (Dublin, 2004).

O'Brien, P., *Havoc: The Auxiliaries in Ireland's War of Independence* (Cork, 2017).

O'Brien, P., 'Masters of chaos: British Special Forces during the Irish War of Independence', *An Cosantóir* (March 2019).

Ó Broin, L., *W.E. Wylie and the Irish Revolution, 1916–1921* (Dublin, 1989).

O'Callaghan, S., *Execution* (London, 1974).

Ó Conchubhair, B. (ed.), *Dublin's Fighting Story, 1916–1921. Told by the Men who Made It* (Cork, 2009) [originally published by *The Kerryman*, 1948].

O'Connor, U., *A Terrible Beauty is Born: The Irish Troubles, 1912–1922* (London, 1975).

O'Connor, U., *Michael Collins and the Troubles: the Struggle for Irish Freedom 1912–1922* (New York, 1996).

O'Donoghue, F., 'Guerilla warfare in Ireland 1919–1921', *An Cosantoir* 23 (1963).

O'Donoghue, F., *No Other Law* (Dublin, 1954, 1986).

O'Halpin, E., 'Sir Warren Fisher and the Coalition, 1919–1922', *Historical Journal* 24 (4) (1981).

O'Halpin, E., 'British intelligence in Ireland 1914–1921', in C. Andrew and D. Dilks (eds), *The Missing Dimension: Government and Intelligence Communities in the Twentieth Century* (Urbana, 1984).

O'Halpin, E., *Decline of the Union: British Government in Ireland, 1892–1920* (Dublin, 1987).

O'Halpin, E., *Head of the Civil Service: A Study of Sir Warren Fisher* (London, 1989).

O'Halpin, E., 'Collins and intelligence, 1919–1923', in G. Doherty and D.

Keogh (eds), *Michael Collins and the Making of the Irish State* (Cork, 1998).

O'Halpin, E., 'Problematic killing during the War of Independence and its aftermath: civilian spies and informers', in J. Kelly and M.A. Lyons (eds), *Death and Dying in Ireland, Britain and Europe: Historical Perspectives* (Dublin, 2013).

O'Halpin, E., 'Counting terror: Bloody Sunday and the dead of the Irish Revolution', in D. Fitzpatrick (ed.), *Terror in Ireland 1916–1923* (Dublin, 2012).

O'Mahony, S., 'Three murders in Dublin Castle' (pamphlet, Dublin, 2000).

O'Mahony, R., 'The sack of Balbriggan and tit-for-tat killing', in D. Fitzpatrick (ed.), *Terror in Ireland* (Dublin, 2012).

O'Malley, C., *The Men Will Talk To Me* (Cork, 2010).

O'Malley, E., *On Another Man's Wound* (Dublin, 1936, 1979).

O'Malley, E., *The Singing Flame* (Dublin, 1978).

O'Malley, E., *Raids and Rallies* (Dublin, 1982).

O'Meara, M., *Bloody Sunday, 1920–1995, A Commemorative Booklet* (Dublin, 1995).

O'Reilly, T., *Rebel Heart: George Lennon Flying Column Commander* (Cork, 2009).

Ó Ruairc, L., 'Did the Black and Tans run from the rifles of the I.R.A.?', *History Ireland* 12 (2) (2004).

Ó Ruairc, P. Óg, 'Terror in Ireland', *History Ireland* 20 (3) (2012).

Ó Ruairc, P. Óg, 'Spies & informers beware', *An Cosantóir* (March 2019).

O'Sullivan, P. and Lee, F., 'The execution of Field Marshal Sir Henry Wilson: the facts', *Sunday Press* (10 August 1958).

Packenham, F., *Peace by Ordeal* (London, 1935).

Paseta, S., *Irish Nationalist Women: 1909–1918* (Cambridge, 2013).

Pattison, G., 'The British army's effectiveness in the Irish Campaign 1919–1921, and the lessons for modern counterinsurgency operations, with special reference to C3I aspects', UK Ministry of Defence (1999).

Pearse, P., 'The Coming Revolution', *Political Writings and Speeches* (Dublin, 1962).

Petter, M., '"Temporary gentlemen" in the aftermath of the Great War: rank, status and the ex-officer problem', *The Historical Journal* 37 (1)

(March 1994).

Phillips, W.A., *The Revolution in Ireland, 1906–1923* (London, 1923).

Pinkman, J.A. (ed. F.E. Maguire), *In the Legion of the Vanguard* (Dublin, 1998).

Polk, W.R., *Violent Politics: A History of Insurgency, Terrorism, and Guerrilla War from the American Revolution to Iraq* (New York, 2007).

Popplewell, R., 'Lacking intelligence: some reflections on recent approaches to British counter-insurgence 1900–1960', *Intelligence and National Security* **10** (2) (1995).

Price, H.E., 'The strategy and tactics of revolutionary terrorism', *Comparative Studies in Society and History* **19** (1) (1977).

Prisk, C.E., 'The umbrella of legitimacy', in M.G. Manwaring (ed.), *Uncomfortable Wars: Toward a New Paradigm of Low Intensity Conflict* (Boulder, CO, 1991).

Putkowski, J.J., 'The best secret service man we had: Jack Burns and the IRA', *Lobster* (1994).

Quinlan, A., 'The mother who turned IRA spy to save her son', *Irish Independent* (25 November 2012).

Quinlan, A., 'Wartime sexual violence against women "ignored"', *Irish Times* (9 July 2018).

Rafter, K., *Sinn Féin 1905–2005: In the Shadow of Gunmen* (Dublin, 2005).

Rast, M., 'Tactics, politics and propaganda in the Irish War of Independence, 1917–1921', unpublished Masters thesis, Georgia State University (2011).

Regan, J., *The Irish Counter-revolution, 1921–1936* (Dublin, 1999).

Regan, J., 'Irish public histories as an historiographical problem', *Irish Historical Studies* **37** (146) (2010).

Regan, J., *Myth and the Irish State* (Sallins, 2013).

Regan, J.M. (ed. J. Augusteijn), *The Memoirs of John M. Regan, A Catholic Officer in the RIC and RUC: 1909–1948* (Dublin, 2007).

Reid, E.N., 'British intelligence operations during the Anglo-Irish War', unpublished Masters dissertation, Central Washington University (2016).

Richardson, M., 'Terrorism: trauma in the excess of affect,' in J.R. Kurtz (ed.), *Cambridge Critical Concepts: Trauma and Literature* (Cambridge, 2018).

Ryan, A., *Comrades: Inside the War of Independence* (Dublin, 2007).

Ryan, B., *A Full Private Remembers the Troubled Times* (Hollyford, 1969).

Ryan, L., '"Drunken Tans": representation of sex and violence in the Anglo-Irish War (1919–1921)', *Feminist Review* 66 (2000).

Ryan, L., 'Furies and die-hards: women and Irish republicanism in the early twentieth century', *Gender and History* 11 (2) (2002).

Ryan, L. and Ward, M. (eds), *Irish Women and Nationalism: Soldiers, New Women and Hags* (Dublin, 2004).

Ryan, M., *The Day Michael Collins was Shot* (Dublin, 1989).

Ryan, M., *Tom Barry: Irish Freedom Fighter* (Cork, 2003).

Ryan, M., *Michael Collins and the Women in His Life* (Dublin, 1996) [republished as *Michael Collins and the Women Who Spied for Ireland* (Cork, 2007)].

Sarat, A., Basler, C. and Dumm, T.L. (eds), *Performances of Violence* (Amherst, 2011).

Schmid, A.P. and Jongman, A.J., *Political Terrorism* (Amsterdam, 1988).

Schwenkenbecher, A., *Terrorism: A Philosophical Inquiry* (New York, 2012).

Seedorf, M.F., 'The Lloyd George government and the Strickland Report on the burning of Cork 1920', *Albion: A Quarterly Journal Concerned with British Studies* 4 (2) (1972).

Seedorf, M., 'Defending reprisals: Sir Hamar Greenwood and the "Troubles", 1920–1921', *Éire-Ireland* 25 (4) (1990).

Sharkey, S., *Ireland and the Iconography of Rape* (London, 1994).

Sharkey, S., 'My role as an intelligence officer with the Third Tipperary Brigade (1919–1921)', *Tipperary Historical Journal* 11 (1998).

Sheehan, T., *Lady Hostage (Mrs Lindsay)* (Dripsey, 1990).

Sheehan, W. (ed.), *British Voices From the Irish War of Independence 1918–1921: The Words of British Servicemen Who Were There* (Doughcloyne, 2007).

Sheehan, W., *Hearts and Mines: The British 5th Division, Ireland, 1920–1922* (Cork, 2009).

Short, K.R.M., *The Dynamite War: Irish-American Bombers in Victorian Britain* (Dublin, 1979).

Silke, A., 'Ferocious times: the IRA, the RIC, and Britain's failure in 1919–1921', *Terrorism and Political Violence* 27 (3) (2016).

Simon, Sir J.A., 'Irish reprisals: Auxiliary Division's record', *The London*

Times (25 April 1921).

Sitaraman, G., 'Counterinsurgence, the War on Terror and the Laws of War', *Virginia Law Review* (2009).

Sloan, G., 'Hide, seek, and negotiate: Alfred Cope and counterintelligence in Ireland, 1919–1921', *Journal of Intelligence and National Security* **33** (2) (2018).

Smith, M., *The Spying Game* (London, 2003).

Smith, S.C., 'General Templer and counter-insurgence in Malaya: hearts and minds, intelligence and propaganda', *Intelligence and National Security* **16** (3) (2001).

Stapleton, W.J., 'A Volunteer's story', *Irish Independent,* 1916 Golden Jubilee Supplement (April 1966).

Stapleton, W.J., 'Michael Collins's Squad', *Capuchin Annual* (1969).

Stepniak (unknown pseudonym), *Underground Russia* (New York, 1892).

Stewart, A.T.Q. (ed.), *Michael Collins: The Secret File* (Belfast, 1997).

Stewart, A.T.Q., *The Shape of Irish History* (Belfast, 2001).

Stewart, S., 'The difference between terrorism and insurgency', *Strategy* (26 June 2014).

Stover, J.D., 'Terror confined? Prison violence in Ireland, 1919–1921', in D. Fitzpatrick (ed.), *Terror in Ireland* (Dublin, 2012).

Street, Major C.J.C. (writing under the pseudonym of 'I.O.'), *The Administration of Ireland, 1920* (New York, 1921; London, 1922).

Street, Major C.J.C., *Ireland in 1921* (New York, 1921; London, 1922).

Stubbs, R., *Hearts and Minds in Guerrilla Warfare: The Malayan Emergency, 1948–1960* (Singapore, 1989).

Sturgis, M. (ed. M. Hopkinson), *The Last Days of Dublin Castle: The Mark Sturgis Diaries* (Dublin, 1999).

Sugg, W., 'British intelligence wiped out', *An Phoblacht* (20 November 1997).

Sugg, W., 'Bloody Sunday', *An Phoblacht* (27 November 1997).

Tait, C., Edwards, D. and Lenihan, P. (eds), *Age of Atrocity—Violence and Political Conflict in Early Modern Ireland* (Dublin, 2010).

Talbot, H., *Michael Collins' Own Story* (London, 1923).

Taylor, R., *Assassination: The Death of Sir Henry Wilson and the Tragedy of Ireland* (London, 1961).

Taylor, R., *Michael Collins* (London, 1958, 1970).

Telfer, K., *The Summer of '45: Stories and Voices from VE Day to VJ Day*

(London, 2015).

Tery, S. (trans. M.G. Rose), 'Raids and reprisals: Ireland: eye-witness (1923)', *Éire-Ireland* 20 (2) (1985)

Thornton, T.P., 'Terror as a weapon of political agitation', in H. Eckstein (ed.), *Internal War: Problems and Approaches* (London, 1964).

Townshend, C., *The British Campaign in Ireland 1919–1921: The Development of Political and Military Policies* (Oxford, 1975).

Townshend, C., 'The IRA and development of guerrilla war', *English Historical Review* 93 (371) (1979).

Townshend, C., 'Bloody Sunday: Michael Collins speaks', *European Studies Review* 9 (1979).

Townshend, C., *Political Violence in Ireland. Government and Resistance since 1848* (Oxford, 1983).

Townshend, C., 'The process of terror in Irish politics', in N. O'Sullivan (ed.), *Terrorism, Ideology and Revolution* (Brighton, 1986).

Townshend, C., 'The culture of paramilitarism in Ireland', in M. Crenshaw (ed.), *Terrorism in Context* (Pennsylvania, 1995).

Townshend, C., *Terrorism: A Very Short Introduction* (Oxford, 2002).

Townshend, C., 'In aid of civil power: Britain, Ireland, and Palestine 1916–1948', in D. Marston and C. Malkasian (eds), *Counterinsurgency in Modern Warfare* (Oxford, 2008).

Townshend, C., 'The Irish War of Independence, context and meaning', in C. Crowe (ed.), *Guide to the Military Service (1916–1923) Pensions Collection* (Dublin, 2012).

Townshend, C., *The Republic: The Fight for Irish Independence, 1918–1923* (London, 2013).

Trautman, W.E., 'Direct action and sabotage (1912)', in S. Salerno (ed.), *Direct Action and Sabotage: Three Classic IWW Pamphlets from the 1910s* (Chicago, 1997).

Twohig, P.J., *Green Tears for Hecuba: Ireland's Fight for Freedom* (Ballincolig, 1994).

Twohig, P.J., *Blood on the Flag* (translation of *B'fhiú an braon fola*, by James (Séamus) Malone) (Cork, 1996).

Urquart, D., *Irish Women's History Reader* (Dublin, 2001).

Valiulis, M.G., *Portrait of a Revolutionary: General Richard Mulcahy and the Founding of the Irish State* (Blackrock, 1992).

Walsh, M., *The News from Ireland: Foreign Correspondents and the Irish Revolution* (New York, 2008).

Walsh, M., *G-2: In Defence of Ireland: Irish Military Intelligence, 1918–1945* (Cork, 2010).

Walsh, P. (ed.), *Ireland (1921), with an introduction to the Anglo-Irish Treaty and the 'Lost World' of Imperial Ireland by Lionel Curtis and Henry Harrison on South Africa and Ireland* (Belfast, 2002).

Walter, E.V., *Terror and Resistance: A Study of Political Violence* (Oxford, 1969).

Ward, M. (ed.), *In Their Own Voice. Women and Irish Nationalism* (Dublin, 1995, 2001).

Ward, M., *Unmanageable Revolutionaries: Women and Irish Nationalism* (London, 1995).

Ward, M., *Hanna Sheehy Skeffington: Suffragette and Sinn Féiner, Her Memoirs and Political Writings* (Dublin, 2015).

Waters, S. (ed. S. Ball), *A Policeman's Ireland: Recollections of Samuel Waters, RIC* (Cork, 1999).

Weinstein, J.M., *Inside Rebellion: The Politics of Insurgent Violence* (Cambridge, 2007).

West, N., *MI5: British Security Service Operations, 1909–1945* (London, 1983).

Wheeler-Bennett, Sir J.W., *John Anderson, Viscount Waverly* (London, 1962).

White, D., 'The Castle Document', *History Ireland* 24 (4) (2016).

White, G. and O'Shea, B., *The Burning of Cork* (Cork, 2006).

White, R.W., 'From gunmen to politicians: the impact of terrorism and political violence on twentieth-century Ireland', *Journal of Conflict Studies* 27 (2) (2007).

Winter, Sir O., *Winter's Tale* (London, 1955).

Winter, Sir O., 'A report on the Intelligence Branch of the Chief of Police, Dublin Castle, from May 1920–July 1921', in P. Hart (ed.) *British Intelligence in Ireland, 1920–1921: The Final Reports* (Cork, 2002).

Wood, E.J., 'Variation in sexual violence during war', *Politics and Society* 34 (3) (2006).

Woodcock, C., *Experiences of an Officer's Wife in Ireland* (London, 1921, 1994).

Yeates, P., '"Oh God, what did I do to deserve this?" The life and death of Detective Sergeant John Barton', *History Ireland* 24 (5) (2016).

Younger, C., *Ireland's Civil War* (New York, 1979).

Index